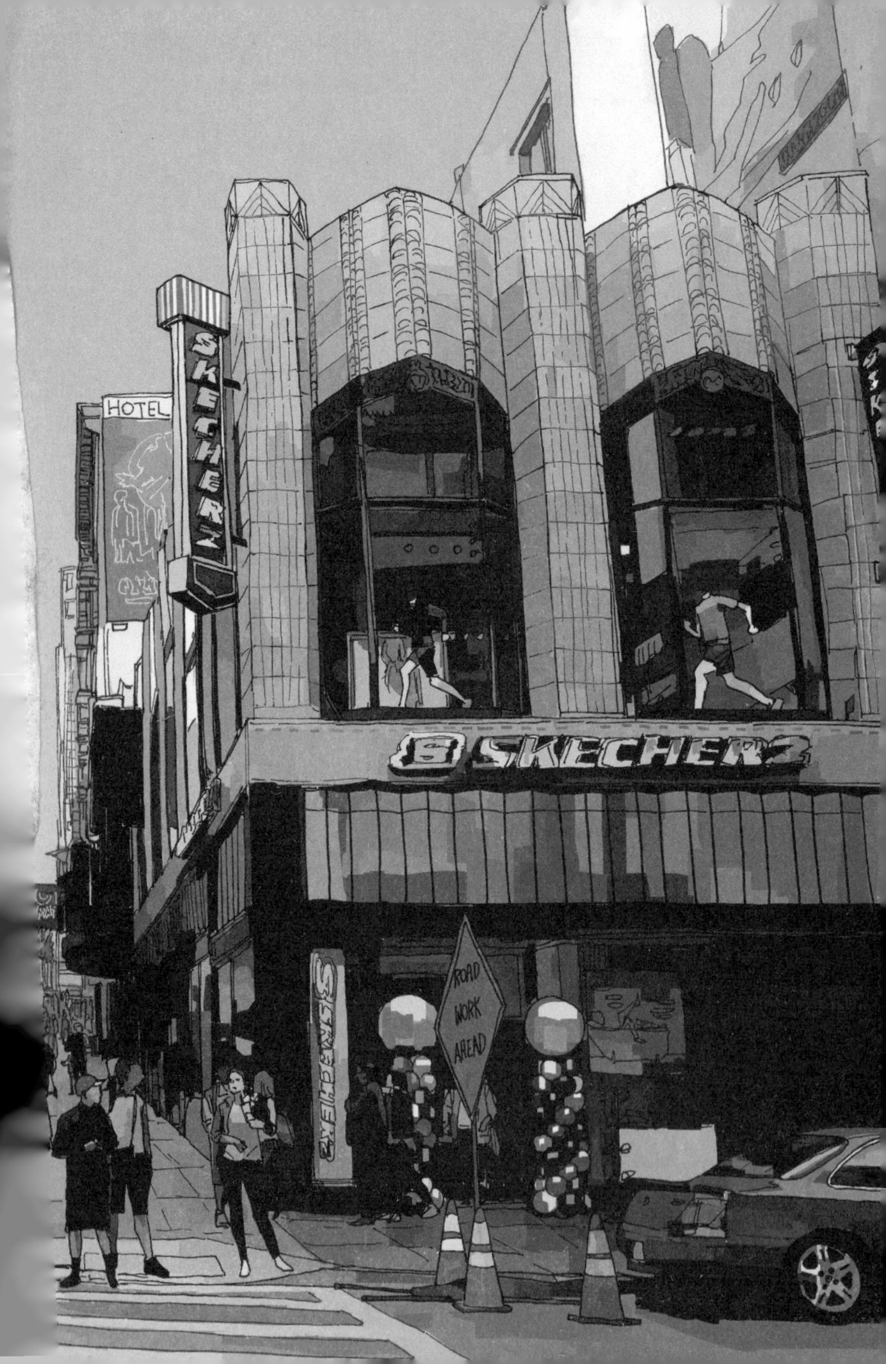
HOTEL
SKECHERS
SKECHERS
SKECHERS
ROAD
WORK
AHEAD

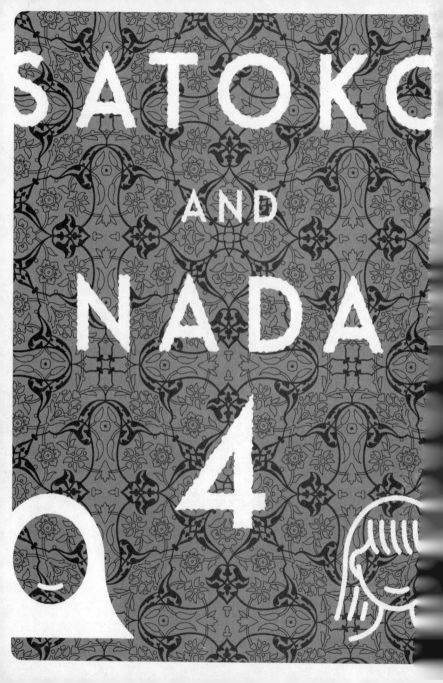

SATOKO
AND
NADA
4

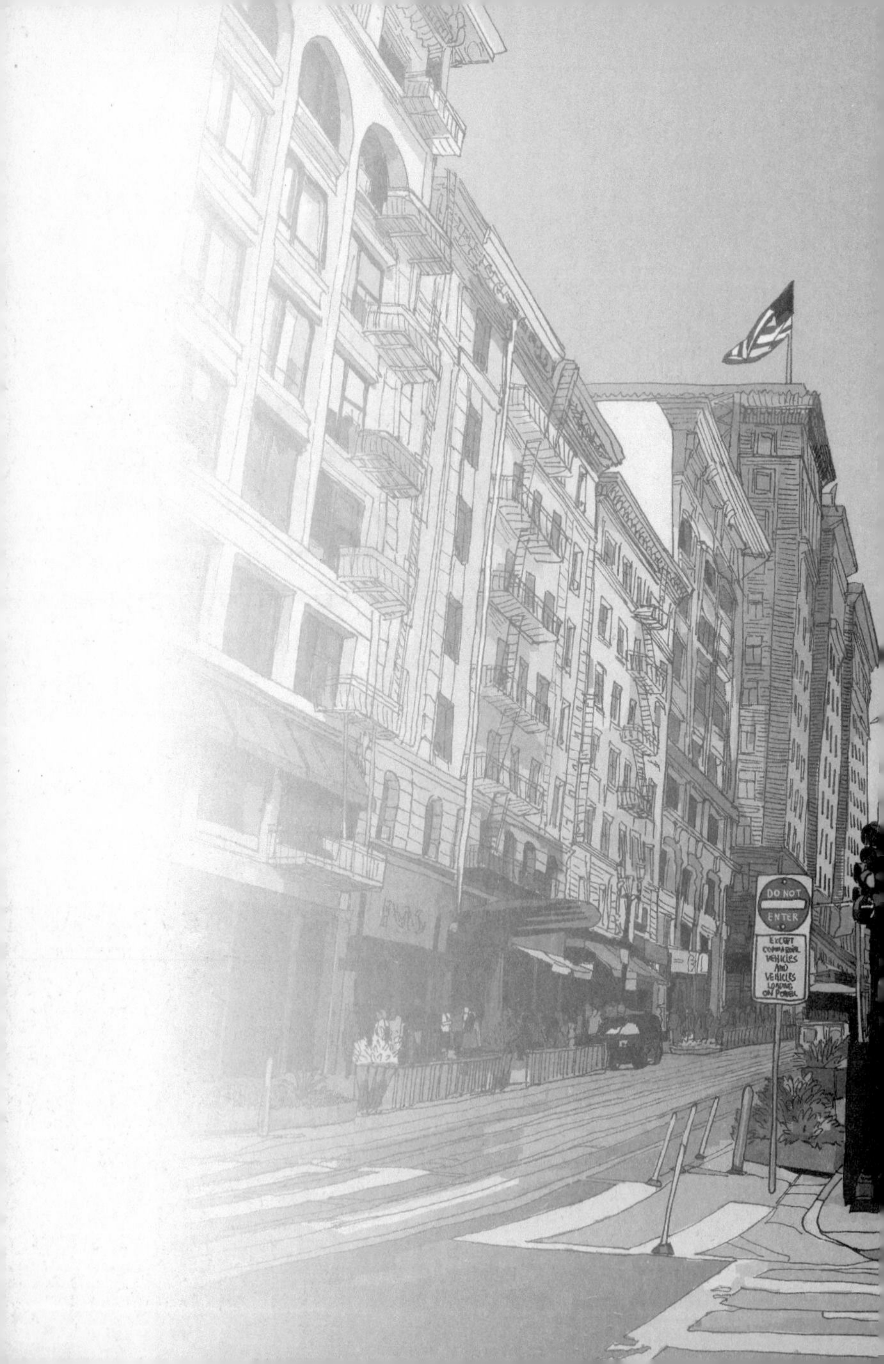
DO NOT
ENTER

SATOKO AND NADA

Presented by Yupechika

BONK

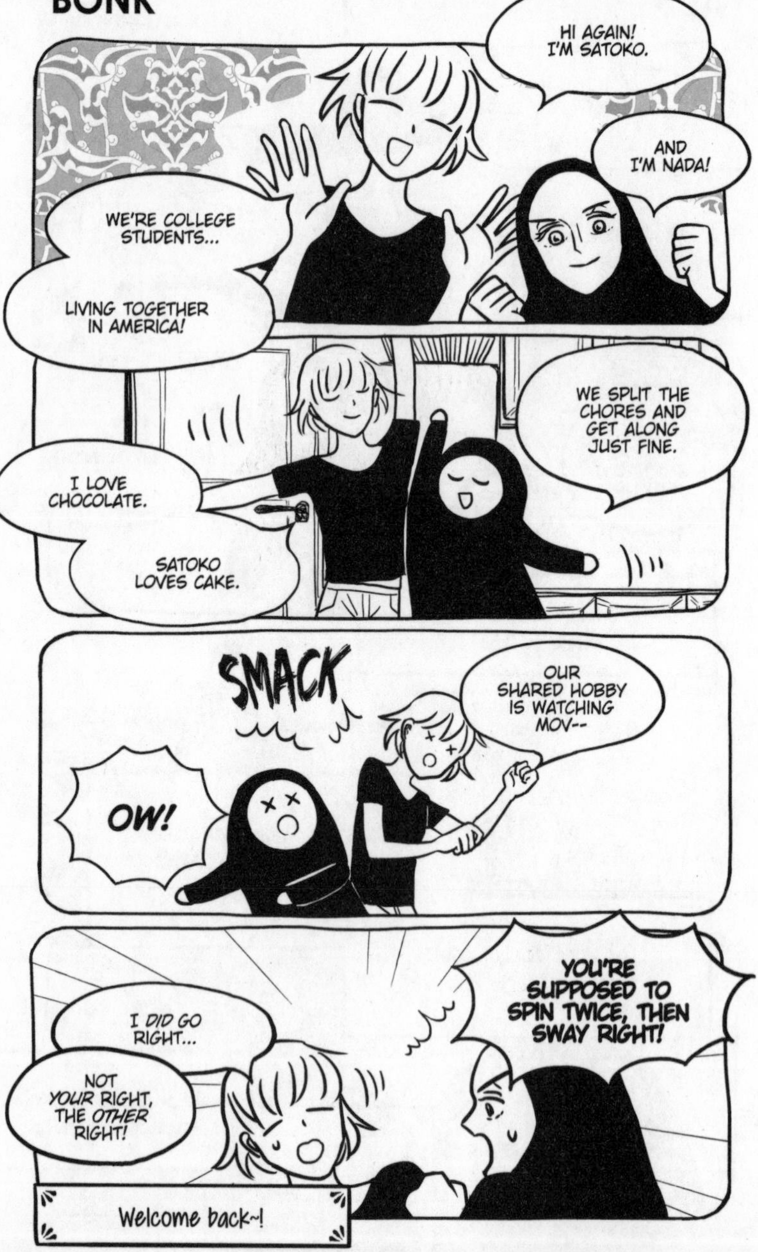
HI AGAIN! I'M SATOKO.
AND I'M NADA!
WE'RE COLLEGE STUDENTS...
LIVING TOGETHER IN AMERICA!
WE SPLIT THE CHORES AND GET ALONG JUST FINE.
I LOVE CHOCOLATE.
SATOKO LOVES CAKE.
OUR SHARED HOBBY IS WATCHING MOV--
SMACK
OW!
YOU'RE SUPPOSED TO SPIN TWICE, THEN SWAY RIGHT!
I *DID* GO RIGHT...
NOT *YOUR* RIGHT, THE *OTHER* RIGHT!
Welcome back~!

AL

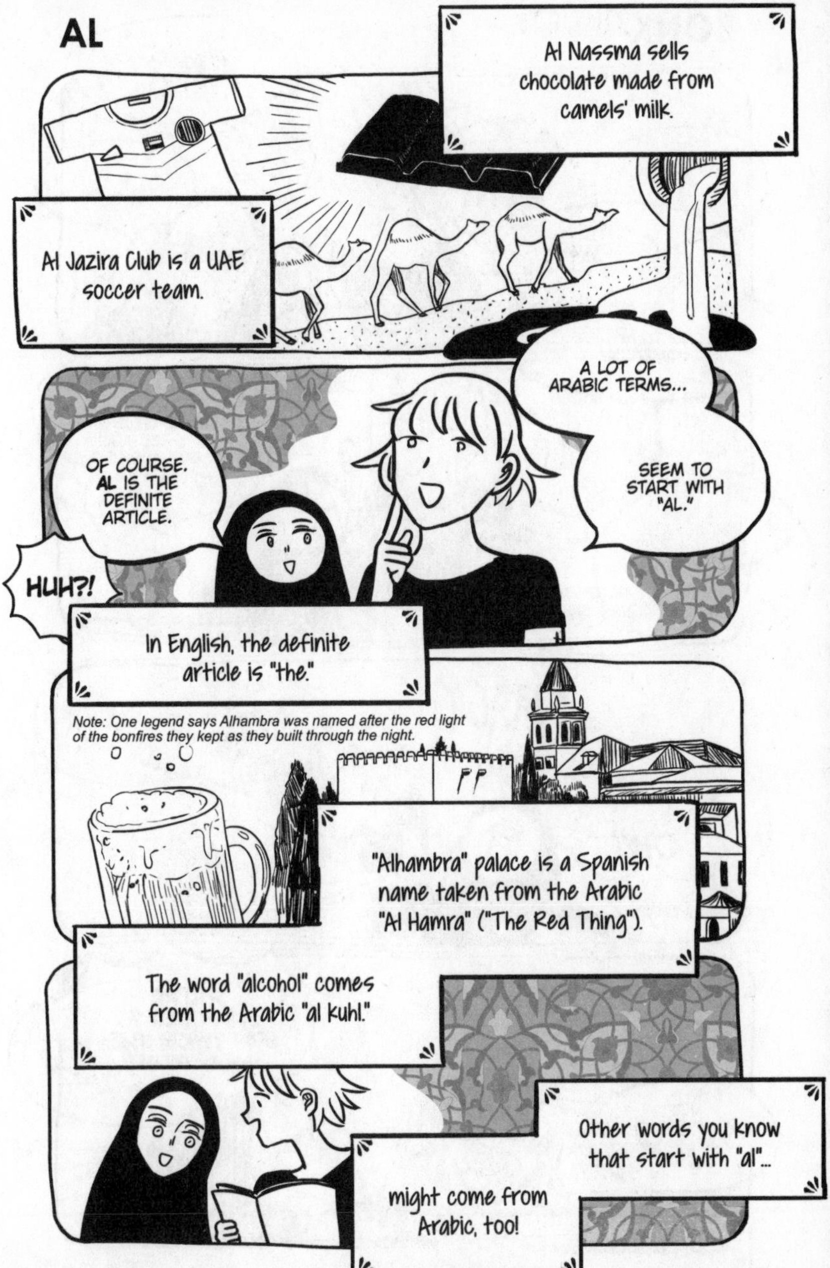

Al Nassma sells chocolate made from camels' milk.
Al Jazira Club is a UAE soccer team.
A LOT OF ARABIC TERMS...
SEEM TO START WITH "AL."
OF COURSE. **AL** IS THE DEFINITE ARTICLE.
HUH?!
In English, the definite article is "the."
Note: One legend says Alhambra was named after the red light of the bonfires they kept as they built through the night.
"Alhambra" palace is a Spanish name taken from the Arabic "Al Hamra" ("The Red Thing").
The word "alcohol" comes from the Arabic "al kuhl."
Other words you know that start with "al"...
might come from Arabic, too!

AUDIOBOOK

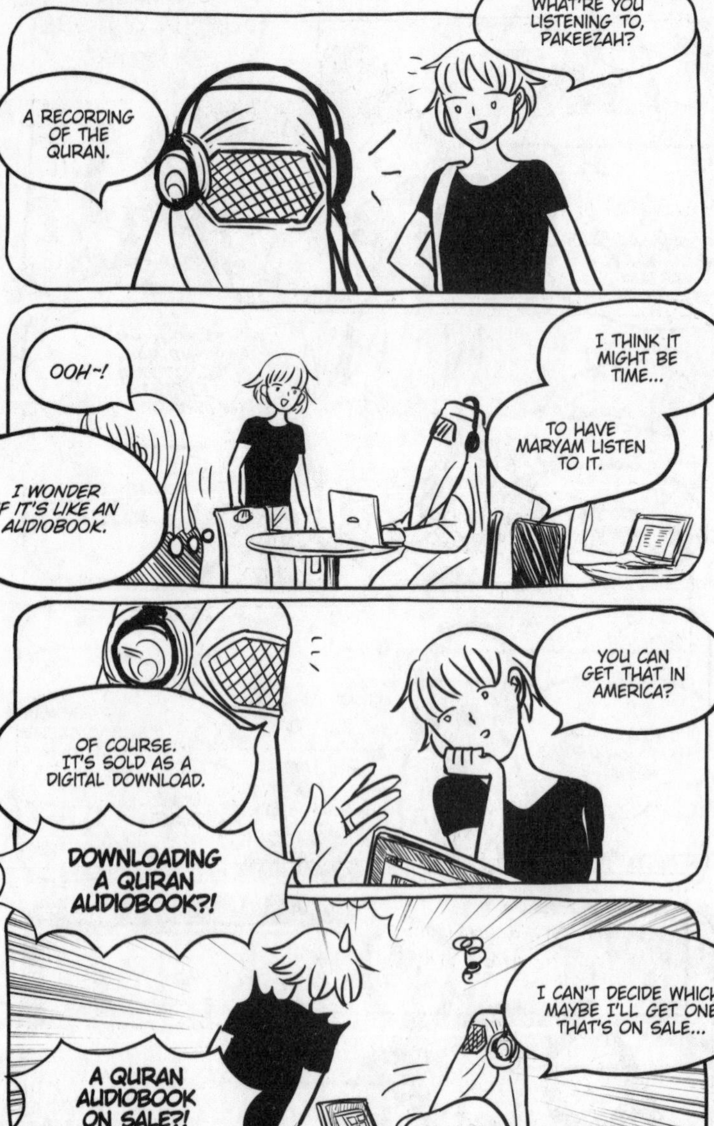
WHAT'RE YOU LISTENING TO, PAKEEZAH?
A RECORDING OF THE QURAN.
I THINK IT MIGHT BE TIME...
TO HAVE MARYAM LISTEN TO IT.
OOH~!
I WONDER IF IT'S LIKE AN AUDIOBOOK.
YOU CAN GET THAT IN AMERICA?
OF COURSE. IT'S SOLD AS A DIGITAL DOWNLOAD.
DOWNLOADING A QURAN AUDIOBOOK?!
I CAN'T DECIDE WHICH. MAYBE I'LL GET ONE THAT'S ON SALE...
A QURAN AUDIOBOOK ON SALE?!
Modern religion.

HANDSOME

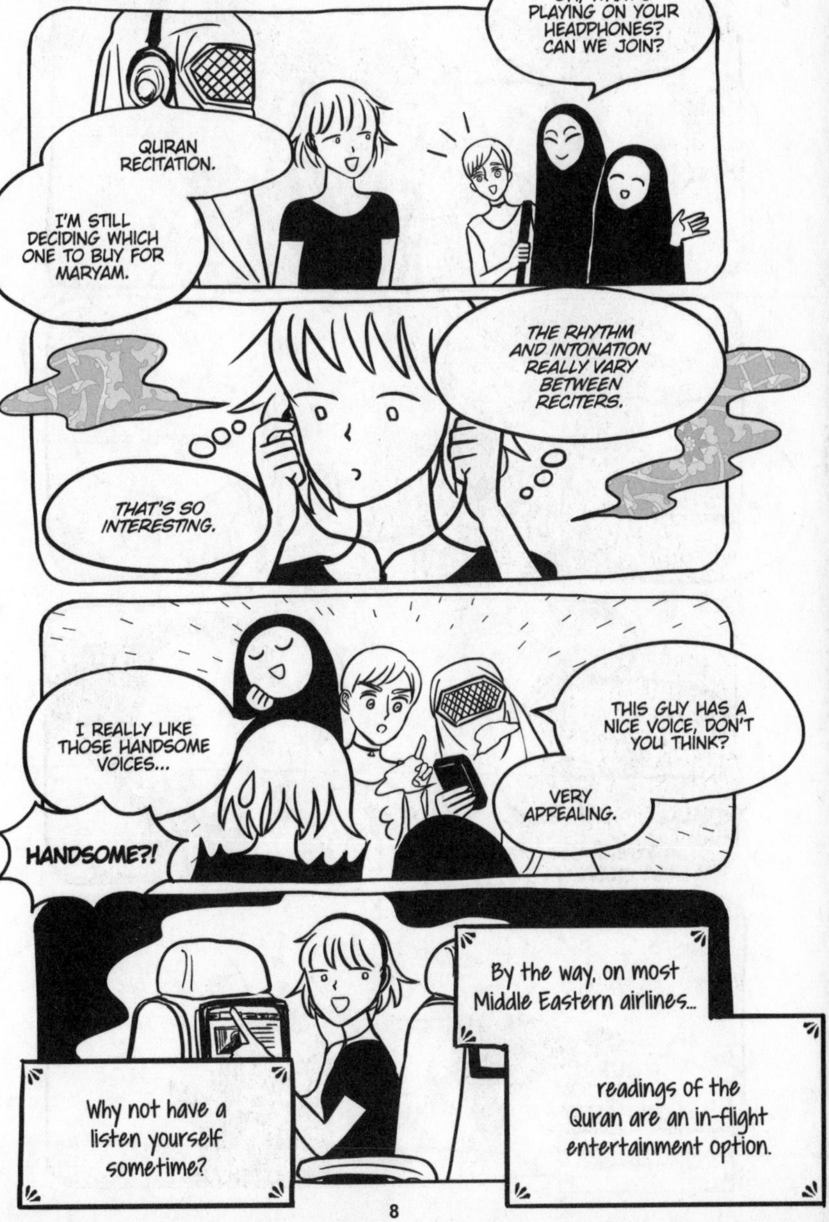
OH, WHAT'S PLAYING ON YOUR HEADPHONES? CAN WE JOIN?
QURAN RECITATION.
I'M STILL DECIDING WHICH ONE TO BUY FOR MARYAM.
THE RHYTHM AND INTONATION REALLY VARY BETWEEN RECITERS.
THAT'S SO INTERESTING.
THIS GUY HAS A NICE VOICE, DON'T YOU THINK?
VERY APPEALING.
I REALLY LIKE THOSE HANDSOME VOICES...
HANDSOME?!
By the way, on most Middle Eastern airlines...
readings of the Quran are an in-flight entertainment option.
Why not have a listen yourself sometime?

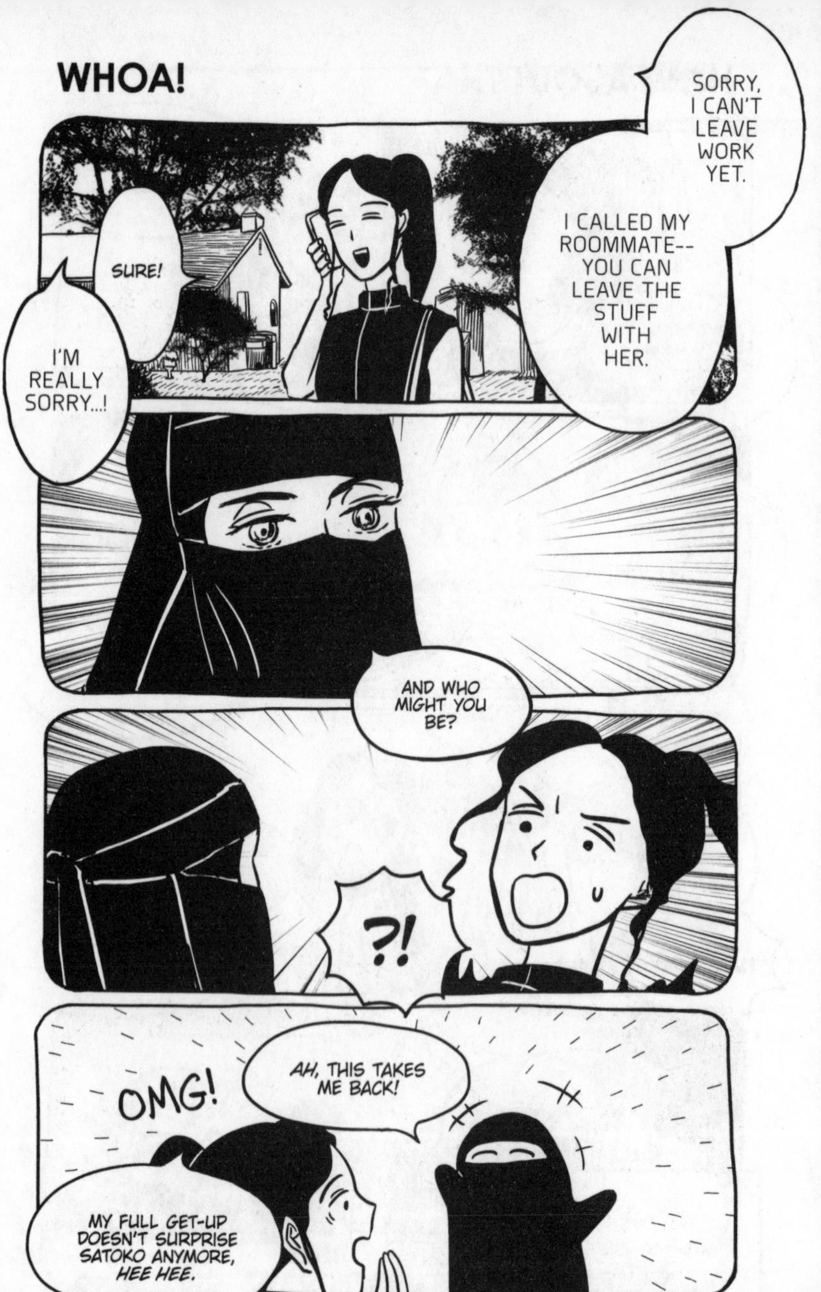
WHOA!
SORRY, I CAN'T LEAVE WORK YET.
I CALLED MY ROOMMATE-- YOU CAN LEAVE THE STUFF WITH HER.
SURE!
I'M REALLY SORRY...!
AND WHO MIGHT YOU BE?
?!
AH, THIS TAKES ME BACK!
OMG!
MY FULL GET-UP DOESN'T SURPRISE SATOKO ANYMORE, *HEE HEE.*

HOW ABOUT THAT

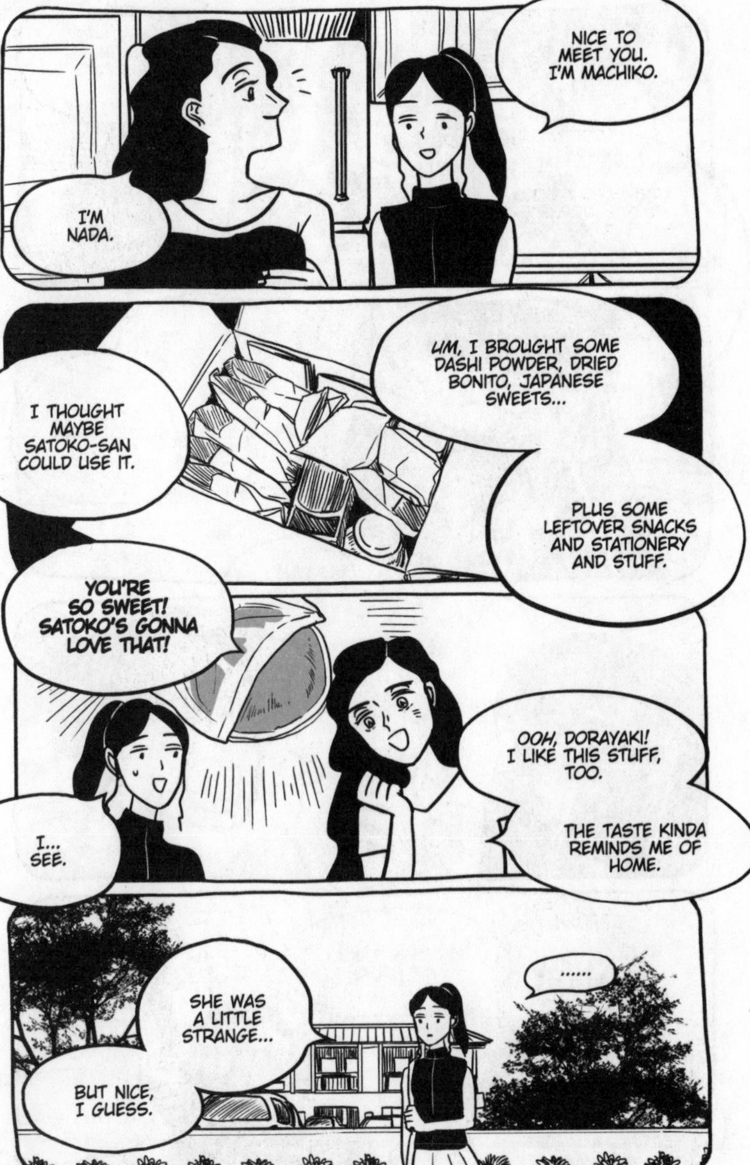

NICE TO MEET YOU. I'M MACHIKO.
I'M NADA.
UM, I BROUGHT SOME DASHI POWDER, DRIED BONITO, JAPANESE SWEETS...
PLUS SOME LEFTOVER SNACKS AND STATIONERY AND STUFF.
I THOUGHT MAYBE SATOKO-SAN COULD USE IT.
YOU'RE SO SWEET! SATOKO'S GONNA LOVE THAT!
OOH, DORAYAKI! I LIKE THIS STUFF, TOO.
THE TASTE KINDA REMINDS ME OF HOME.
I... SEE.
......
SHE WAS A LITTLE STRANGE...
BUT NICE, I GUESS.

LET'S GO TOGETHER

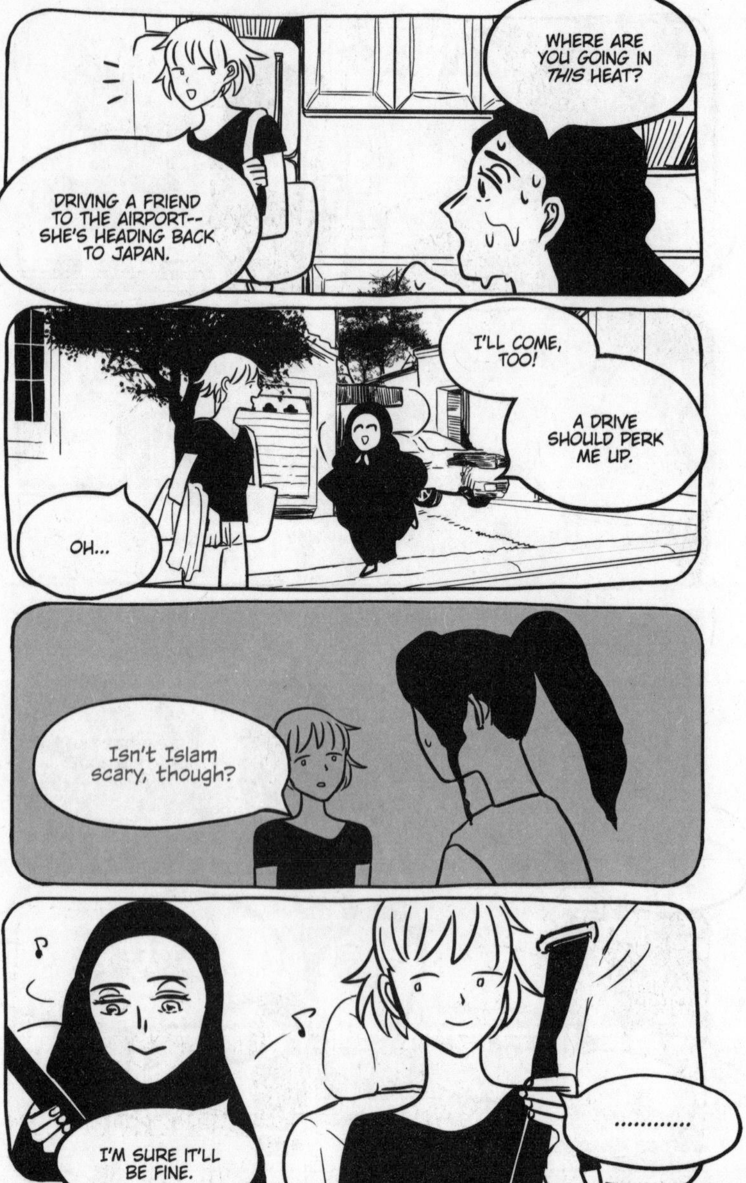
WHERE ARE YOU GOING IN *THIS* HEAT?
DRIVING A FRIEND TO THE AIRPORT--SHE'S HEADING BACK TO JAPAN.
I'LL COME, TOO!
A DRIVE SHOULD PERK ME UP.
OH...
Isn't Islam scary, though?
....
I'M SURE IT'LL BE FINE.

CONFUSION

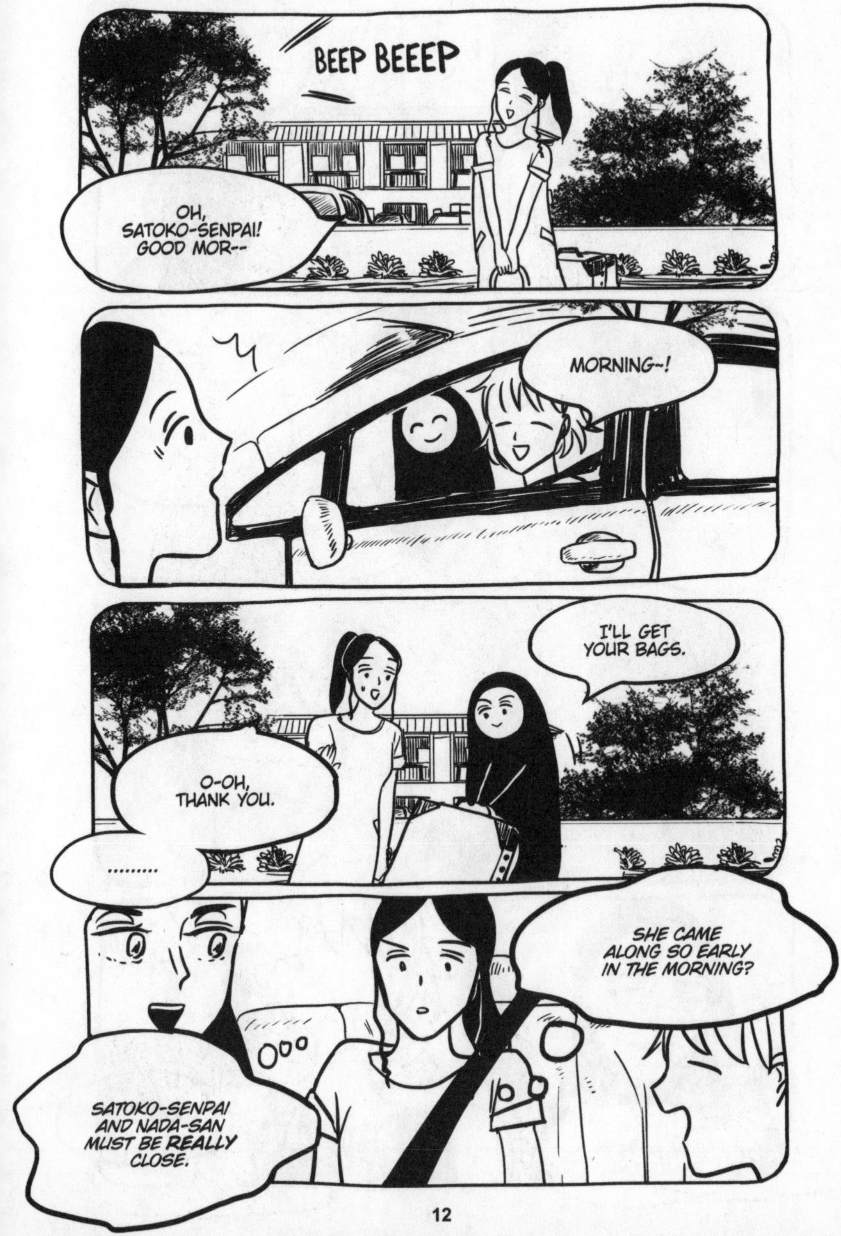

BEEP BEEEP
OH, SATOKO-SENPAI! GOOD MOR--
MORNING~!
I'LL GET YOUR BAGS.
O-OH, THANK YOU.
....
SHE CAME ALONG SO EARLY IN THE MORNING?
SATOKO-SENPAI AND NADA-SAN MUST BE REALLY CLOSE.

MACHIKO

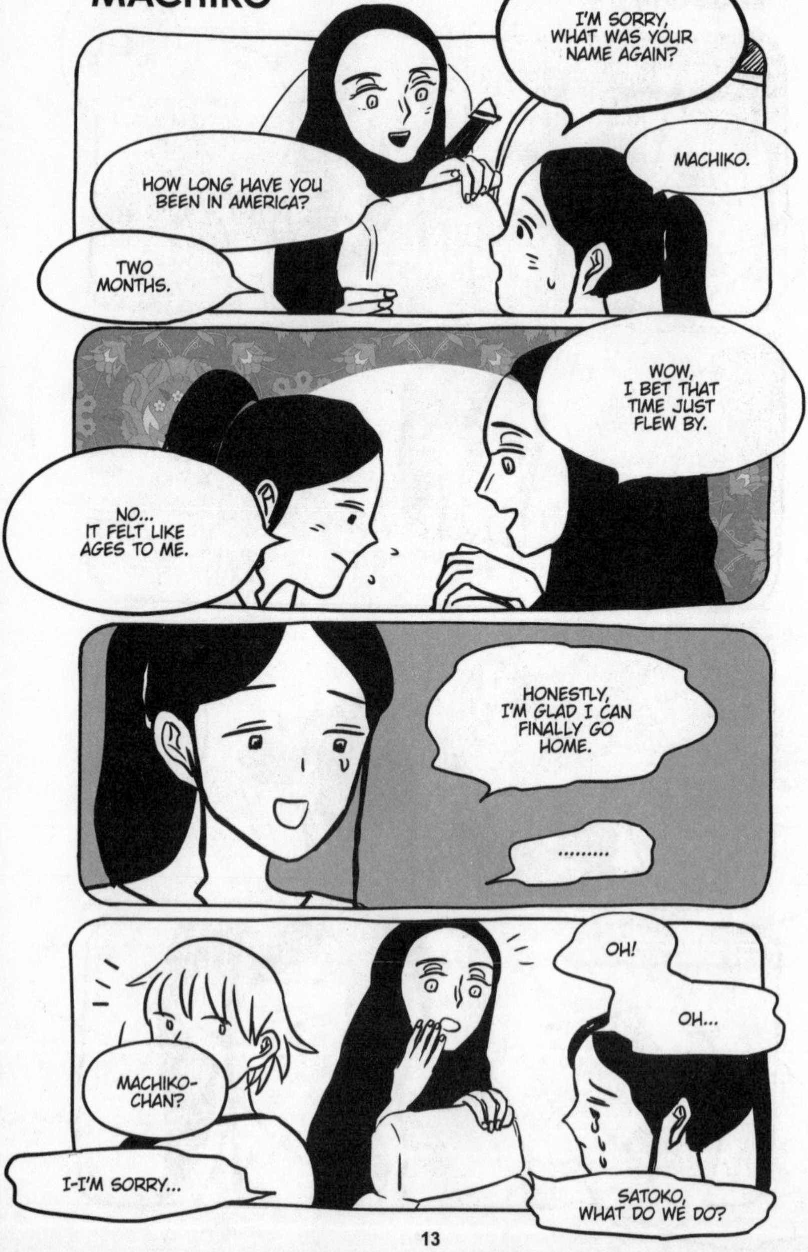

I'M SORRY, WHAT WAS YOUR NAME AGAIN?
MACHIKO.
HOW LONG HAVE YOU BEEN IN AMERICA?
TWO MONTHS.
WOW, I BET THAT TIME JUST FLEW BY.
NO... IT FELT LIKE AGES TO ME.
HONESTLY, I'M GLAD I CAN FINALLY GO HOME.
....
OH!
OH...
MACHIKO-CHAN?
I-I'M SORRY...
SATOKO, WHAT DO WE DO?

LESSON

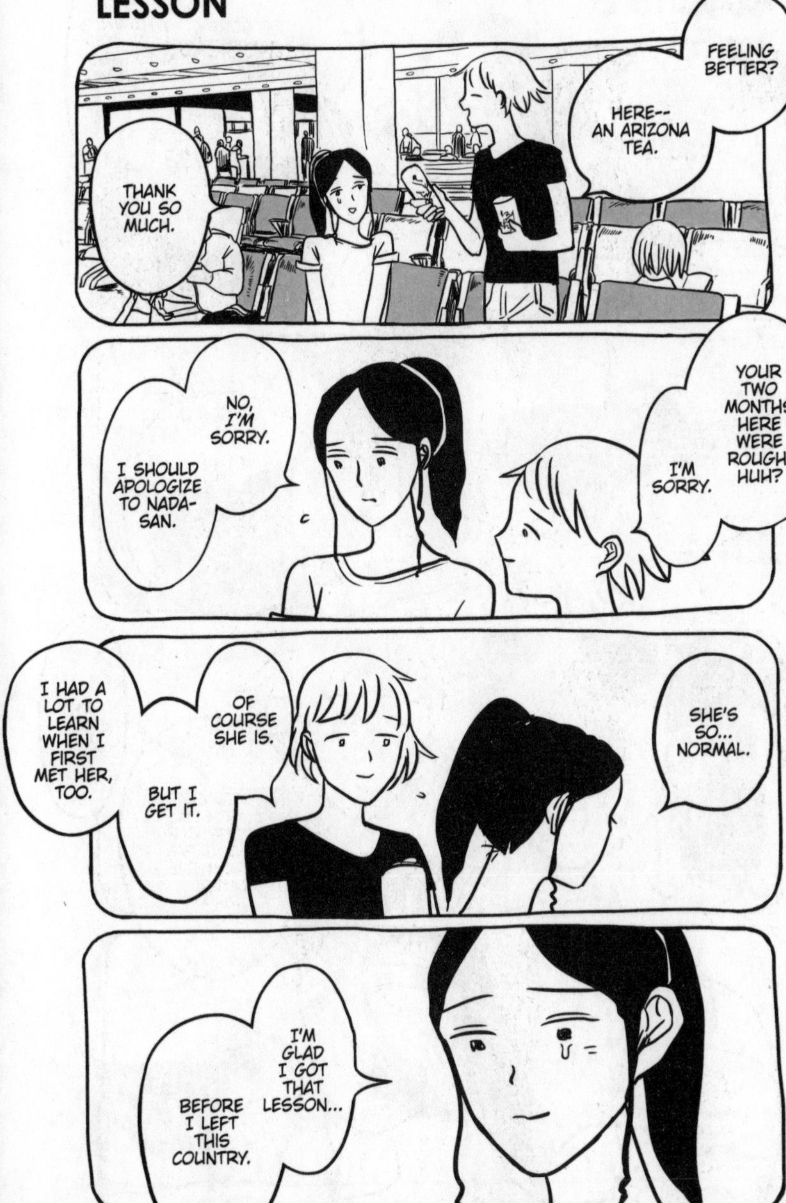
FEELING BETTER?
HERE-- AN ARIZONA TEA.
THANK YOU SO MUCH.
YOUR TWO MONTHS HERE WERE ROUGH, HUH?
I'M SORRY.
NO, *I'M* SORRY.
I SHOULD APOLOGIZE TO NADA-SAN.
SHE'S SO... NORMAL.
OF COURSE SHE IS.
BUT I GET IT.
I HAD A LOT TO LEARN WHEN I FIRST MET HER, TOO.
I'M GLAD I GOT THAT LESSON...
BEFORE I LEFT THIS COUNTRY.

IDEAL

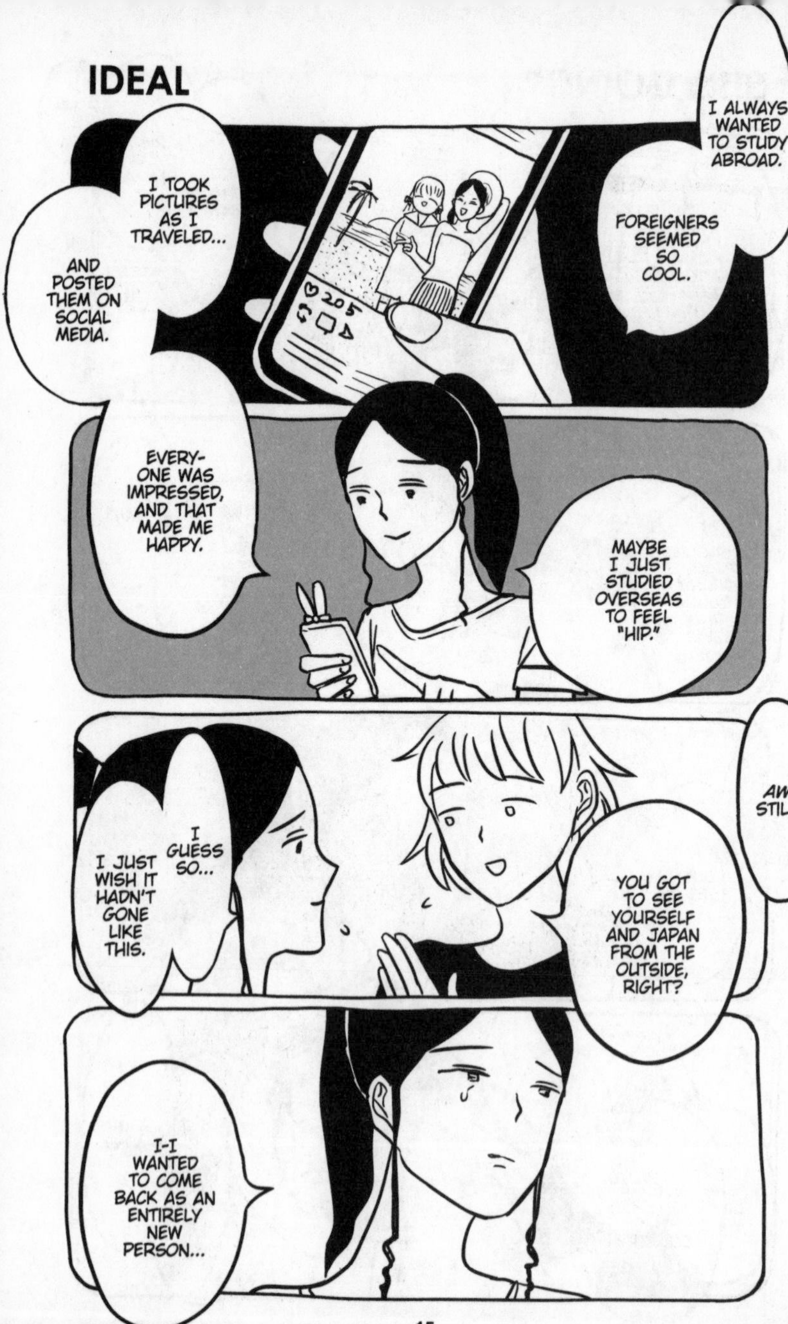

I ALWAYS WANTED TO STUDY ABROAD.
FOREIGNERS SEEMED SO COOL.
I TOOK PICTURES AS I TRAVELED...
AND POSTED THEM ON SOCIAL MEDIA.
205
EVERY-ONE WAS IMPRESSED, AND THAT MADE ME HAPPY.
MAYBE I JUST STUDIED OVERSEAS TO FEEL "HIP."
AW. STILL!
YOU GOT TO SEE YOURSELF AND JAPAN FROM THE OUTSIDE, RIGHT?
I GUESS SO...
I JUST WISH IT HADN'T GONE LIKE THIS.
I-I WANTED TO COME BACK AS AN ENTIRELY NEW PERSON...

STILL GOING?

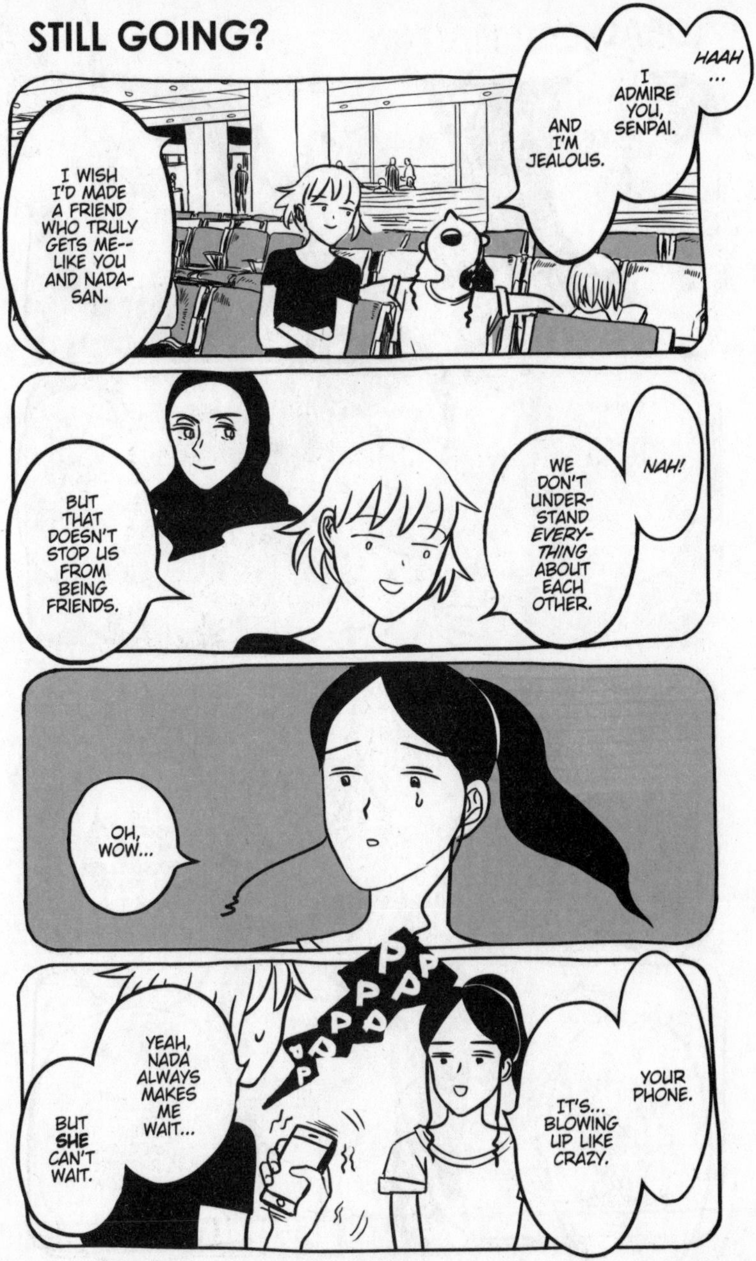
HAAH ...
I ADMIRE YOU, SENPAI.
AND I'M JEALOUS.
I WISH I'D MADE A FRIEND WHO TRULY GETS ME-- LIKE YOU AND NADA-SAN.
NAH!
WE DON'T UNDER-STAND *EVERY-THING* ABOUT EACH OTHER.
BUT THAT DOESN'T STOP US FROM BEING FRIENDS.
OH, WOW...
YOUR PHONE.
IT'S... BLOWING UP LIKE CRAZY.
PPPPPPPPPP
YEAH, NADA ALWAYS MAKES ME WAIT...
BUT **SHE** CAN'T WAIT.

ALL ABOUT NADA

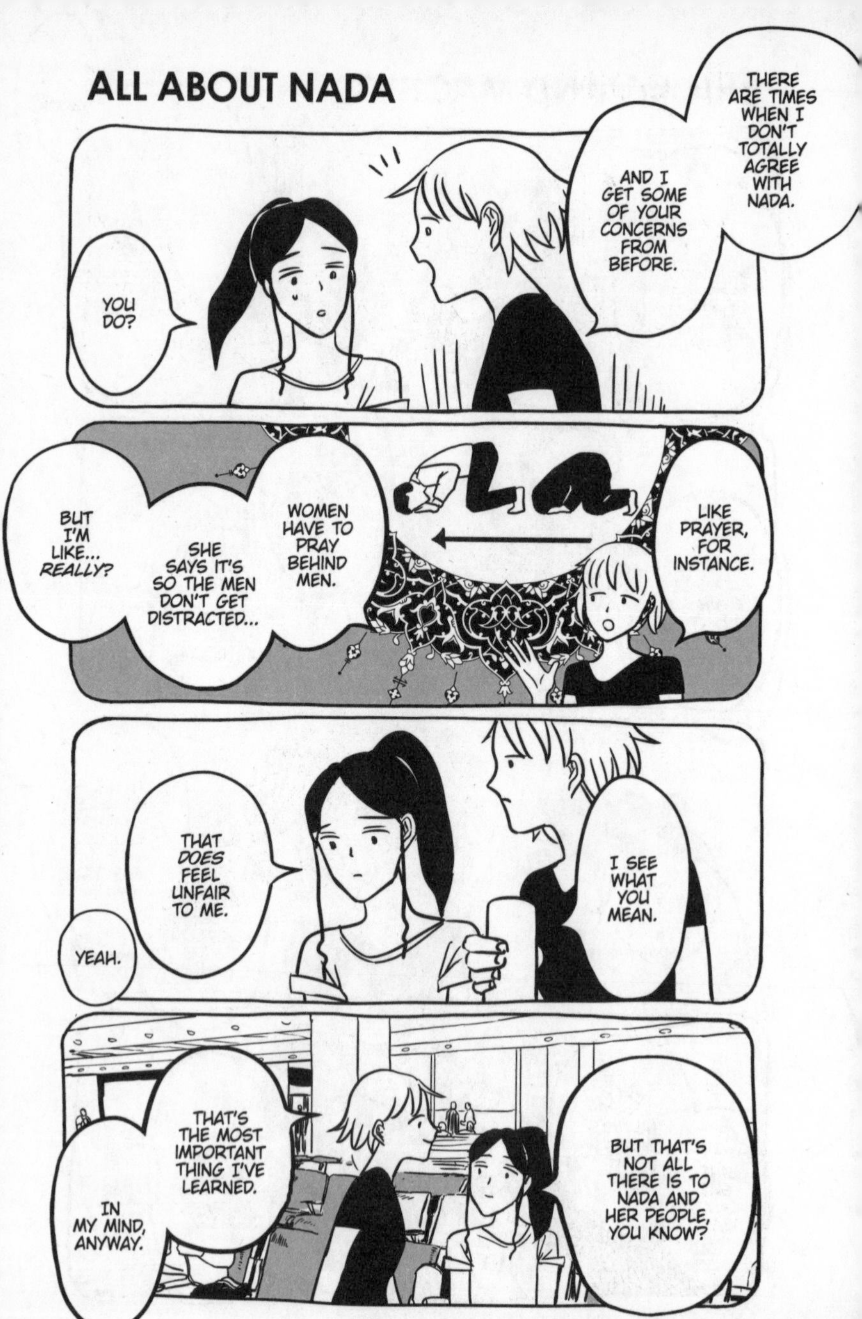
THERE ARE TIMES WHEN I DON'T TOTALLY AGREE WITH NADA.
AND I GET SOME OF YOUR CONCERNS FROM BEFORE.
YOU DO?
LIKE PRAYER, FOR INSTANCE.
La
WOMEN HAVE TO PRAY BEHIND MEN.
SHE SAYS IT'S SO THE MEN DON'T GET DISTRACTED...
BUT I'M LIKE... *REALLY?*
I SEE WHAT YOU MEAN.
THAT *DOES* FEEL UNFAIR TO ME.
YEAH.
BUT THAT'S NOT ALL THERE IS TO NADA AND HER PEOPLE, YOU KNOW?
THAT'S THE MOST IMPORTANT THING I'VE LEARNED.
IN MY MIND, ANYWAY.

SATOKO AND MACHIKO

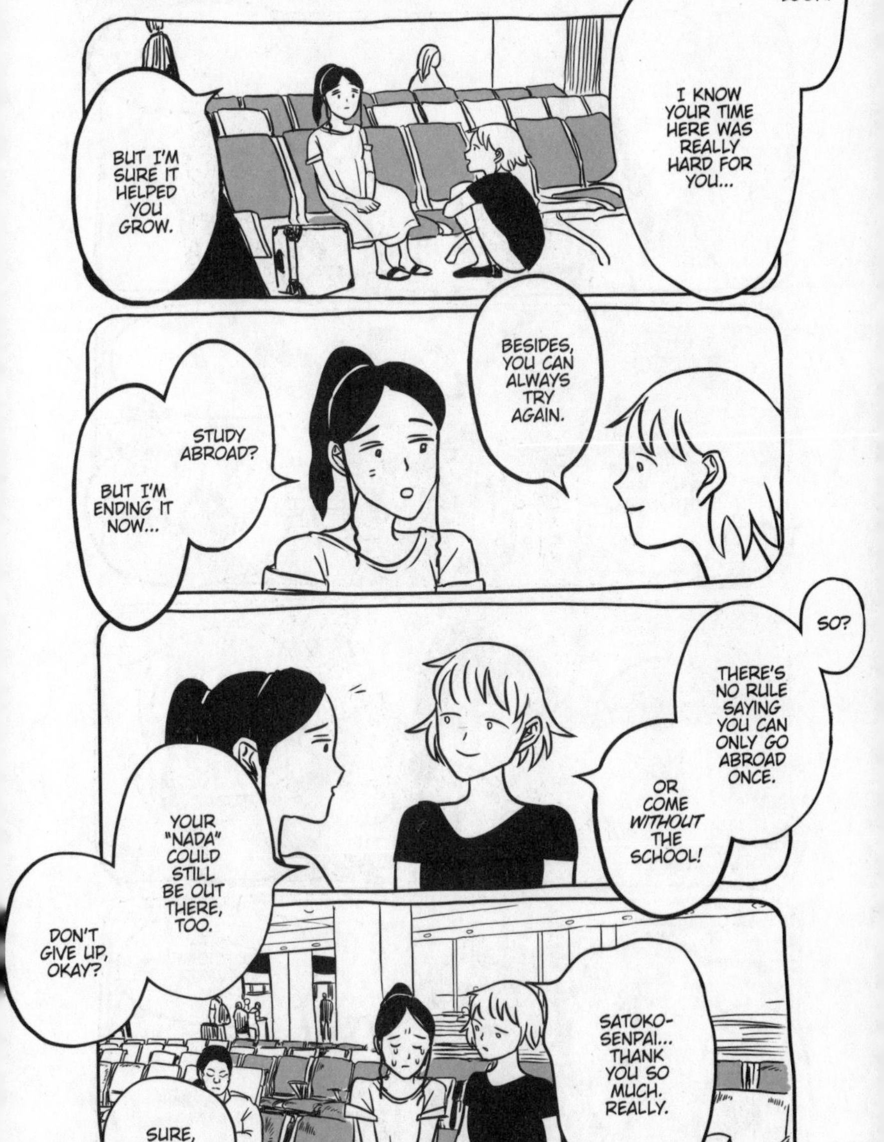
LOOK.
I KNOW YOUR TIME HERE WAS REALLY HARD FOR YOU...
BUT I'M SURE IT HELPED YOU GROW.
BESIDES, YOU CAN ALWAYS TRY AGAIN.
STUDY ABROAD?
BUT I'M ENDING IT NOW...
SO?
THERE'S NO RULE SAYING YOU CAN ONLY GO ABROAD ONCE.
OR COME *WITHOUT* THE SCHOOL!
YOUR "NADA" COULD STILL BE OUT THERE, TOO.
DON'T GIVE UP, OKAY?
SATOKO-SENPAI... THANK YOU SO MUCH. REALLY.
SURE, MACHIKO-CHAN.

MANY FORMS

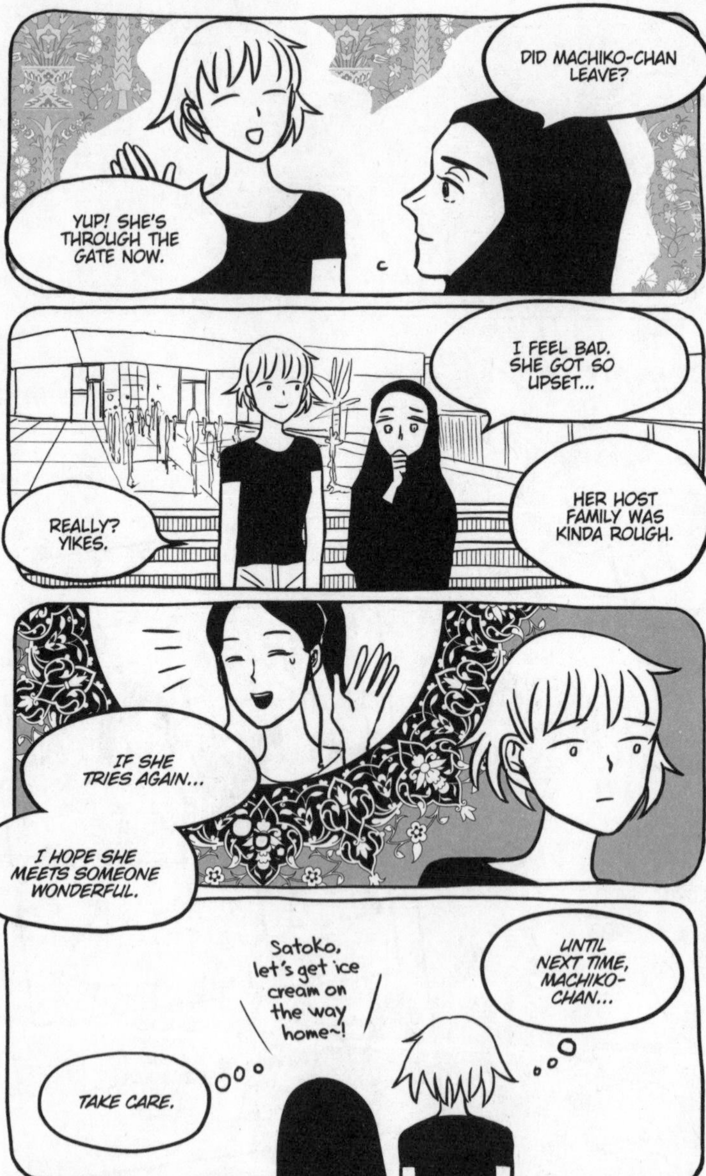
DID MACHIKO-CHAN LEAVE?
YUP! SHE'S THROUGH THE GATE NOW.
I FEEL BAD. SHE GOT SO UPSET...
HER HOST FAMILY WAS KINDA ROUGH.
REALLY? YIKES.
IF SHE TRIES AGAIN...
I HOPE SHE MEETS SOMEONE WONDERFUL.
UNTIL NEXT TIME, MACHIKO-CHAN...
Satoko, let's get ice cream on the way home~!
TAKE CARE.

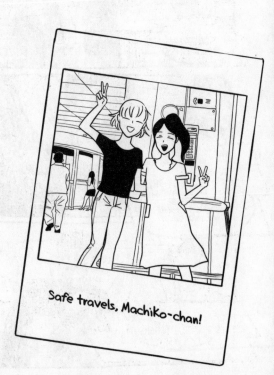

Safe travels, Machiko-chan!

ADVICE

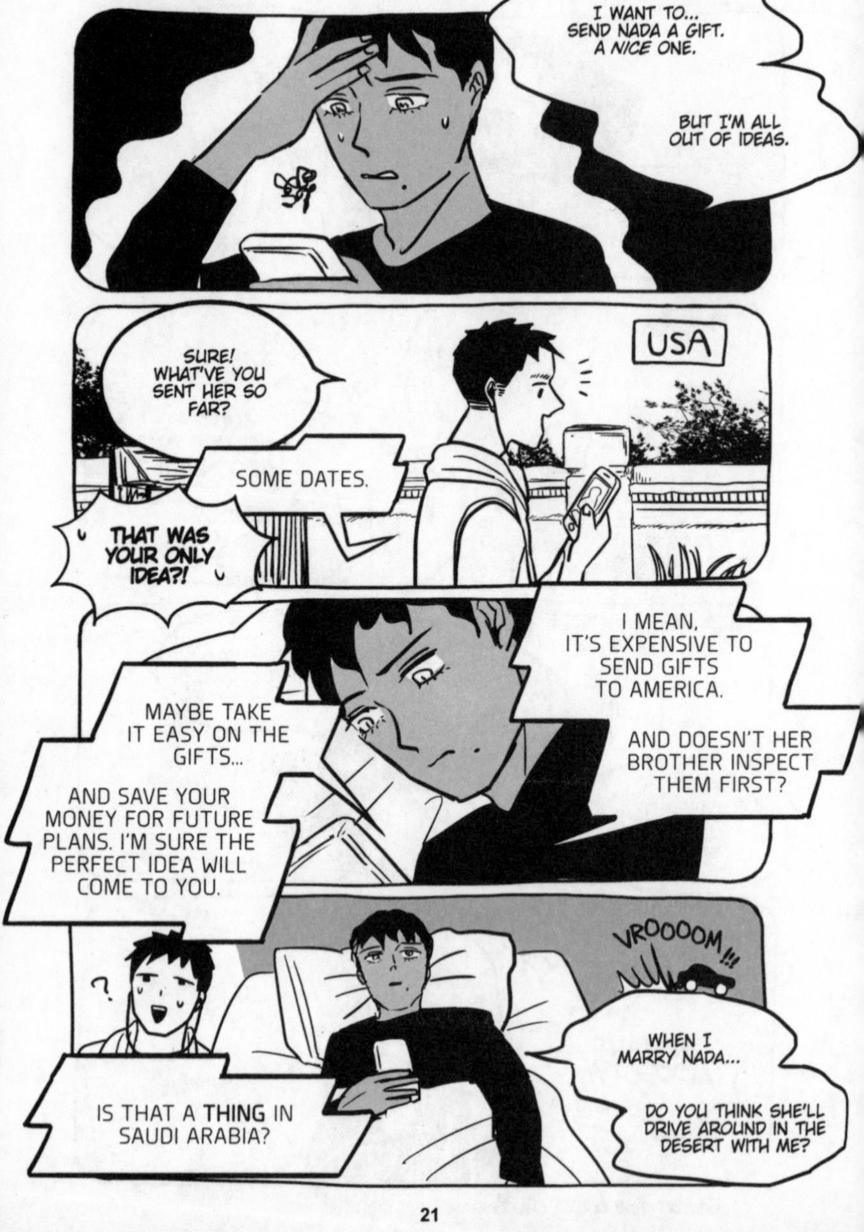
I WANT TO... SEND NADA A GIFT. A *NICE* ONE.
BUT I'M ALL OUT OF IDEAS.
USA
SURE! WHAT'VE YOU SENT HER SO FAR?
SOME DATES.
THAT WAS YOUR ONLY IDEA?!
I MEAN, IT'S EXPENSIVE TO SEND GIFTS TO AMERICA.
AND DOESN'T HER BROTHER INSPECT THEM FIRST?
MAYBE TAKE IT EASY ON THE GIFTS...
AND SAVE YOUR MONEY FOR FUTURE PLANS. I'M SURE THE PERFECT IDEA WILL COME TO YOU.
VROOOOM!!!
WHEN I MARRY NADA...
DO YOU THINK SHE'LL DRIVE AROUND IN THE DESERT WITH ME?
?
IS THAT A **THING** IN SAUDI ARABIA?

LIFE HACKS

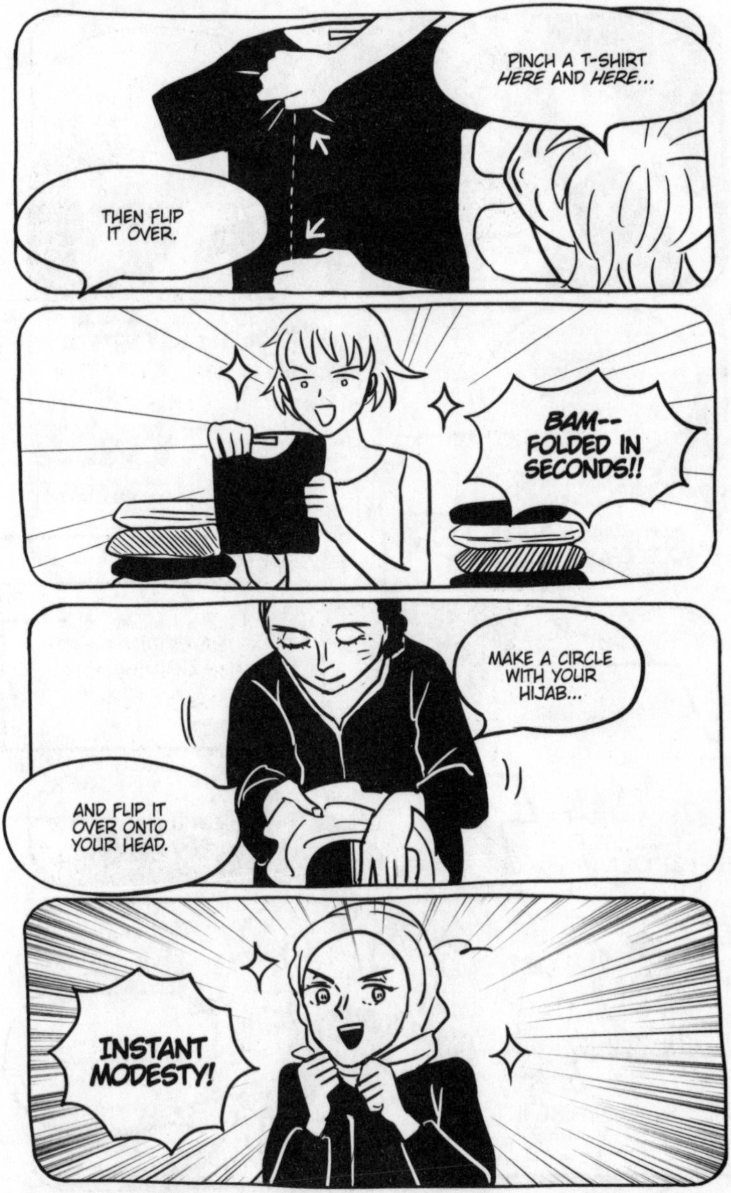
PINCH A T-SHIRT *HERE* AND *HERE*...
THEN FLIP IT OVER.
BAM-- FOLDED IN SECONDS!!
MAKE A CIRCLE WITH YOUR HIJAB...
AND FLIP IT OVER ONTO YOUR HEAD.
INSTANT MODESTY!

Great for a girl on the go!

NUMBER OF MINARETS

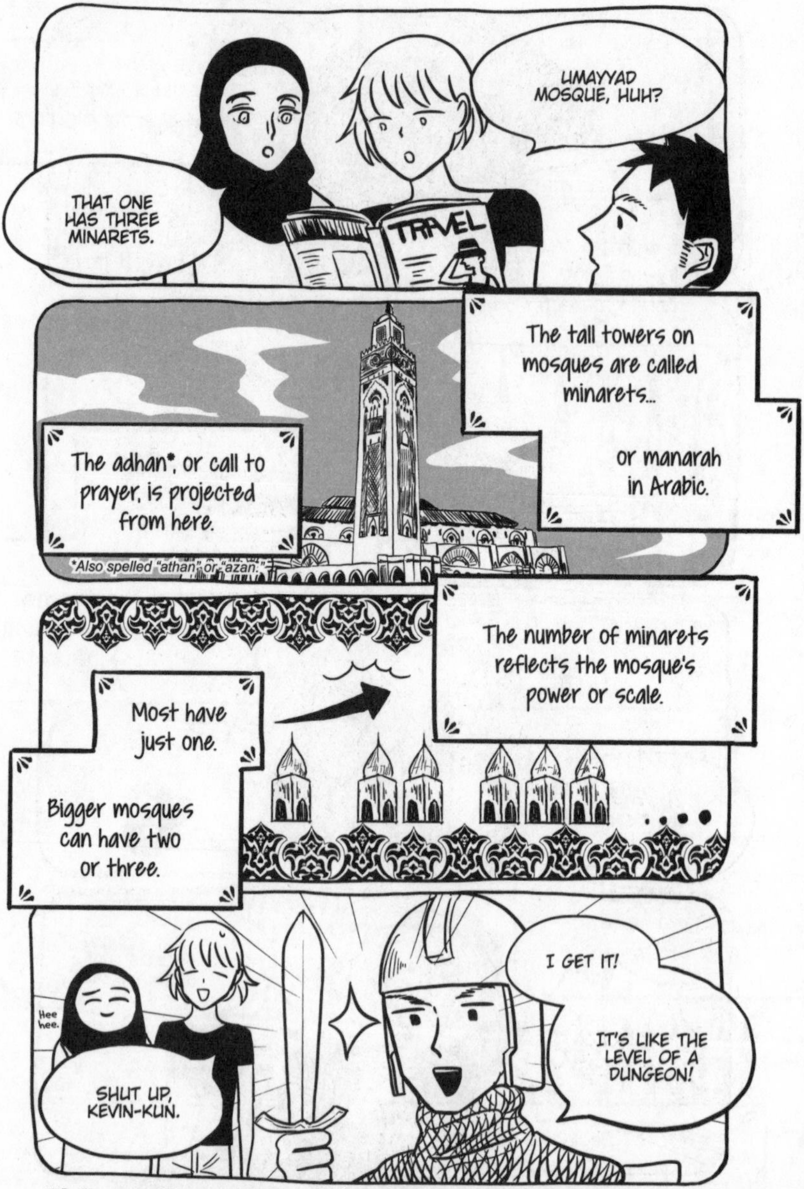
UMAYYAD MOSQUE, HUH?
THAT ONE HAS THREE MINARETS.
TRAVEL
The tall towers on mosques are called minarets...
or manarah in Arabic.
The adhan*, or call to prayer, is projected from here.
*Also spelled "athan" or "azan."
The number of minarets reflects the mosque's power or scale.
Most have just one.
Bigger mosques can have two or three.
I GET IT!
IT'S LIKE THE LEVEL OF A DUNGEON!
Hee hee.
SHUT UP, KEVIN-KUN.

※ By the way, a mosque is usually called a "masjid" (meaning "a place of prostration") in Arabic.

SENSITIVE

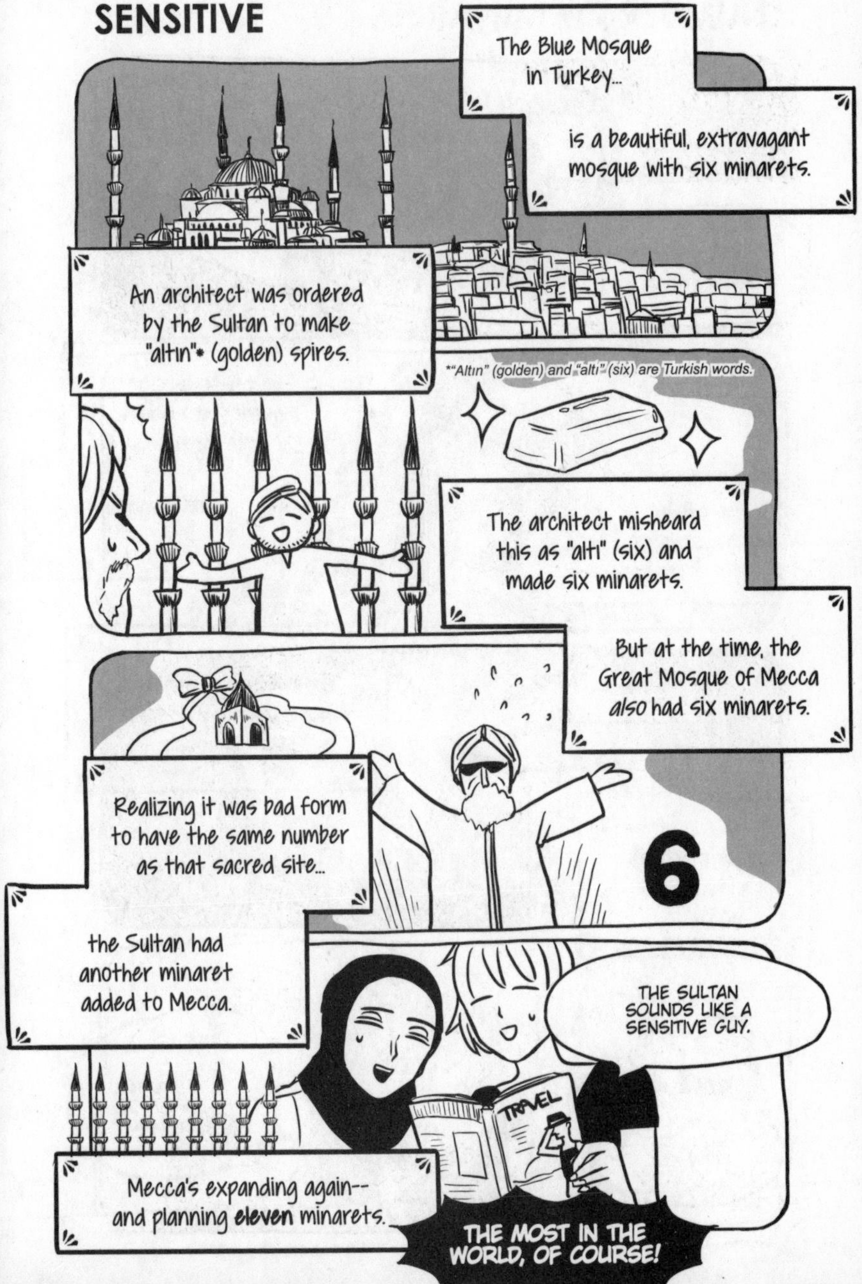
The Blue Mosque in Turkey...
is a beautiful, extravagant mosque with six minarets.
An architect was ordered by the Sultan to make "altın"* (golden) spires.
*"Altın" (golden) and "altı" (six) are Turkish words.
The architect misheard this as "altı" (six) and made six minarets.
But at the time, the Great Mosque of Mecca also had six minarets.
6
Realizing it was bad form to have the same number as that sacred site...
the Sultan had another minaret added to Mecca.
THE SULTAN SOUNDS LIKE A SENSITIVE GUY.
TRAVEL
Mecca's expanding again--and planning **eleven** minarets.
THE MOST IN THE WORLD, OF COURSE!

CAT

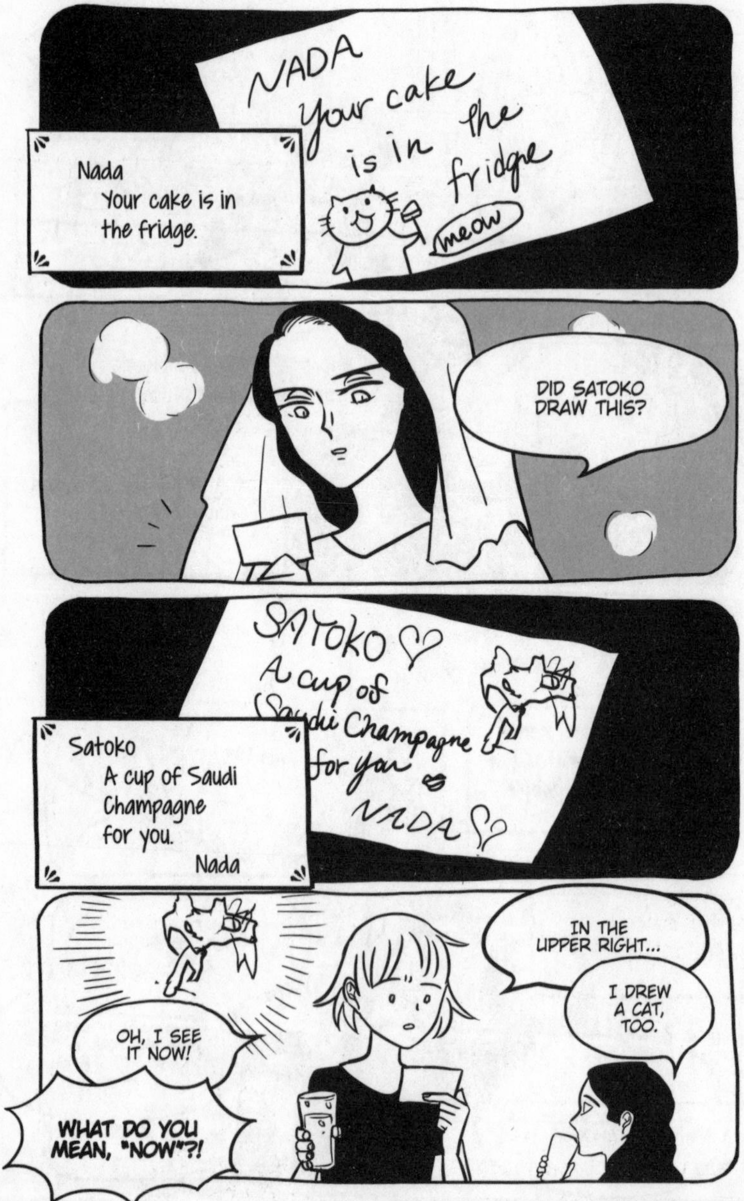
NADA
Your cake
is in the
fridge
meow
Nada
Your cake is in
the fridge.
DID SATOKO DRAW THIS?
SATOKO
A cup of
Champagne
for you
NADA
Satoko
A cup of Saudi
Champagne
for you.
Nada
IN THE UPPER RIGHT...
I DREW A CAT, TOO.
OH, I SEE IT NOW!
WHAT DO YOU MEAN, "NOW"?!

ART LESSONS

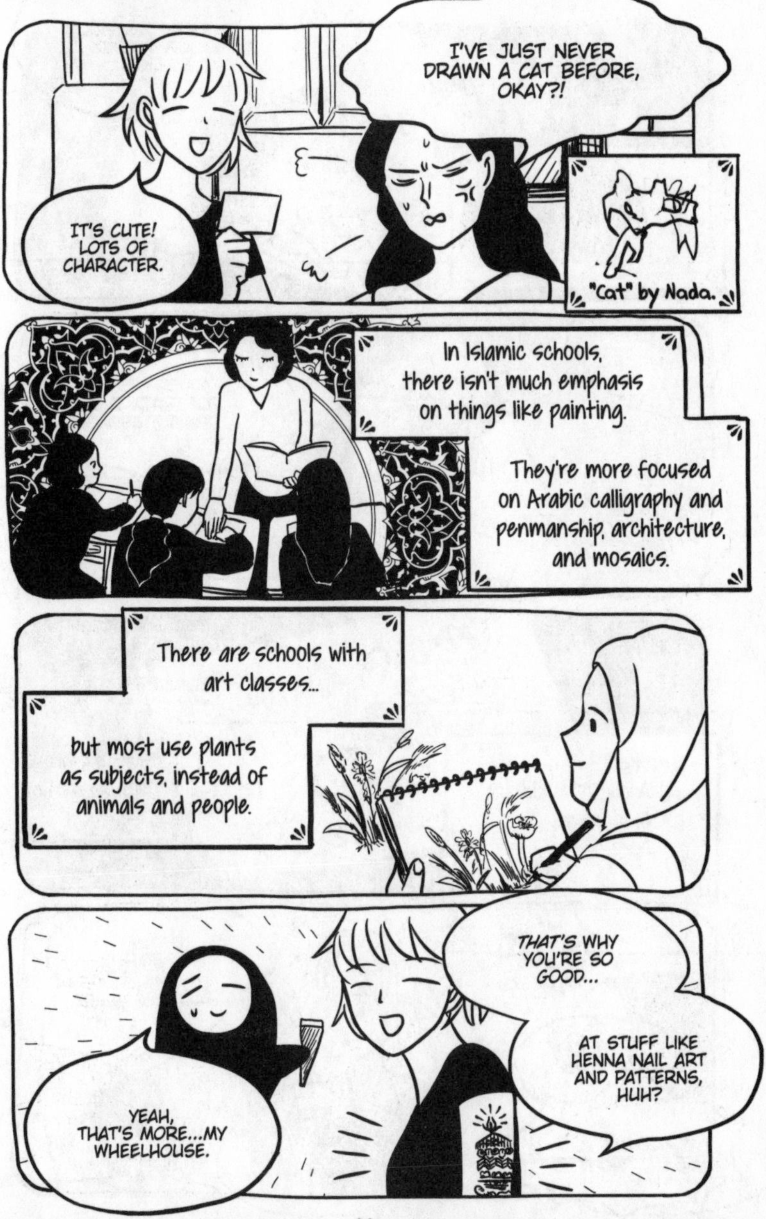
I'VE JUST NEVER DRAWN A CAT BEFORE, OKAY?!
"Cat" by Nada.
IT'S CUTE! LOTS OF CHARACTER.
In Islamic schools, there isn't much emphasis on things like painting.
They're more focused on Arabic calligraphy and penmanship, architecture, and mosaics.
There are schools with art classes...
but most use plants as subjects, instead of animals and people.
THAT'S WHY YOU'RE SO GOOD...
AT STUFF LIKE HENNA NAIL ART AND PATTERNS, HUH?
YEAH, THAT'S MORE...MY WHEELHOUSE.

IDOLATRY

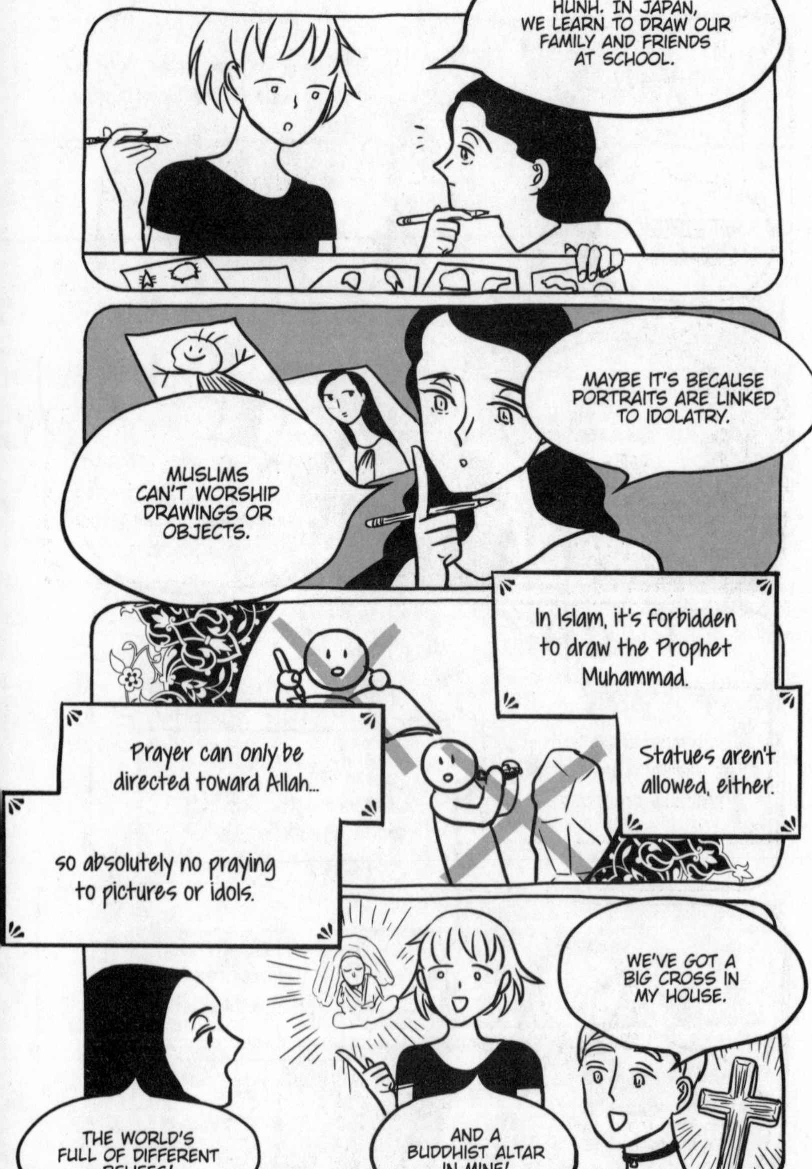
HUNH. IN JAPAN, WE LEARN TO DRAW OUR FAMILY AND FRIENDS AT SCHOOL.
MAYBE IT'S BECAUSE PORTRAITS ARE LINKED TO IDOLATRY.
MUSLIMS CAN'T WORSHIP DRAWINGS OR OBJECTS.
In Islam, it's forbidden to draw the Prophet Muhammad.
Statues aren't allowed, either.
Prayer can only be directed toward Allah...
so absolutely no praying to pictures or idols.
WE'VE GOT A BIG CROSS IN MY HOUSE.
AND A BUDDHIST ALTAR IN MINE!
THE WORLD'S FULL OF DIFFERENT BELIEFS!

DESTRUCTION

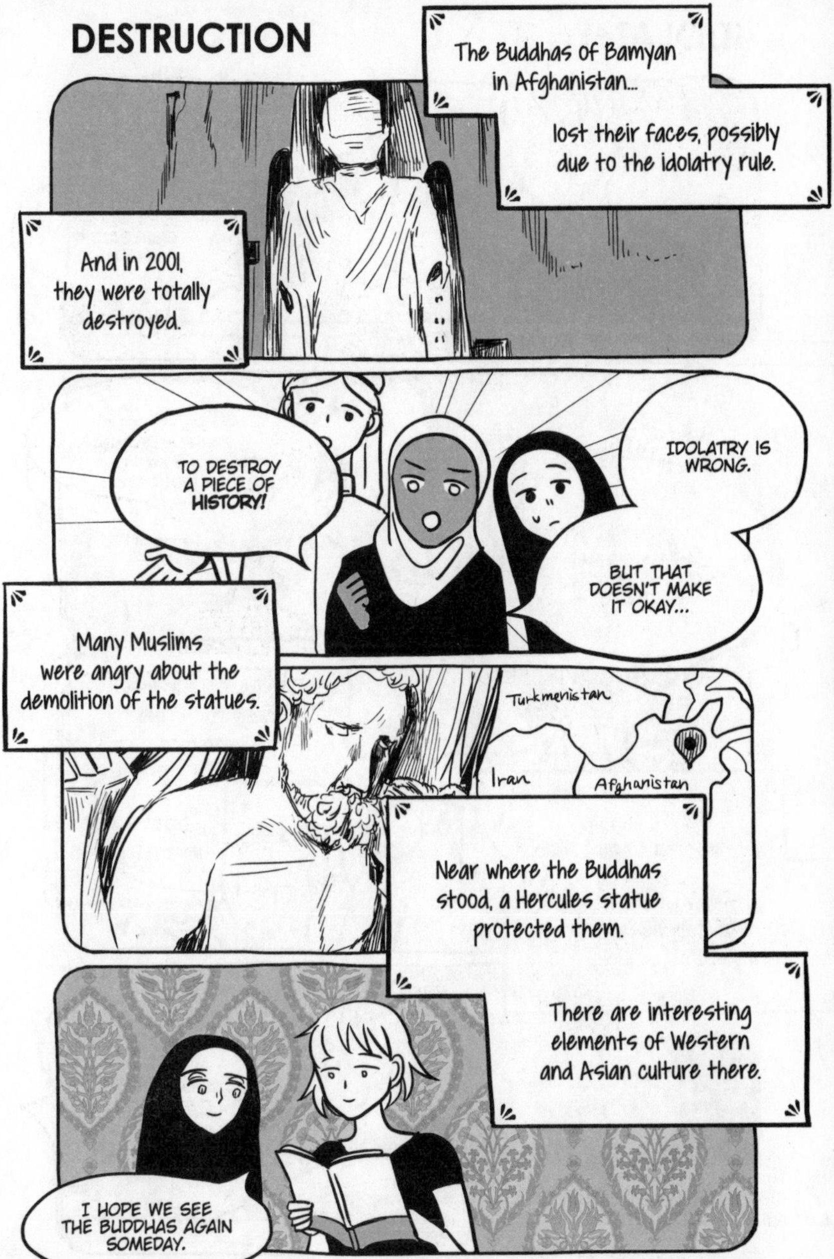
The Buddhas of Bamyan in Afghanistan...
lost their faces, possibly due to the idolatry rule.
And in 2001, they were totally destroyed.
IDOLATRY IS WRONG.
BUT THAT DOESN'T MAKE IT OKAY...
TO DESTROY A PIECE OF **HISTORY!**
Many Muslims were angry about the demolition of the statues.
Turkmenistan
Iran
Afghanistan
Near where the Buddhas stood, a Hercules statue protected them.
There are interesting elements of Western and Asian culture there.
I HOPE WE SEE THE BUDDHAS AGAIN SOMEDAY.

BEWITCHING

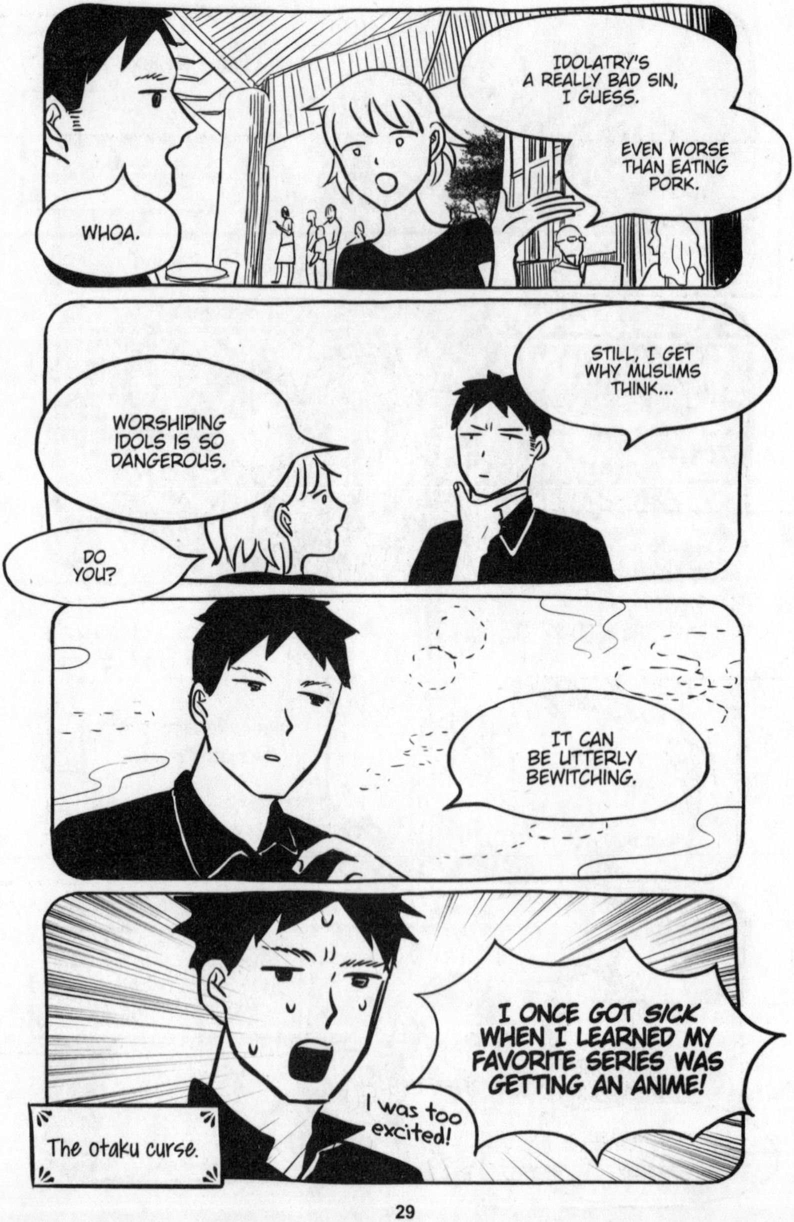
IDOLATRY'S A REALLY BAD SIN, I GUESS.
EVEN WORSE THAN EATING PORK.
WHOA.
STILL, I GET WHY MUSLIMS THINK...
WORSHIPING IDOLS IS SO DANGEROUS.
DO YOU?
IT CAN BE UTTERLY BEWITCHING.
I ONCE GOT *SICK* WHEN I LEARNED MY FAVORITE SERIES WAS GETTING AN ANIME!
I was too excited!
The otaku curse.

ARABIC CALLIGRAPHY

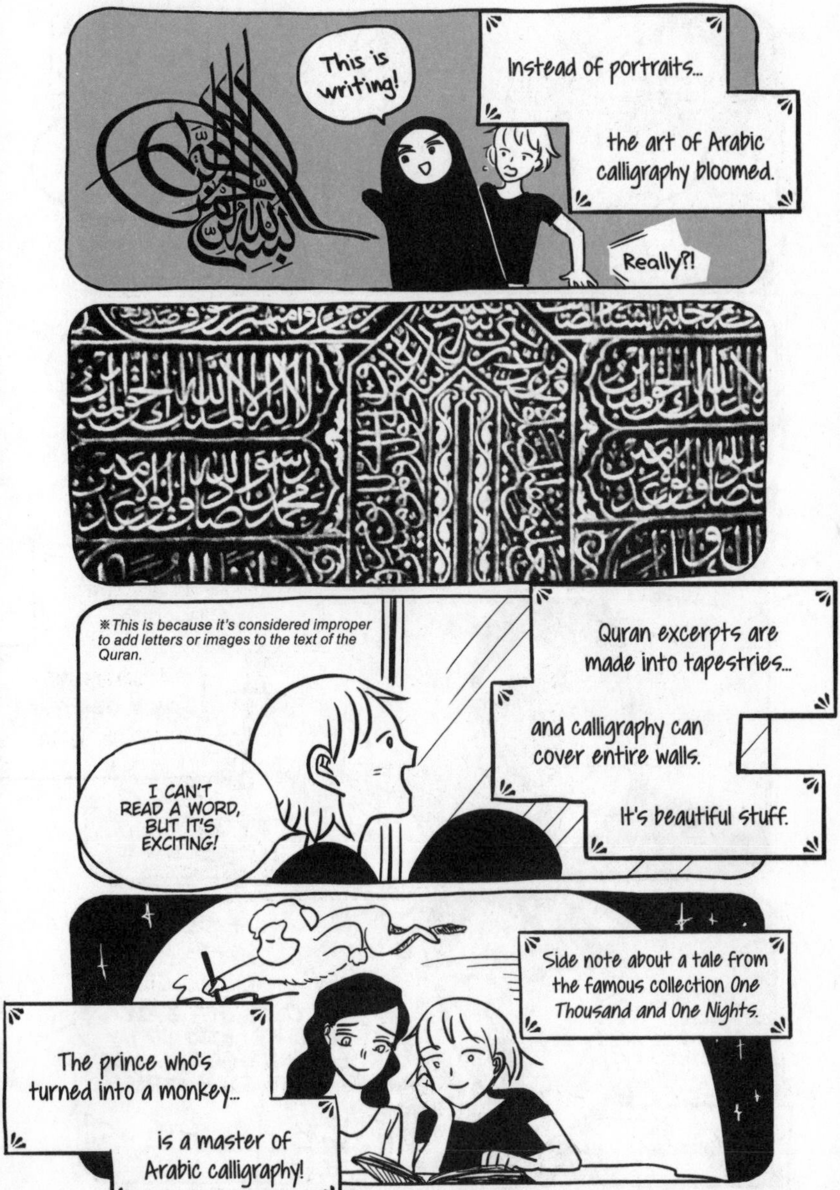
This is writing!
Instead of portraits...
the art of Arabic calligraphy bloomed.
Really?!
※This is because it's considered improper to add letters or images to the text of the Quran.
I CAN'T READ A WORD, BUT IT'S EXCITING!
Quran excerpts are made into tapestries...
and calligraphy can cover entire walls.
It's beautiful stuff.
The prince who's turned into a monkey...
is a master of Arabic calligraphy!
Side note about a tale from the famous collection One Thousand and One Nights.

IT'S ALL WRITING

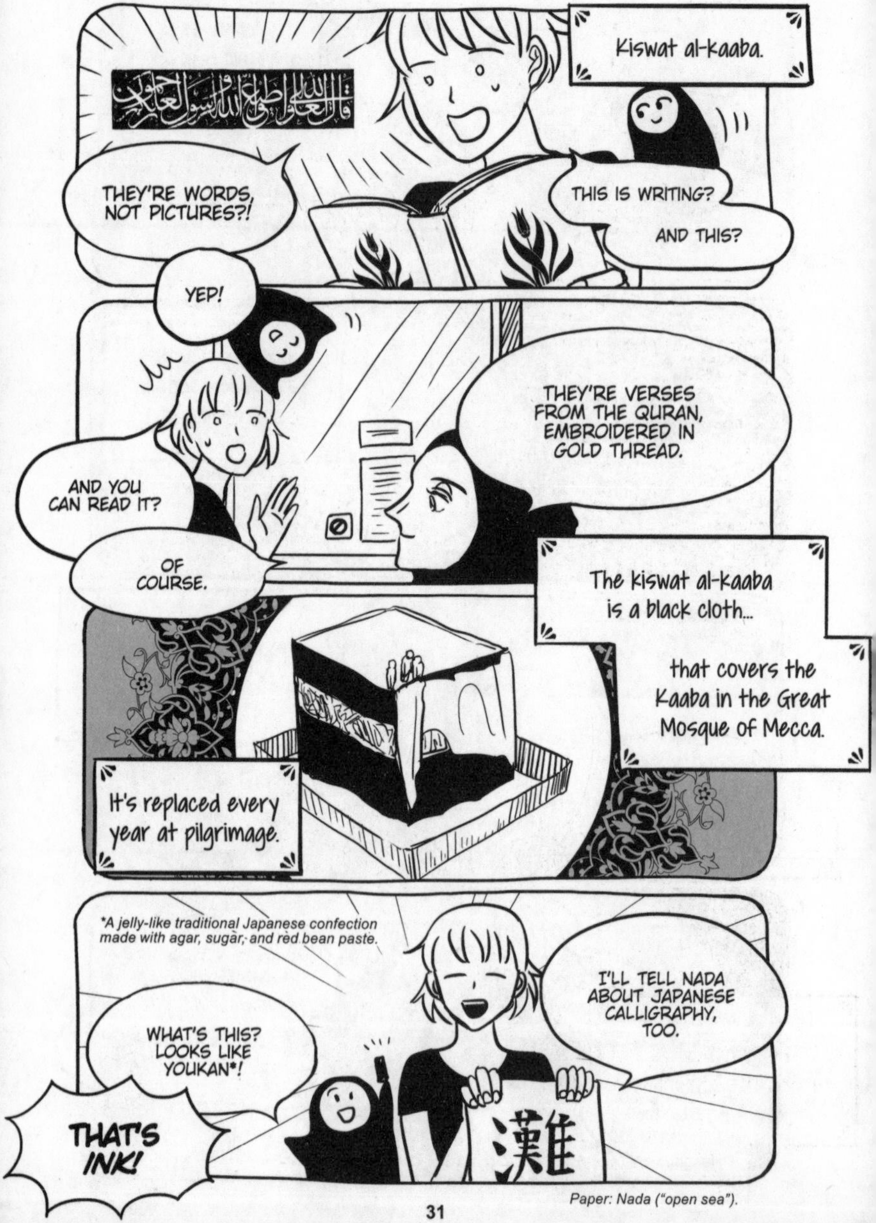
Kiswat al-kaaba.
THIS IS WRITING?
AND THIS?
THEY'RE WORDS, NOT PICTURES?!
YEP!
THEY'RE VERSES FROM THE QURAN, EMBROIDERED IN GOLD THREAD.
AND YOU CAN READ IT?
OF COURSE.
The kiswat al-kaaba is a black cloth...
that covers the Kaaba in the Great Mosque of Mecca.
It's replaced every year at pilgrimage.
I'LL TELL NADA ABOUT JAPANESE CALLIGRAPHY, TOO.
WHAT'S THIS? LOOKS LIKE YOUKAN*!
THAT'S INK!
灘
*A jelly-like traditional Japanese confection made with agar, sugar, and red bean paste.

Paper: Nada ("open sea").

DOGU

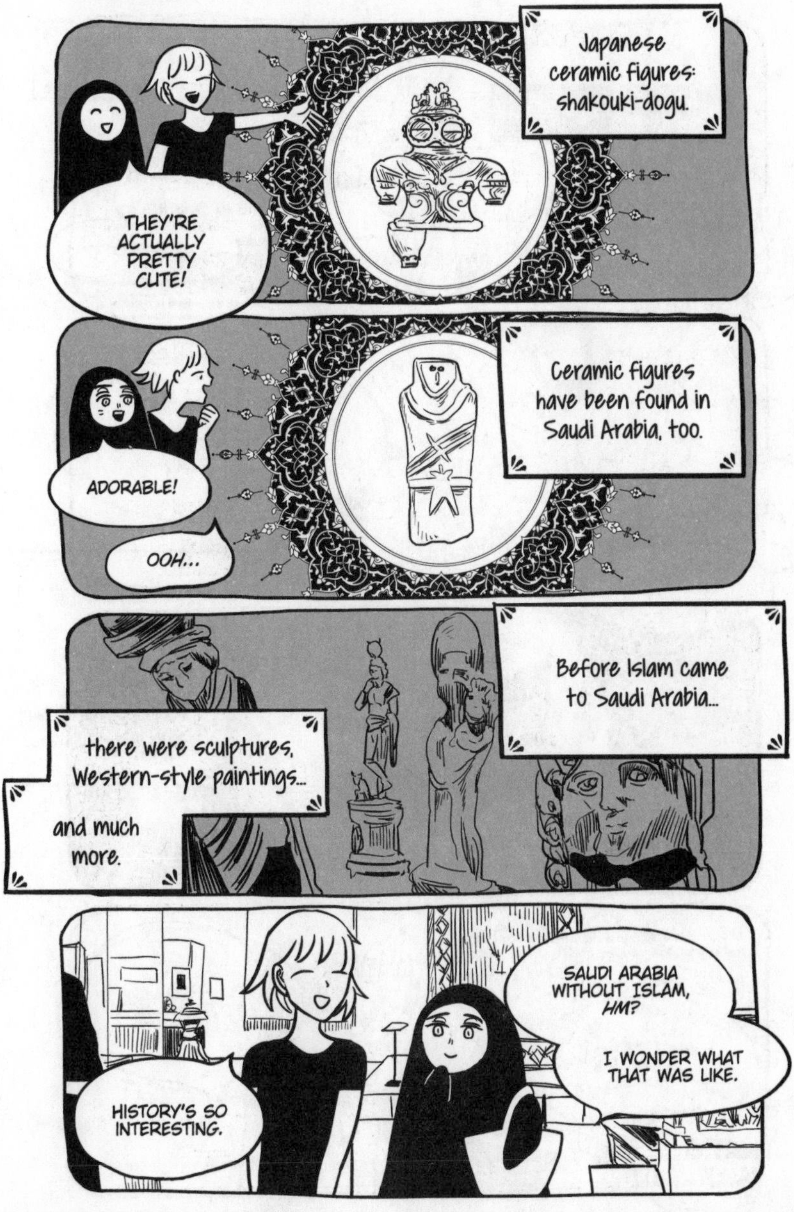

Japanese ceramic figures: shakouki-dogu.
THEY'RE ACTUALLY PRETTY CUTE!
Ceramic figures have been found in Saudi Arabia, too.
ADORABLE!
OOH...
Before Islam came to Saudi Arabia...
there were sculptures, Western-style paintings...
and much more.
SAUDI ARABIA WITHOUT ISLAM, *HM?*
I WONDER WHAT THAT WAS LIKE.
HISTORY'S SO INTERESTING.

TIP

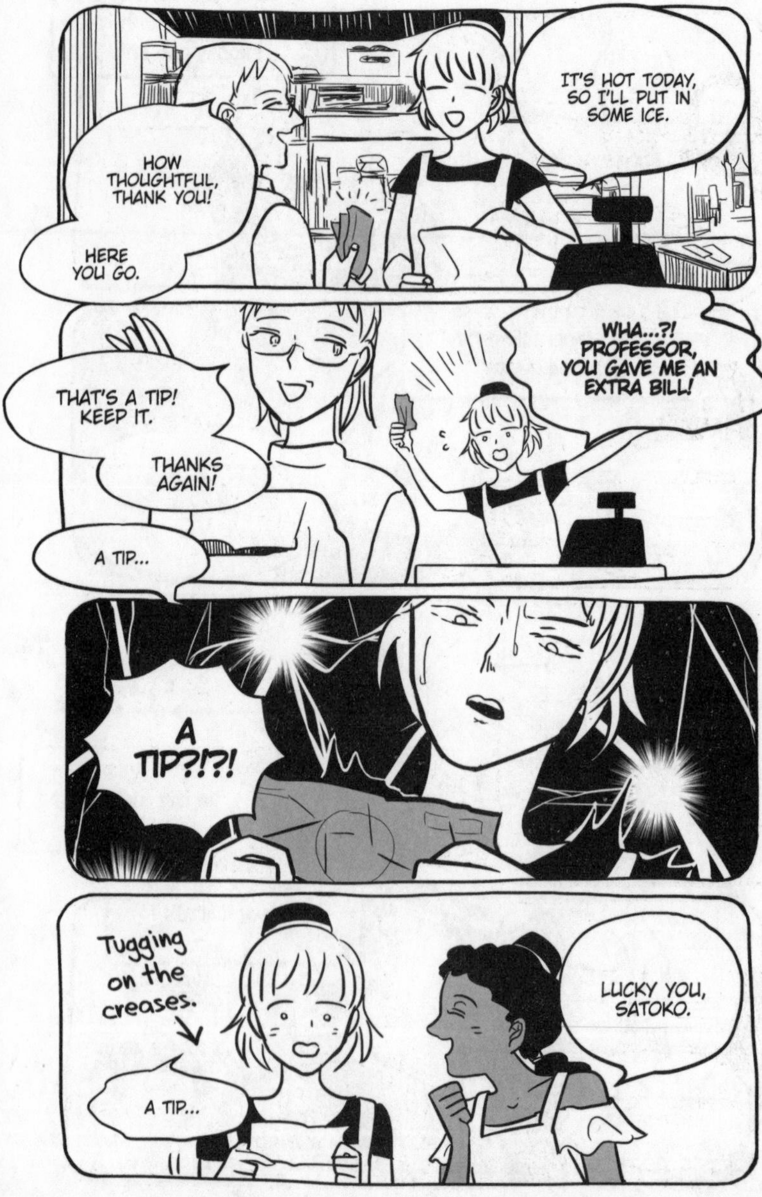
IT'S HOT TODAY, SO I'LL PUT IN SOME ICE.
HOW THOUGHTFUL, THANK YOU!
HERE YOU GO.
WHA...?! PROFESSOR, YOU GAVE ME AN EXTRA BILL!
THAT'S A TIP! KEEP IT.
THANKS AGAIN!
A TIP...
A TIP?!?!
LUCKY YOU, SATOKO.
Tugging on the creases.
A TIP...

TIP 2

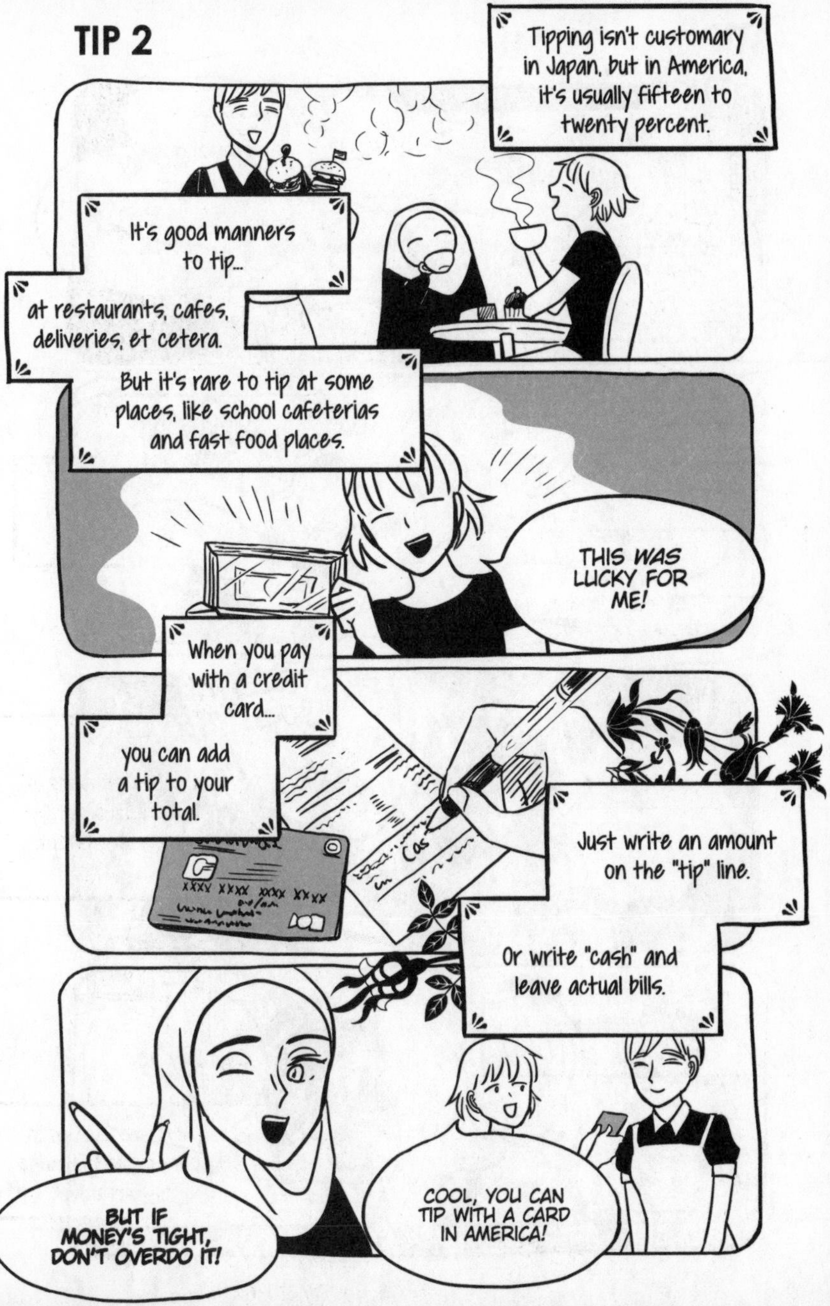

Tipping isn't customary in Japan, but in America, it's usually fifteen to twenty percent.
It's good manners to tip...
at restaurants, cafes, deliveries, et cetera.
But it's rare to tip at some places, like school cafeterias and fast food places.
THIS WAS LUCKY FOR ME!
When you pay with a credit card...
you can add a tip to your total.
Just write an amount on the "tip" line.
Or write "cash" and leave actual bills.
COOL, YOU CAN TIP WITH A CARD IN AMERICA!
BUT IF MONEY'S TIGHT, DON'T OVERDO IT!

TIP 3

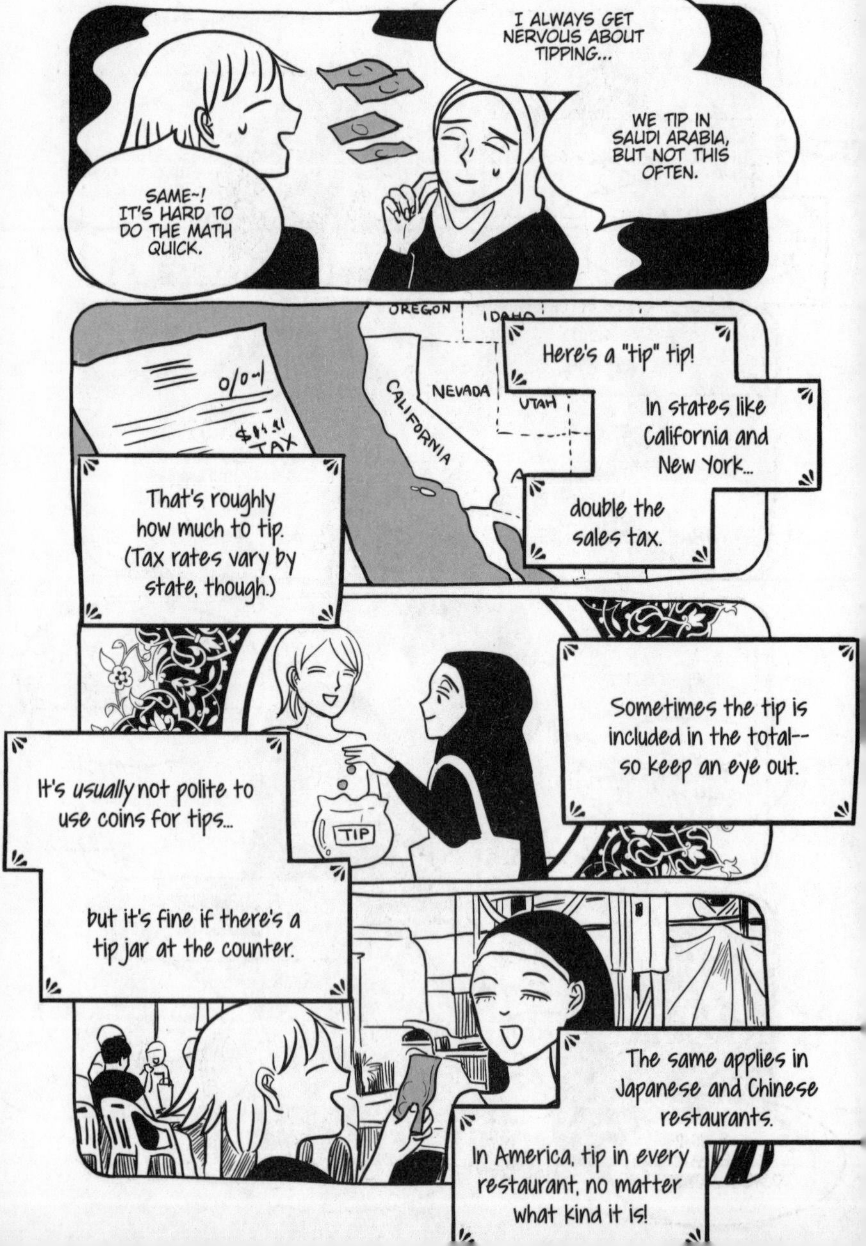
I ALWAYS GET NERVOUS ABOUT TIPPING...
WE TIP IN SAUDI ARABIA, BUT NOT THIS OFTEN.
SAME~! IT'S HARD TO DO THE MATH QUICK.
Here's a "tip" tip!
In states like California and New York...
double the sales tax.
OREGON
NEVADA
UTAH
CALIFORNIA
TAX
That's roughly how much to tip. (Tax rates vary by state, though.)
Sometimes the tip is included in the total--so keep an eye out.
It's *usually* not polite to use coins for tips...
TIP
but it's fine if there's a tip jar at the counter.
The same applies in Japanese and Chinese restaurants.
In America, tip in every restaurant, no matter what kind it is!

DECISION

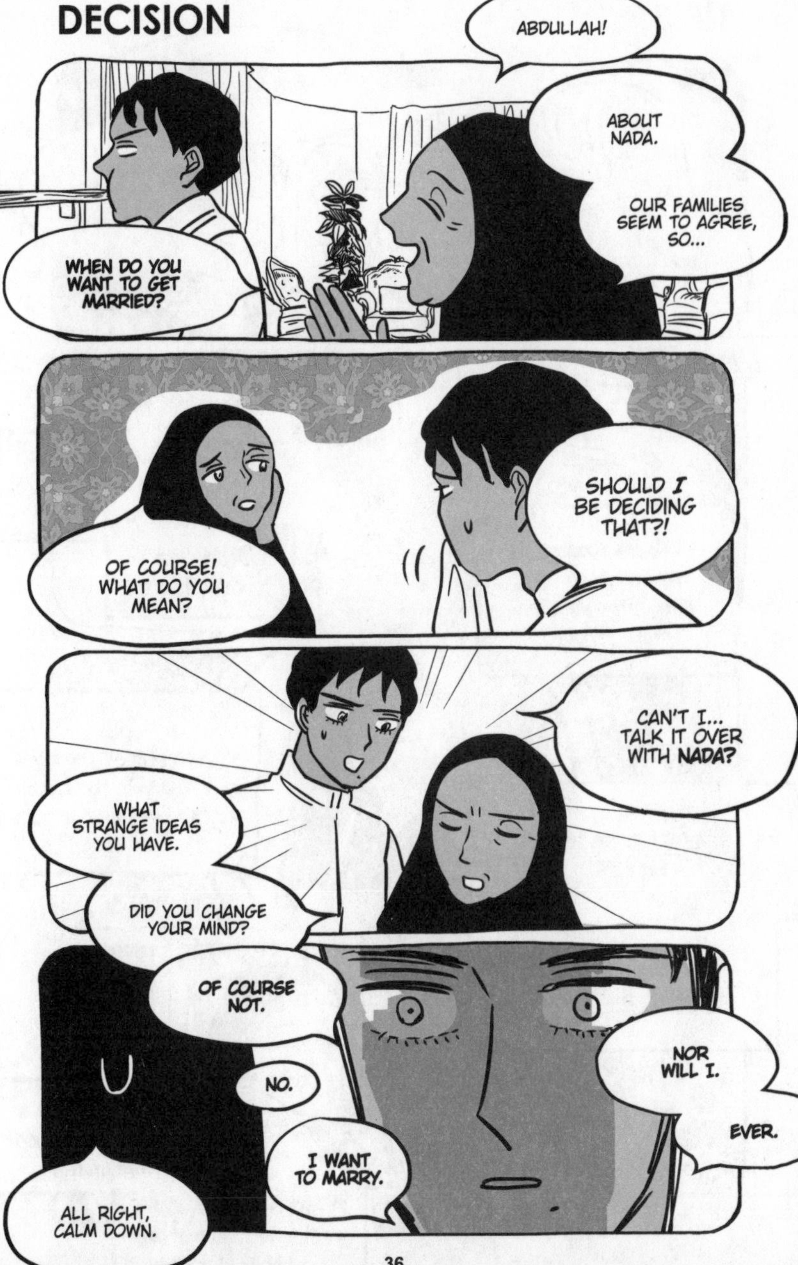

ABDULLAH!
ABOUT NADA.
OUR FAMILIES SEEM TO AGREE, SO...
WHEN DO YOU WANT TO GET MARRIED?
SHOULD *I* BE DECIDING THAT?!
OF COURSE! WHAT DO YOU MEAN?
CAN'T I... TALK IT OVER WITH NADA?
WHAT STRANGE IDEAS YOU HAVE.
DID YOU CHANGE YOUR MIND?
OF COURSE NOT.
NOR WILL I.
EVER.
NO.
I WANT TO MARRY.
ALL RIGHT, CALM DOWN.

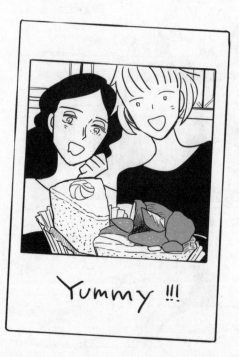

Yummy !!!

FOR THE SHAWFA

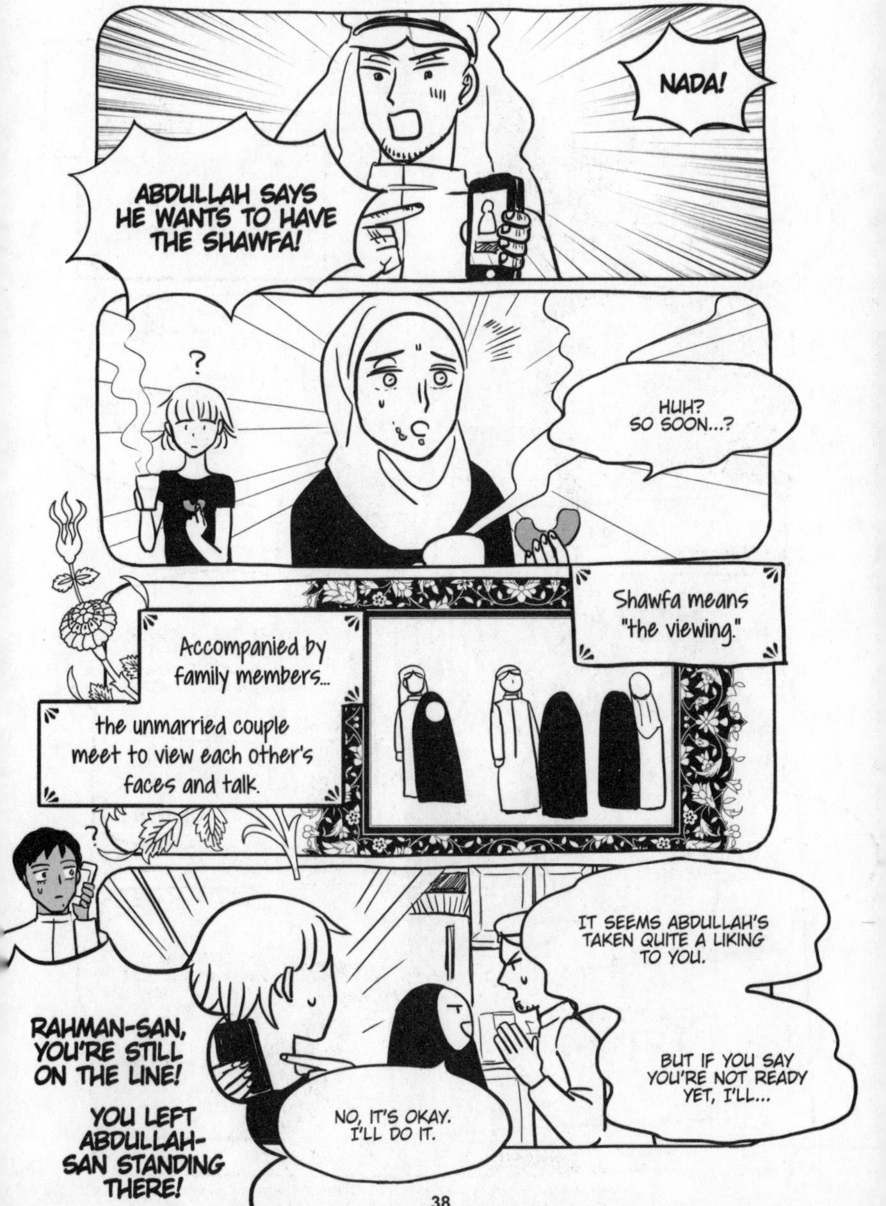
NADA!
ABDULLAH SAYS HE WANTS TO HAVE THE SHAWFA!
HUH? SO SOON...?
Shawfa means "the viewing."
Accompanied by family members...
the unmarried couple meet to view each other's faces and talk.
IT SEEMS ABDULLAH'S TAKEN QUITE A LIKING TO YOU.
BUT IF YOU SAY YOU'RE NOT READY YET, I'LL...
NO, IT'S OKAY. I'LL DO IT.
RAHMAN-SAN, YOU'RE STILL ON THE LINE!
YOU LEFT ABDULLAH-SAN STANDING THERE!

A PROMISE

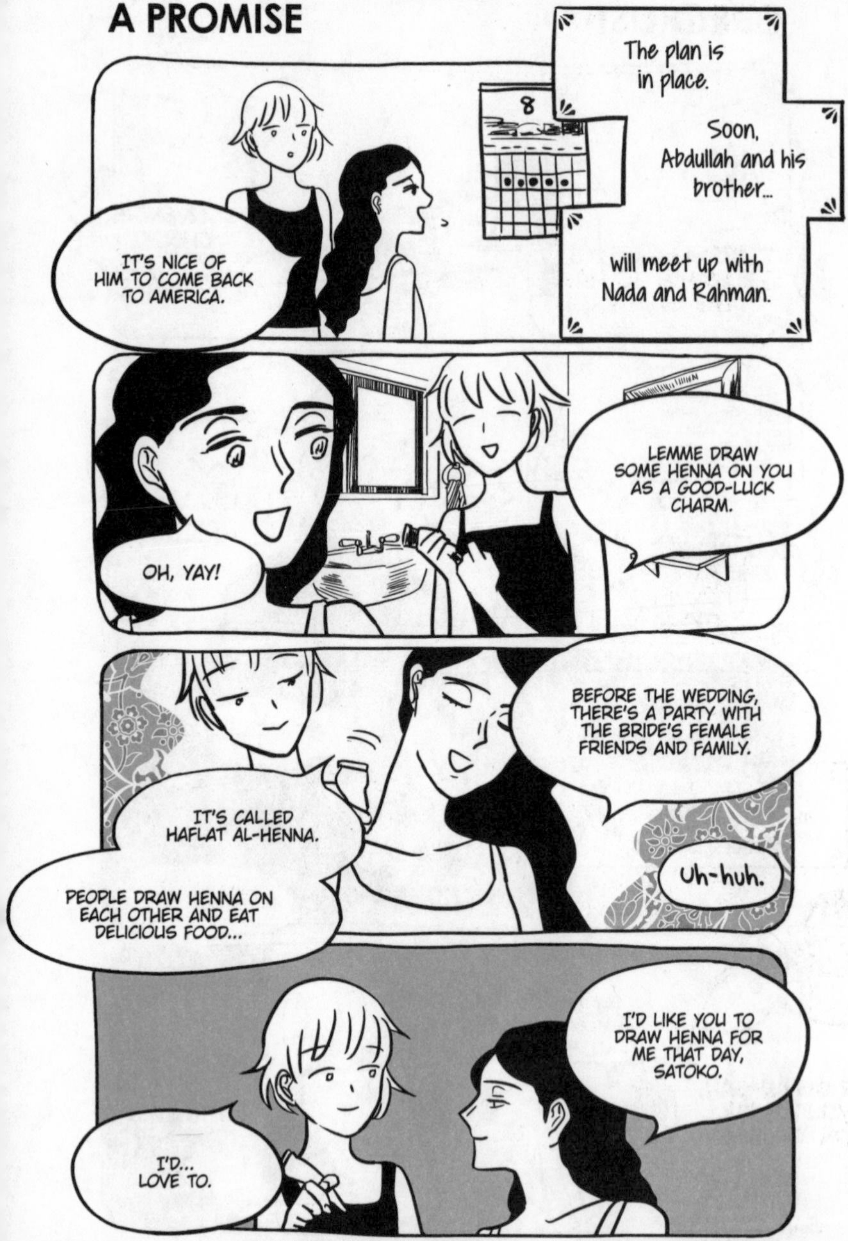

The plan is in place.
Soon, Abdullah and his brother...
will meet up with Nada and Rahman.
IT'S NICE OF HIM TO COME BACK TO AMERICA.
LEMME DRAW SOME HENNA ON YOU AS A GOOD-LUCK CHARM.
OH, YAY!
BEFORE THE WEDDING, THERE'S A PARTY WITH THE BRIDE'S FEMALE FRIENDS AND FAMILY.
IT'S CALLED HAFLAT AL-HENNA.
PEOPLE DRAW HENNA ON EACH OTHER AND EAT DELICIOUS FOOD...
Uh-huh.
I'D LIKE YOU TO DRAW HENNA FOR ME THAT DAY, SATOKO.
I'D... LOVE TO.

As per tradition, a happily married woman applies the henna to the bride's hands and feet, so current Satoko wouldn't qualify for that part.

CHECKLIST

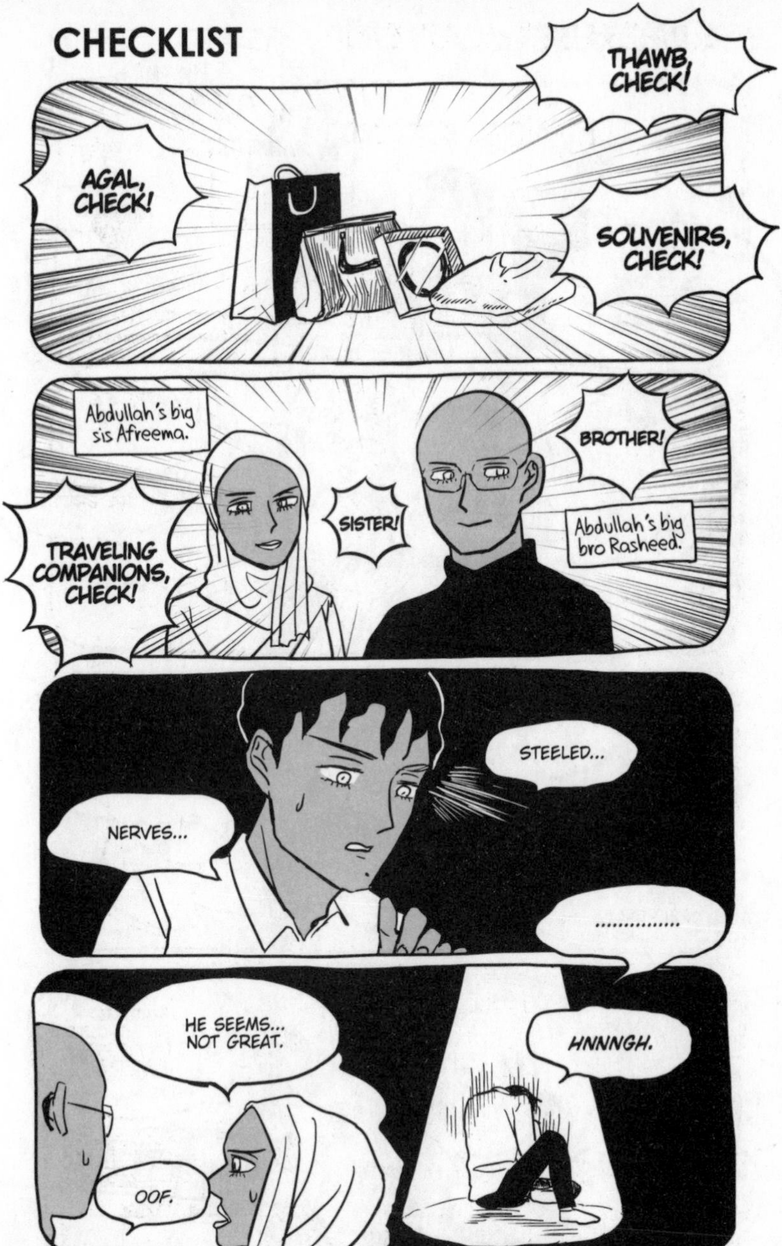

THAWB, CHECK!
SOUVENIRS, CHECK!
AGAL, CHECK!
BROTHER!
Abdullah's big bro Rasheed.
SISTER!
Abdullah's big sis Afreema.
TRAVELING COMPANIONS, CHECK!
STEELED...
NERVES...
....
HNNNGH.
HE SEEMS... NOT GREAT.
OOF.

THE PERFECT SOUVENIR

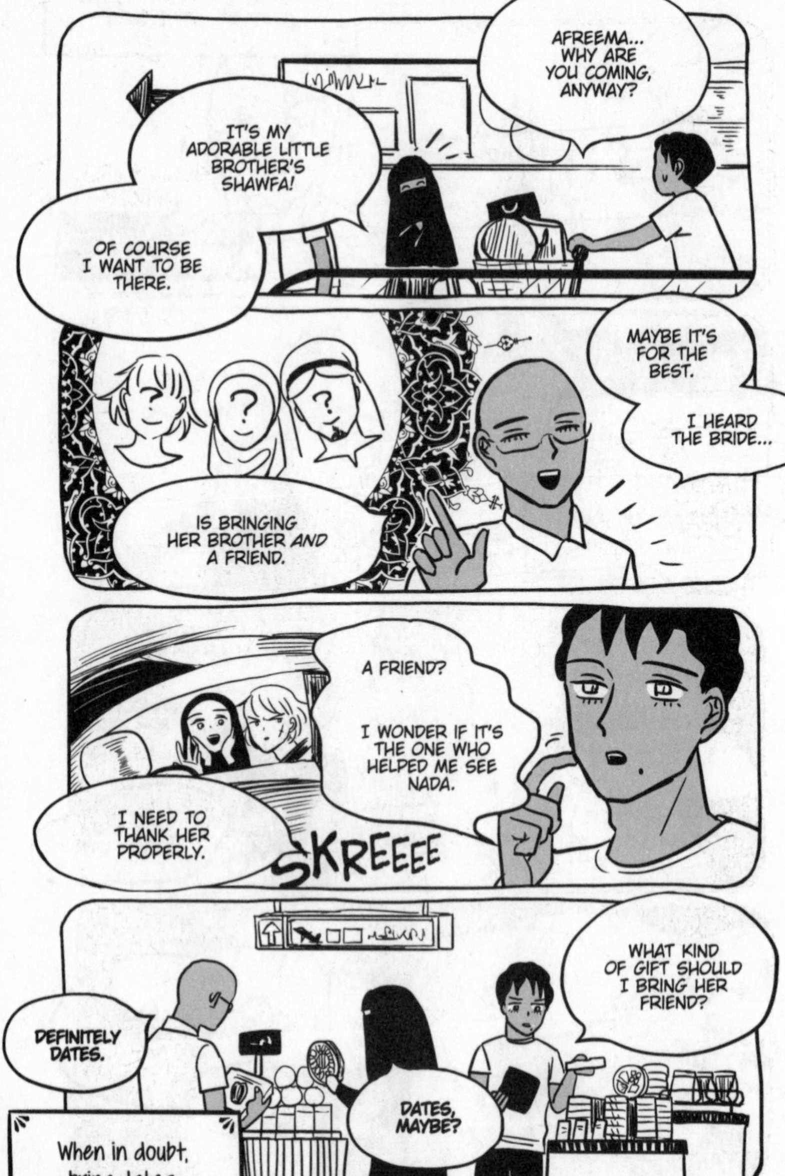
AFREEMA... WHY ARE YOU COMING, ANYWAY?
IT'S MY ADORABLE LITTLE BROTHER'S SHAWFA!
OF COURSE I WANT TO BE THERE.
MAYBE IT'S FOR THE BEST.
I HEARD THE BRIDE...
IS BRINGING HER BROTHER *AND* A FRIEND.
A FRIEND?
I WONDER IF IT'S THE ONE WHO HELPED ME SEE NADA.
I NEED TO THANK HER PROPERLY.
SKREEEE
WHAT KIND OF GIFT SHOULD I BRING HER FRIEND?
DATES, MAYBE?
DEFINITELY DATES.
When in doubt, bring dates.

SHAWFA SHOWDOWN

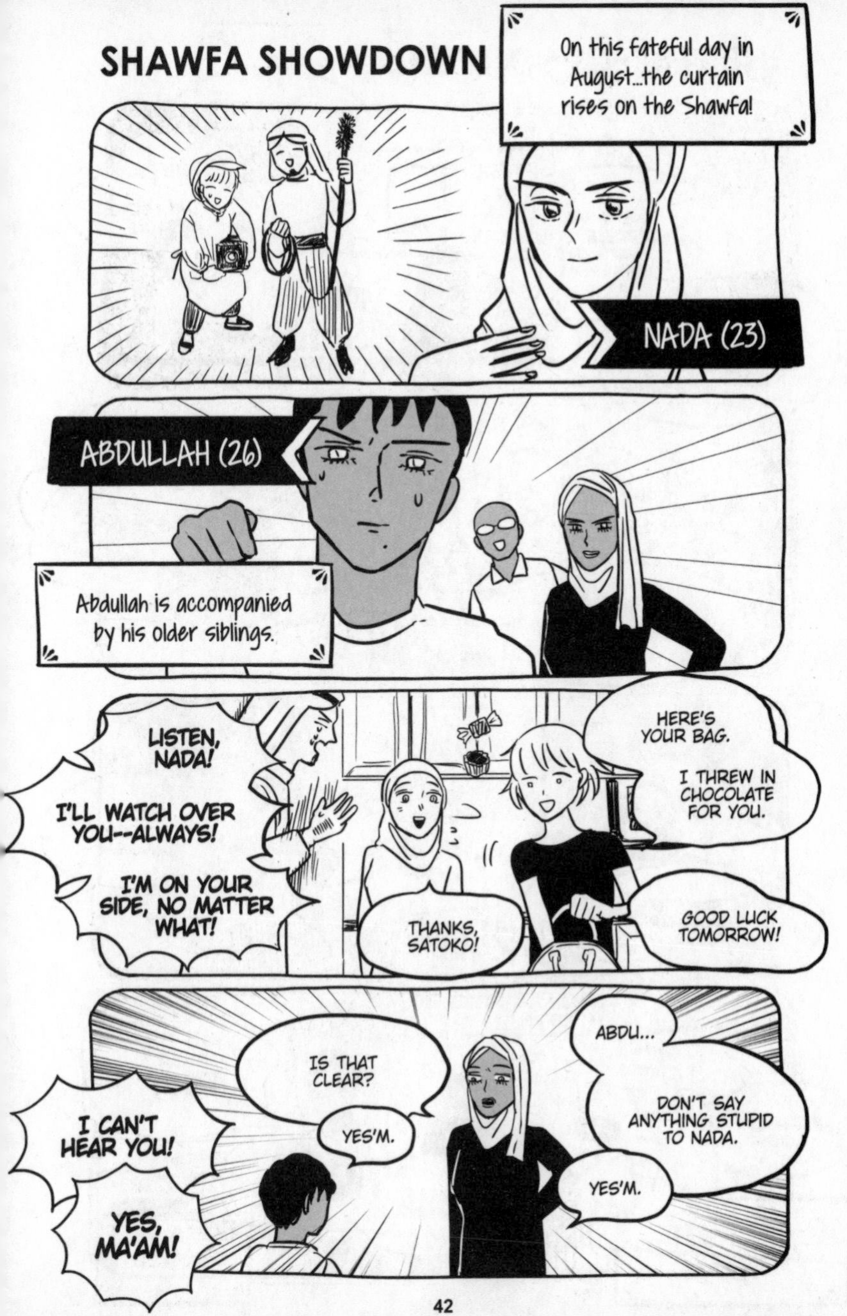
On this fateful day in August...the curtain rises on the Shawfa!
NADA (23)
ABDULLAH (26)
Abdullah is accompanied by his older siblings.
HERE'S YOUR BAG.
I THREW IN CHOCOLATE FOR YOU.
GOOD LUCK TOMORROW!
THANKS, SATOKO!
LISTEN, NADA!
I'LL WATCH OVER YOU--ALWAYS!
I'M ON YOUR SIDE, NO MATTER WHAT!
ABDU...
DON'T SAY ANYTHING STUPID TO NADA.
YES'M.
IS THAT CLEAR?
YES'M.
I CAN'T HEAR YOU!
YES, MA'AM!

SHAWFA SHOWDOWN 2

That day...

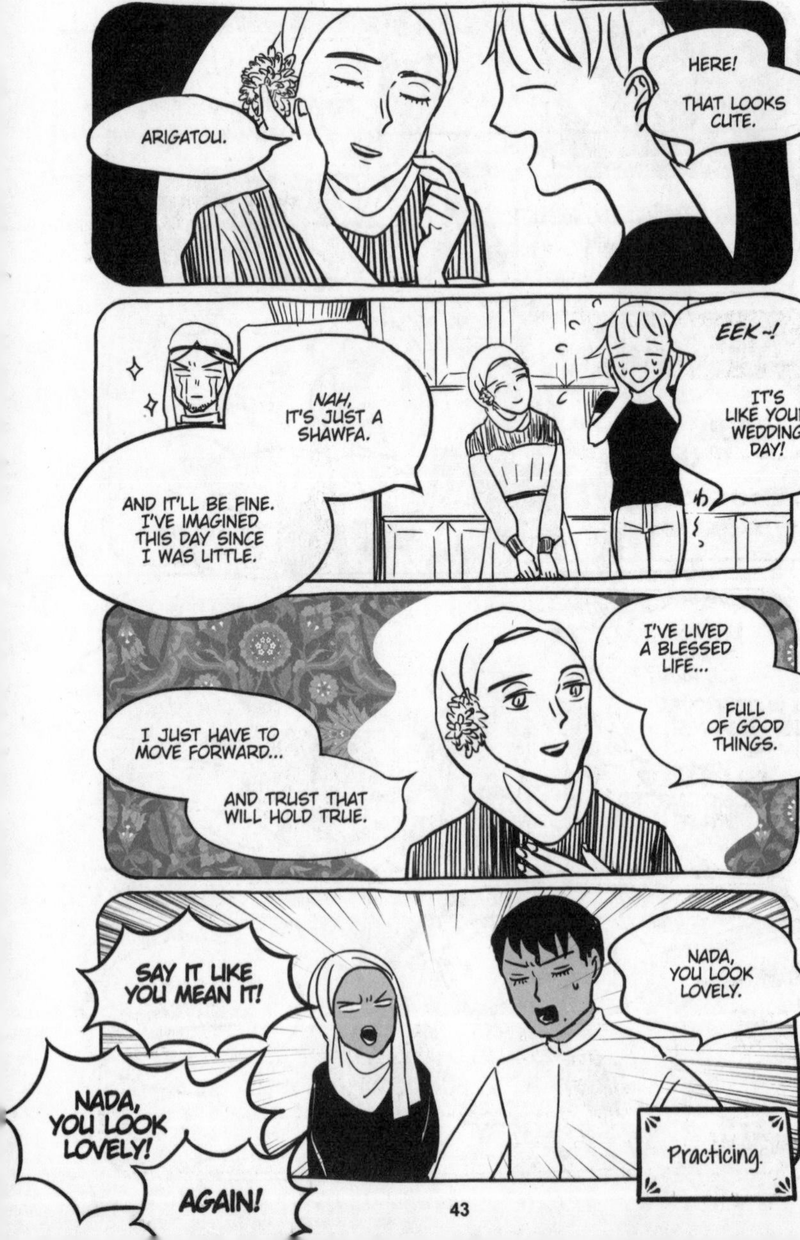
HERE! THAT LOOKS CUTE.
ARIGATOU.
EEK~! IT'S LIKE YOUR WEDDING DAY!
NAH, IT'S JUST A SHAWFA.
AND IT'LL BE FINE. I'VE IMAGINED THIS DAY SINCE I WAS LITTLE.
I'VE LIVED A BLESSED LIFE... FULL OF GOOD THINGS.
I JUST HAVE TO MOVE FORWARD...
AND TRUST THAT WILL HOLD TRUE.
NADA, YOU LOOK LOVELY.
SAY IT LIKE YOU MEAN IT!
Practicing.
NADA, YOU LOOK LOVELY!
AGAIN!

NICE TO MEET YOU!

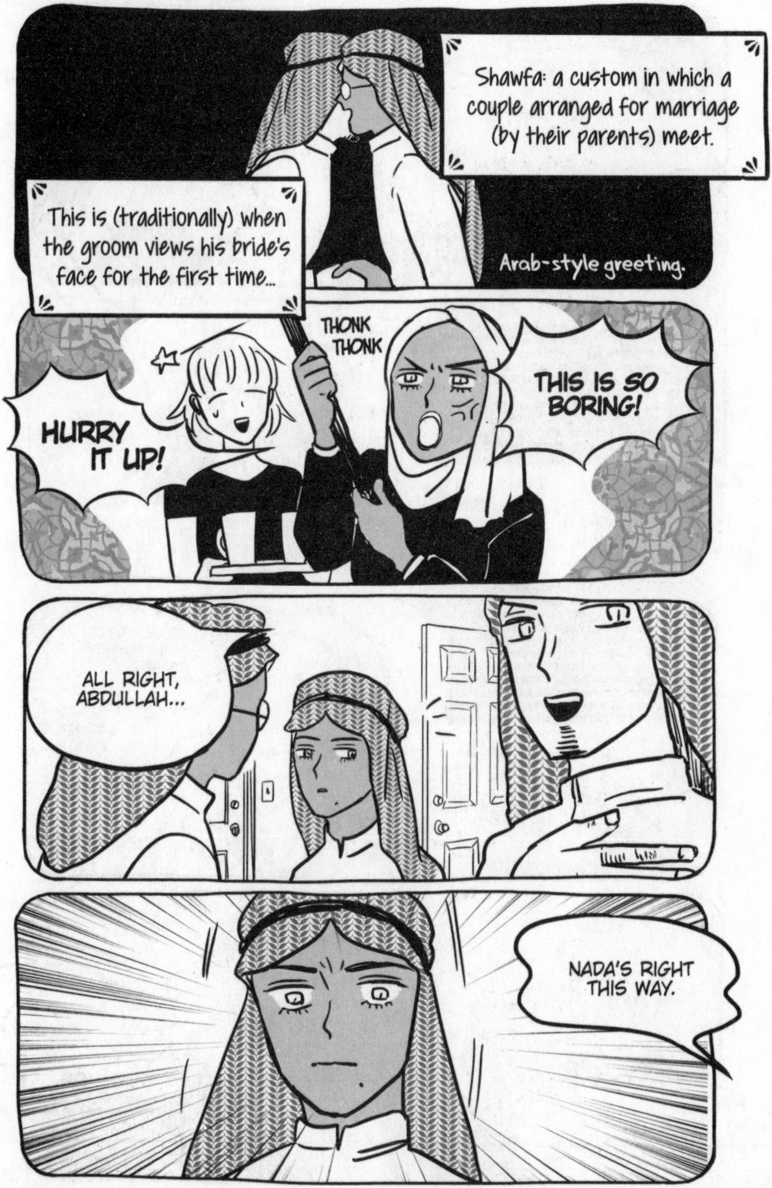
Shawfa: a custom in which a couple arranged for marriage (by their parents) meet.
This is (traditionally) when the groom views his bride's face for the first time...
Arab-style greeting.
THIS IS SO BORING!
THONK THONK
HURRY IT UP!
ALL RIGHT, ABDULLAH...
NADA'S RIGHT THIS WAY.

FACE TO FACE

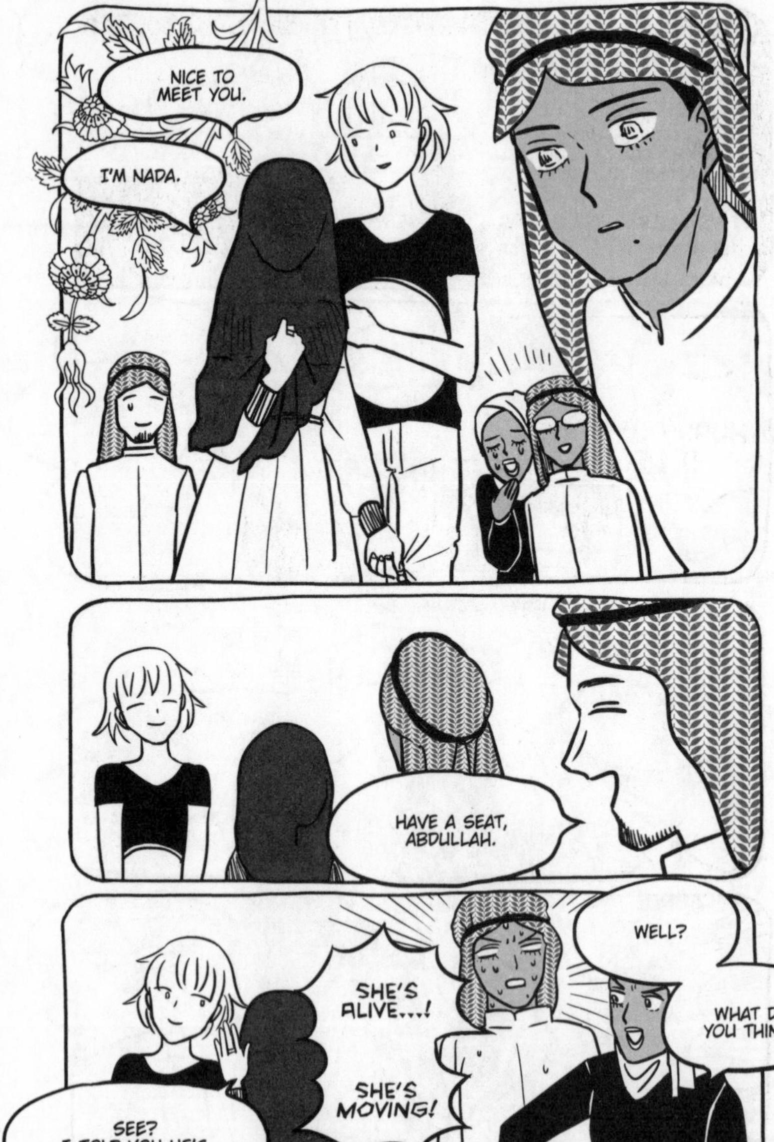

NICE TO MEET YOU.
I'M NADA.
HAVE A SEAT, ABDULLAH.
WELL?
WHAT DO YOU THINK?
SHE'S ALIVE...!
SHE'S MOVING!
SEE? I TOLD YOU HE'S A SWEETIE.

MEETING

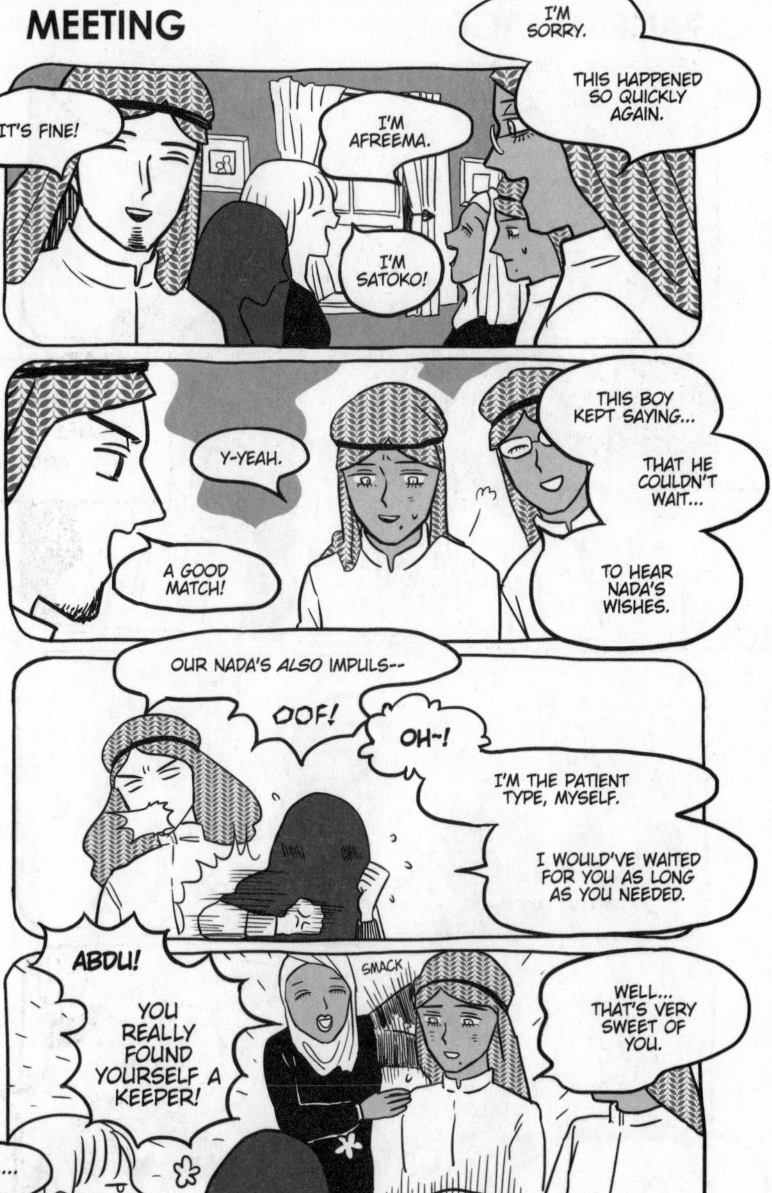
I'M SORRY.
THIS HAPPENED SO QUICKLY AGAIN.
I'M AFREEMA.
I'M SATOKO!
IT'S FINE!
THIS BOY KEPT SAYING...
THAT HE COULDN'T WAIT...
TO HEAR NADA'S WISHES.
Y-YEAH.
A GOOD MATCH!
OUR NADA'S *ALSO* IMPULS--
OOF!
OH~!
I'M THE PATIENT TYPE, MYSELF.
I WOULD'VE WAITED FOR YOU AS LONG AS YOU NEEDED.
WELL... THAT'S VERY SWEET OF YOU.
SMACK
ABDU!
YOU REALLY FOUND YOURSELF A KEEPER!
....

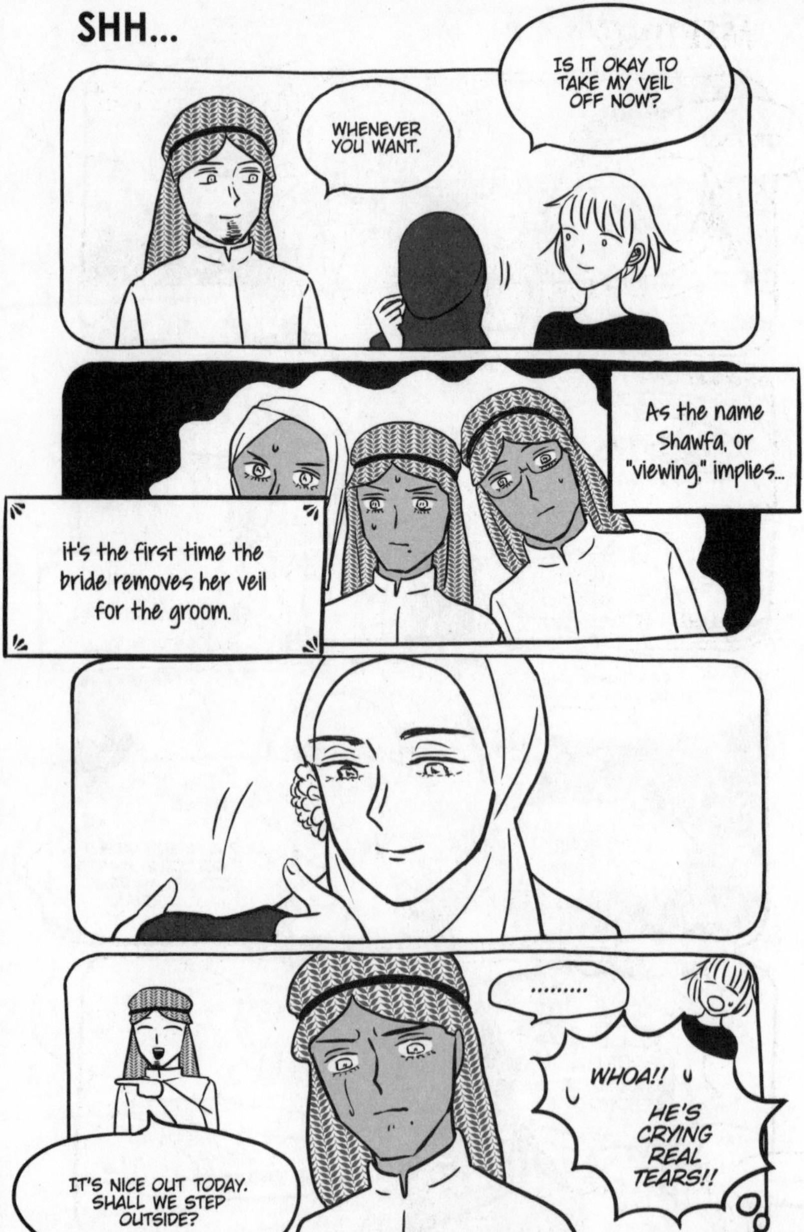
SHH...
IS IT OKAY TO TAKE MY VEIL OFF NOW?
WHENEVER YOU WANT.
As the name Shawfa, or "viewing," implies...
it's the first time the bride removes her veil for the groom.
....
WHOA!!
HE'S CRYING REAL TEARS!!
IT'S NICE OUT TODAY. SHALL WE STEP OUTSIDE?

TELL ME MORE

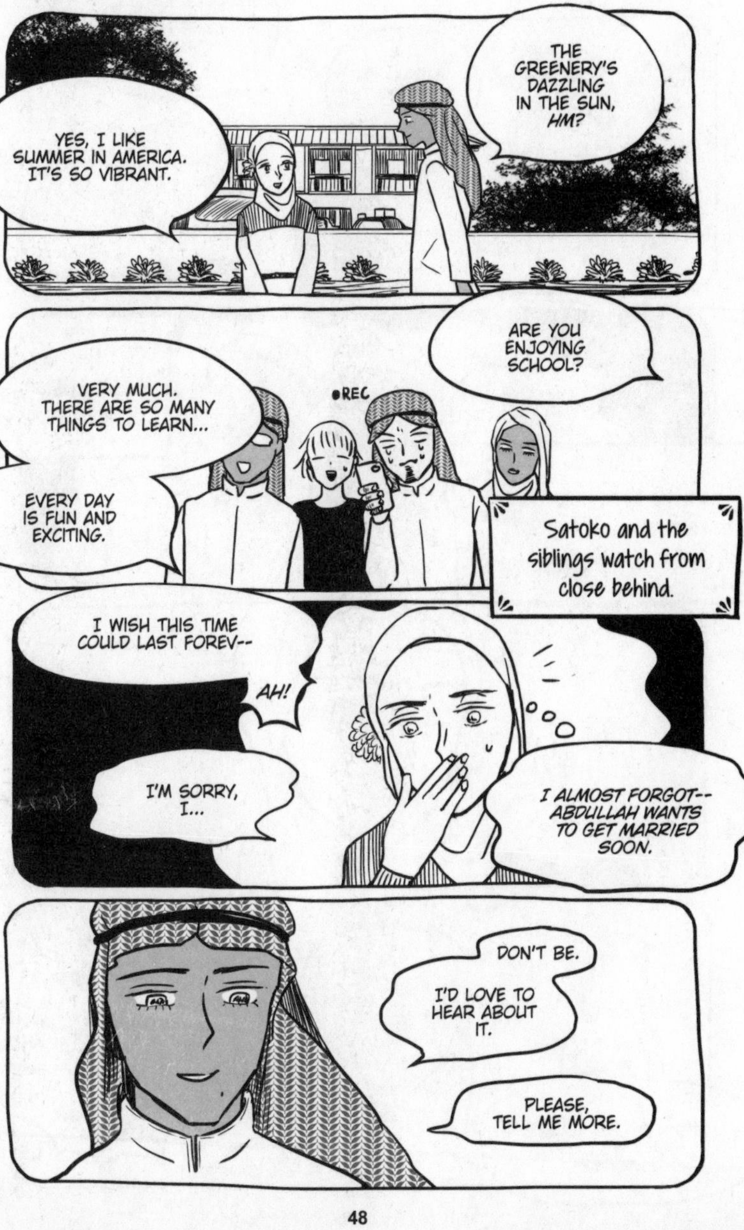
THE GREENERY'S DAZZLING IN THE SUN, *HM?*
YES, I LIKE SUMMER IN AMERICA. IT'S SO VIBRANT.
ARE YOU ENJOYING SCHOOL?
●REC
VERY MUCH. THERE ARE SO MANY THINGS TO LEARN...
EVERY DAY IS FUN AND EXCITING.
Satoko and the siblings watch from close behind.
I WISH THIS TIME COULD LAST FOREV--
AH!
I ALMOST FORGOT--ABDULLAH WANTS TO GET MARRIED SOON.
I'M SORRY, I...
DON'T BE.
I'D LOVE TO HEAR ABOUT IT.
PLEASE, TELL ME MORE.

REAL TALK

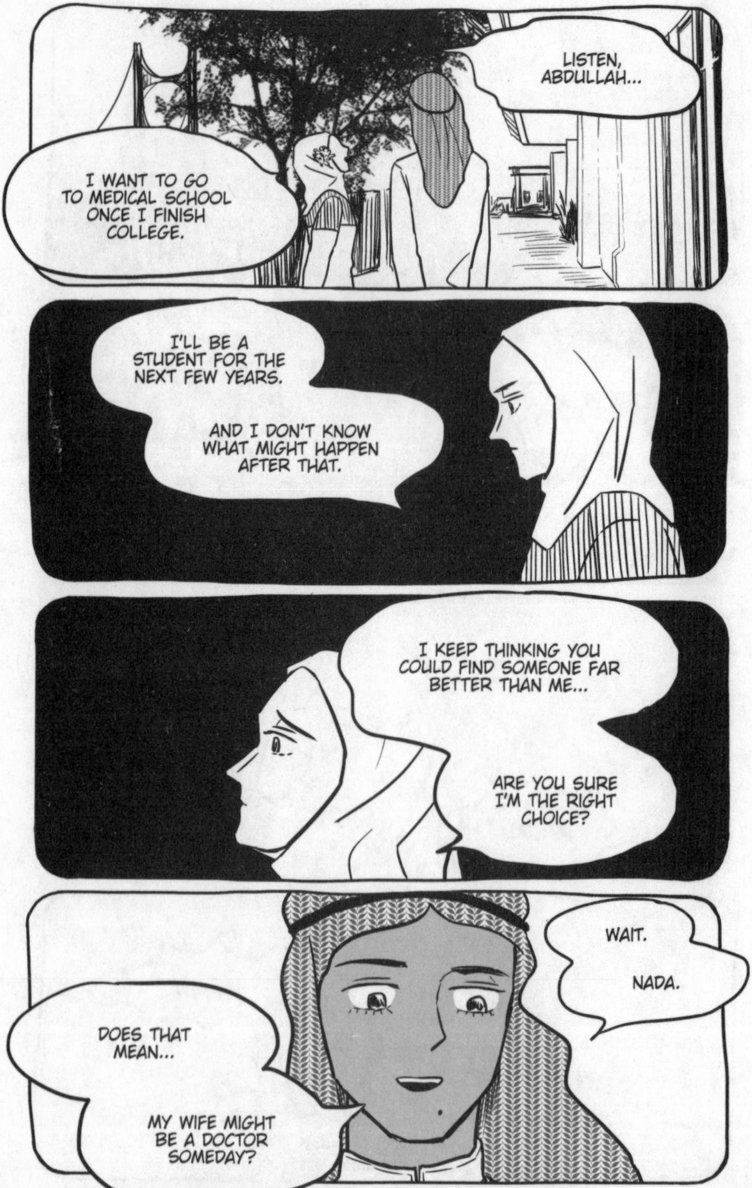
LISTEN, ABDULLAH...
I WANT TO GO TO MEDICAL SCHOOL ONCE I FINISH COLLEGE.
I'LL BE A STUDENT FOR THE NEXT FEW YEARS.
AND I DON'T KNOW WHAT MIGHT HAPPEN AFTER THAT.
I KEEP THINKING YOU COULD FIND SOMEONE FAR BETTER THAN ME...
ARE YOU SURE I'M THE RIGHT CHOICE?
WAIT.
NADA.
DOES THAT MEAN...
MY WIFE MIGHT BE A DOCTOR SOMEDAY?

GUST OF WIND

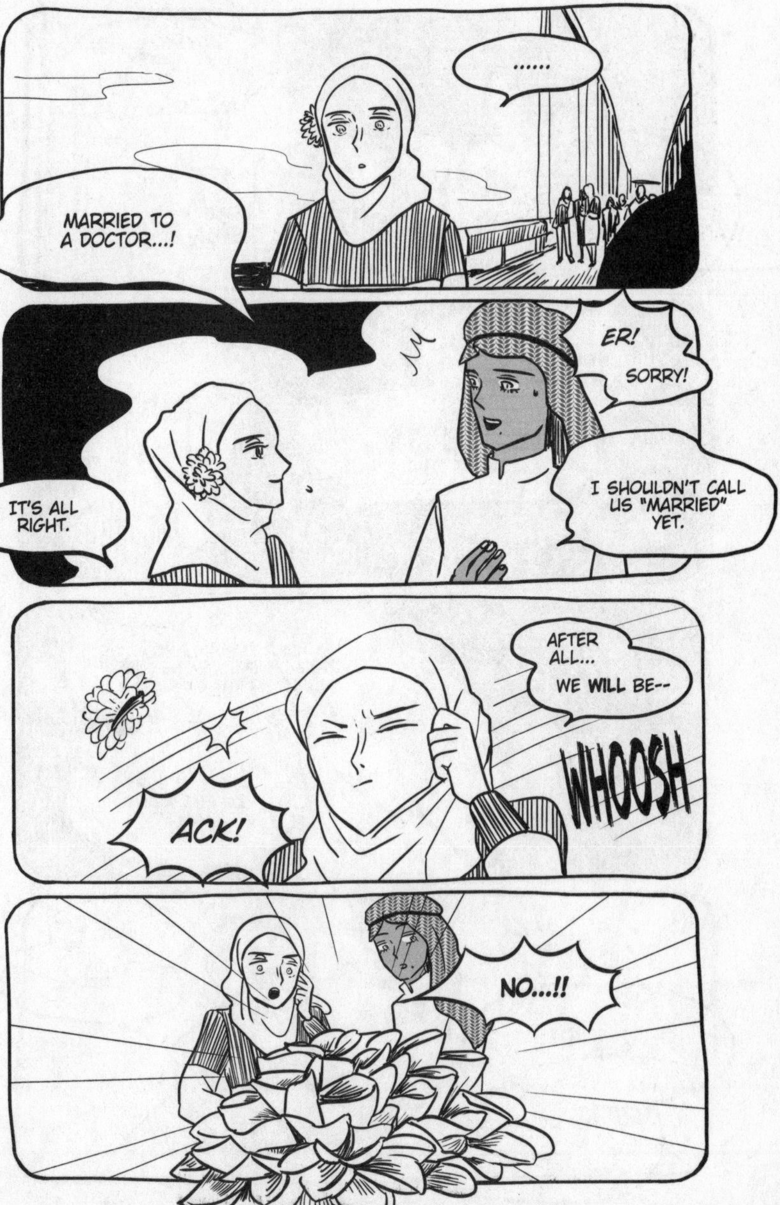
......
MARRIED TO A DOCTOR...!
ER!
SORRY!
I SHOULDN'T CALL US "MARRIED" YET.
IT'S ALL RIGHT.
AFTER ALL...
WE WILL BE--
WHOOSH
ACK!
NO...!!

ON THE BRIDGE

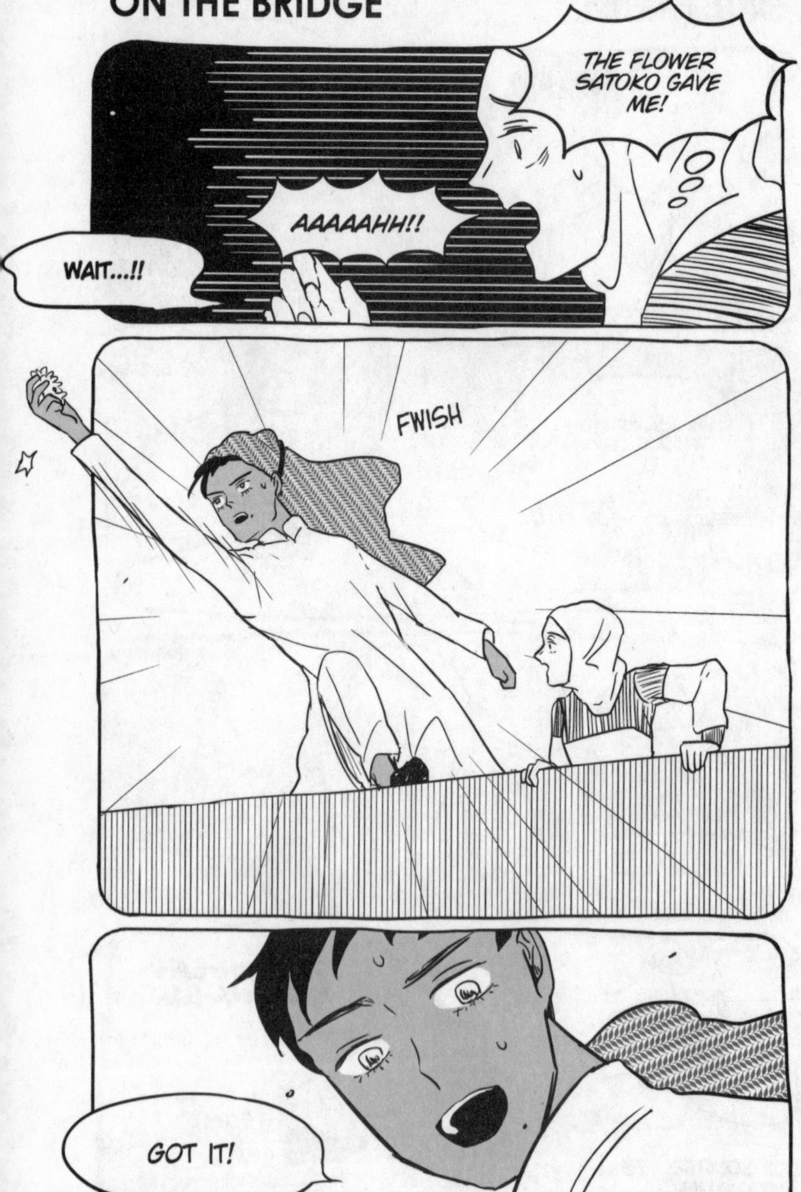
THE FLOWER SATOKO GAVE ME!
AAAAAHH!!
WAIT...!!
FWISH
GOT IT!

TRUE FACE

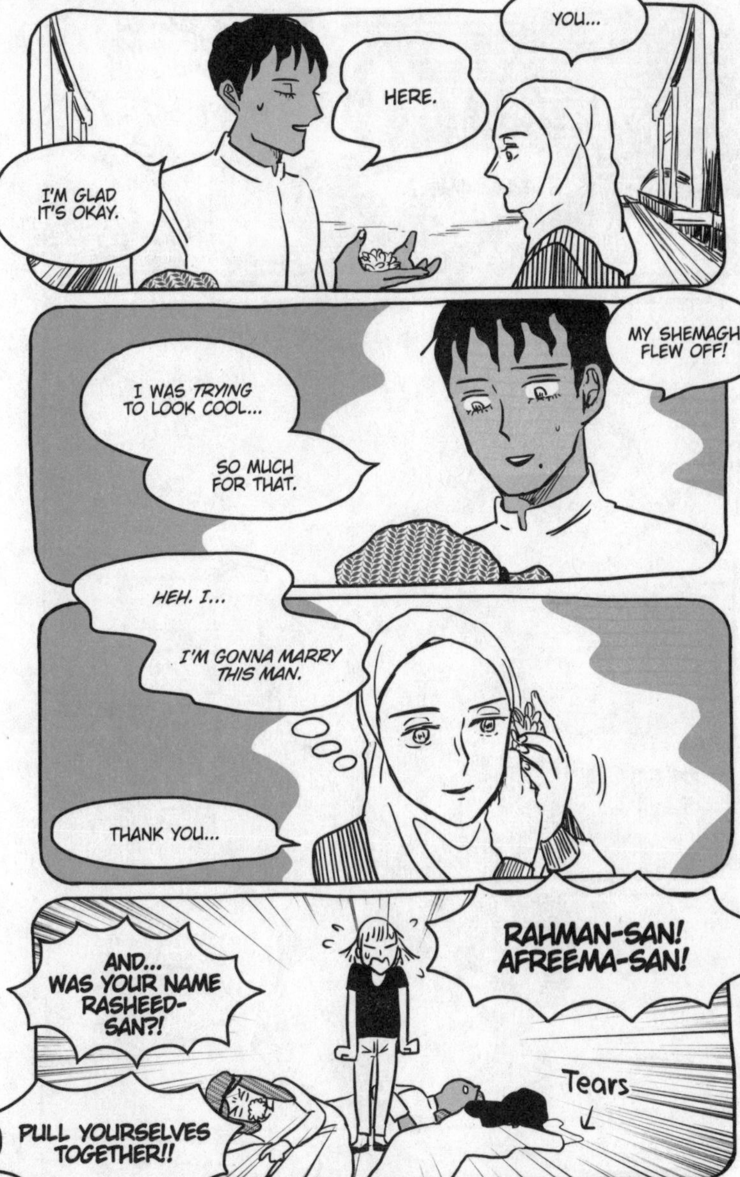
YOU...
HERE.
I'M GLAD IT'S OKAY.
MY SHEMAGH FLEW OFF!
I WAS *TRYING* TO LOOK COOL...
SO MUCH FOR THAT.
HEH. I...
I'M GONNA MARRY THIS MAN.
THANK YOU...
RAHMAN-SAN! AFREEMA-SAN!
AND... WAS YOUR NAME RASHEED-SAN?!
Tears
PULL YOURSELVES TOGETHER!!

DREAMS

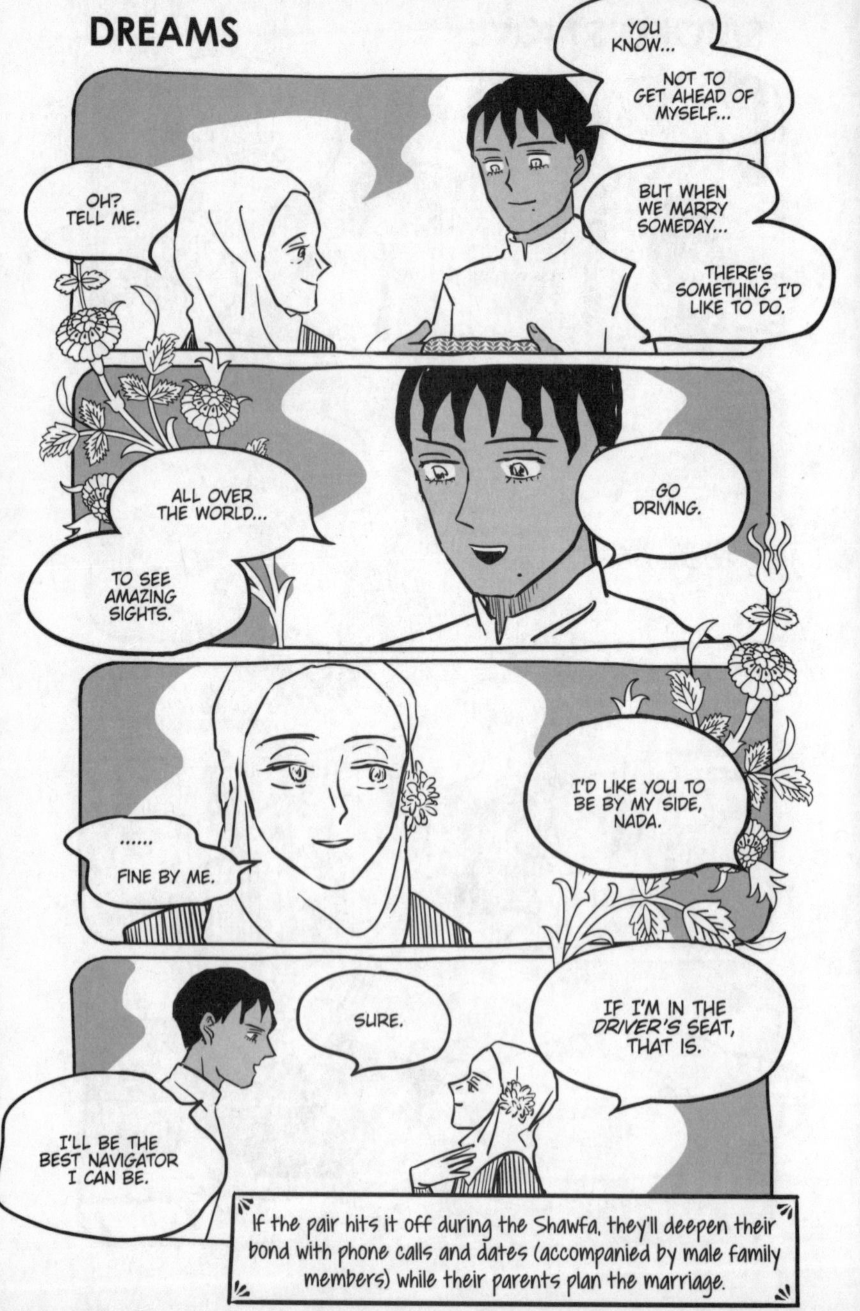

YOU KNOW...
NOT TO GET AHEAD OF MYSELF...
BUT WHEN WE MARRY SOMEDAY...
THERE'S SOMETHING I'D LIKE TO DO.
OH? TELL ME.
GO DRIVING.
ALL OVER THE WORLD...
TO SEE AMAZING SIGHTS.
I'D LIKE YOU TO BE BY MY SIDE, NADA.
......
FINE BY ME.
IF I'M IN THE *DRIVER'S* SEAT, THAT IS.
SURE.
I'LL BE THE BEST NAVIGATOR I CAN BE.
If the pair hits it off during the Shawfa, they'll deepen their bond with phone calls and dates (accompanied by male family members) while their parents plan the marriage.

SATOKO'S MOVE

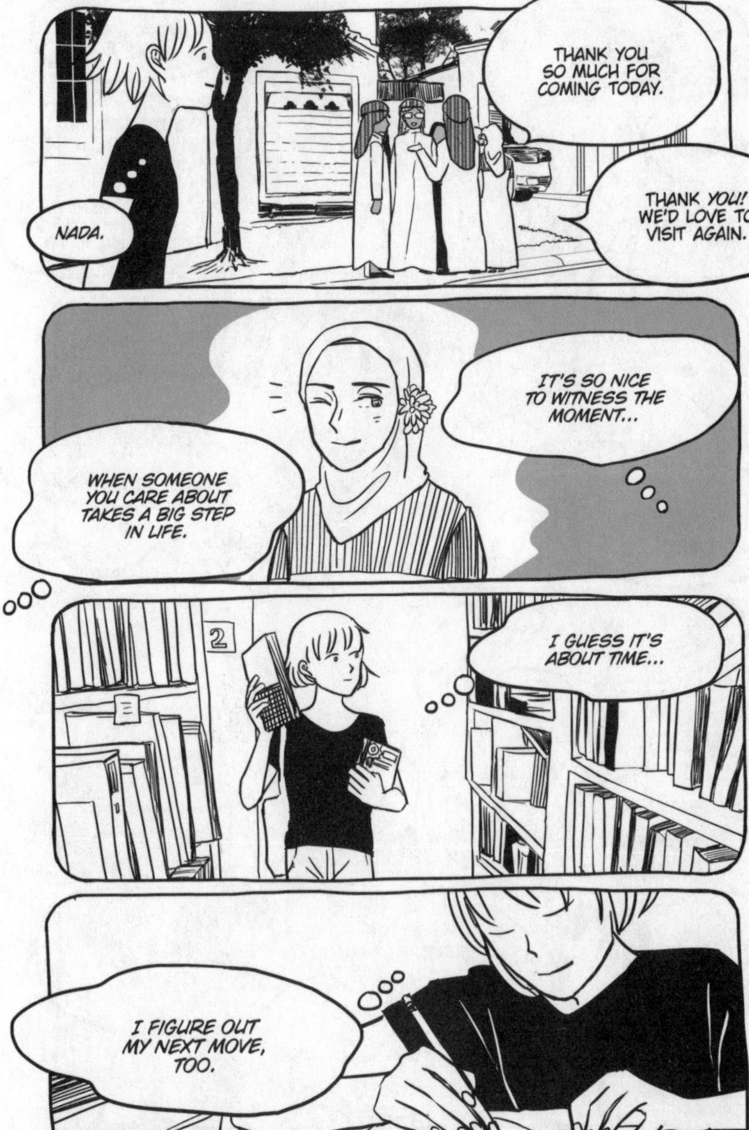
THANK YOU SO MUCH FOR COMING TODAY.
THANK YOU! WE'D LOVE TO VISIT AGAIN.
NADA.
IT'S SO NICE TO WITNESS THE MOMENT...
WHEN SOMEONE YOU CARE ABOUT TAKES A BIG STEP IN LIFE.
I GUESS IT'S ABOUT TIME...
I FIGURE OUT MY NEXT MOVE, TOO.

SIBLINGS

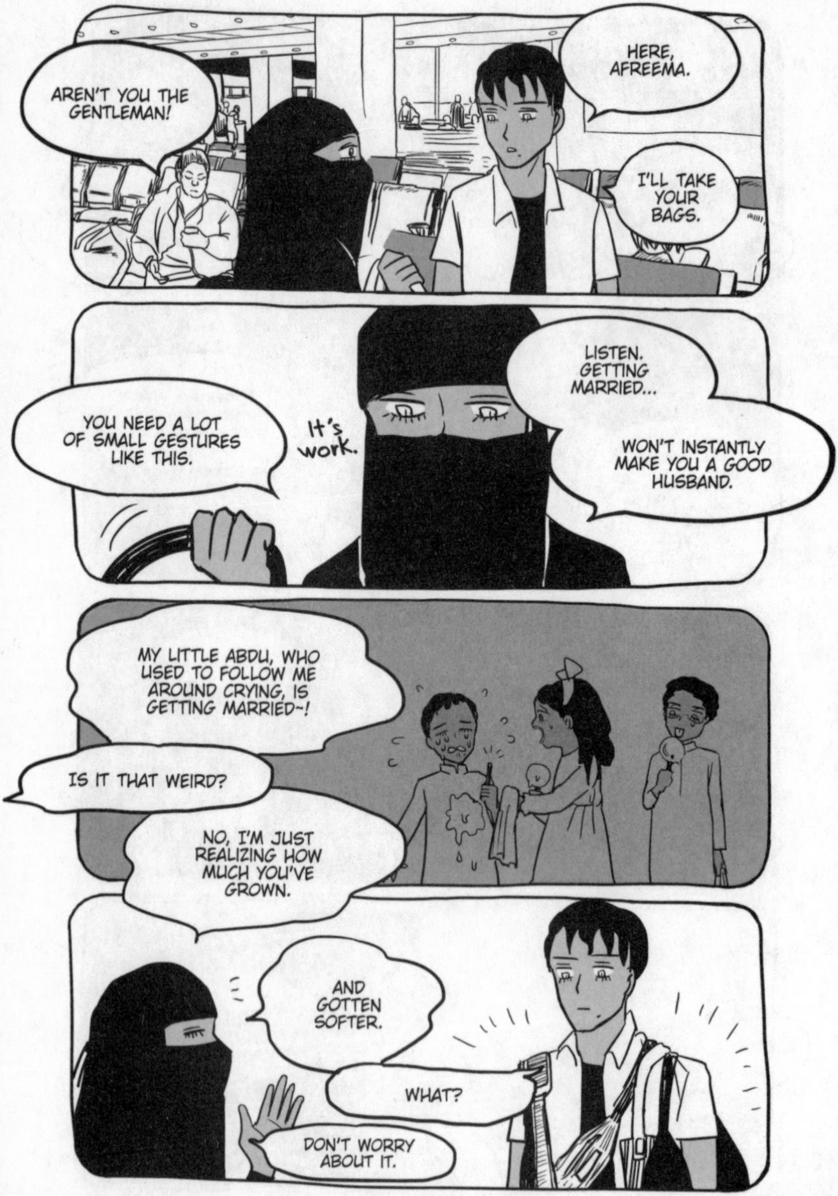
HERE, AFREEMA.
I'LL TAKE YOUR BAGS.
AREN'T YOU THE GENTLEMAN!
LISTEN. GETTING MARRIED...
WON'T INSTANTLY MAKE YOU A GOOD HUSBAND.
It's work.
YOU NEED A LOT OF SMALL GESTURES LIKE THIS.
MY LITTLE ABDU, WHO USED TO FOLLOW ME AROUND CRYING, IS GETTING MARRIED~!
IS IT THAT WEIRD?
NO, I'M JUST REALIZING HOW MUCH YOU'VE GROWN.
AND GOTTEN SOFTER.
WHAT?
DON'T WORRY ABOUT IT.

SHADOWS

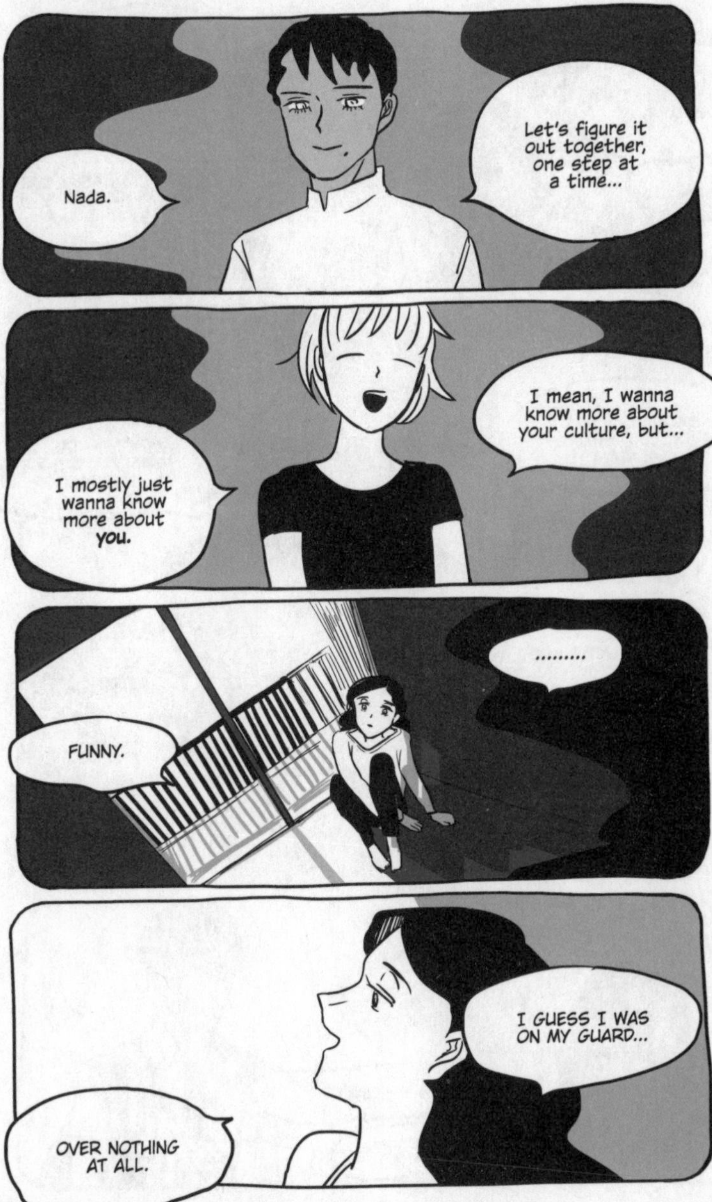
Let's figure it out together, one step at a time...
Nada.
I mean, I wanna know more about your culture, but...
I mostly just wanna know more about **you.**
....
FUNNY.
I GUESS I WAS ON MY GUARD...
OVER NOTHING AT ALL.

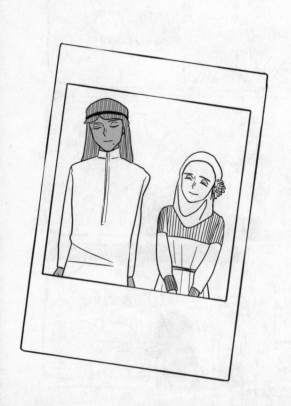

I

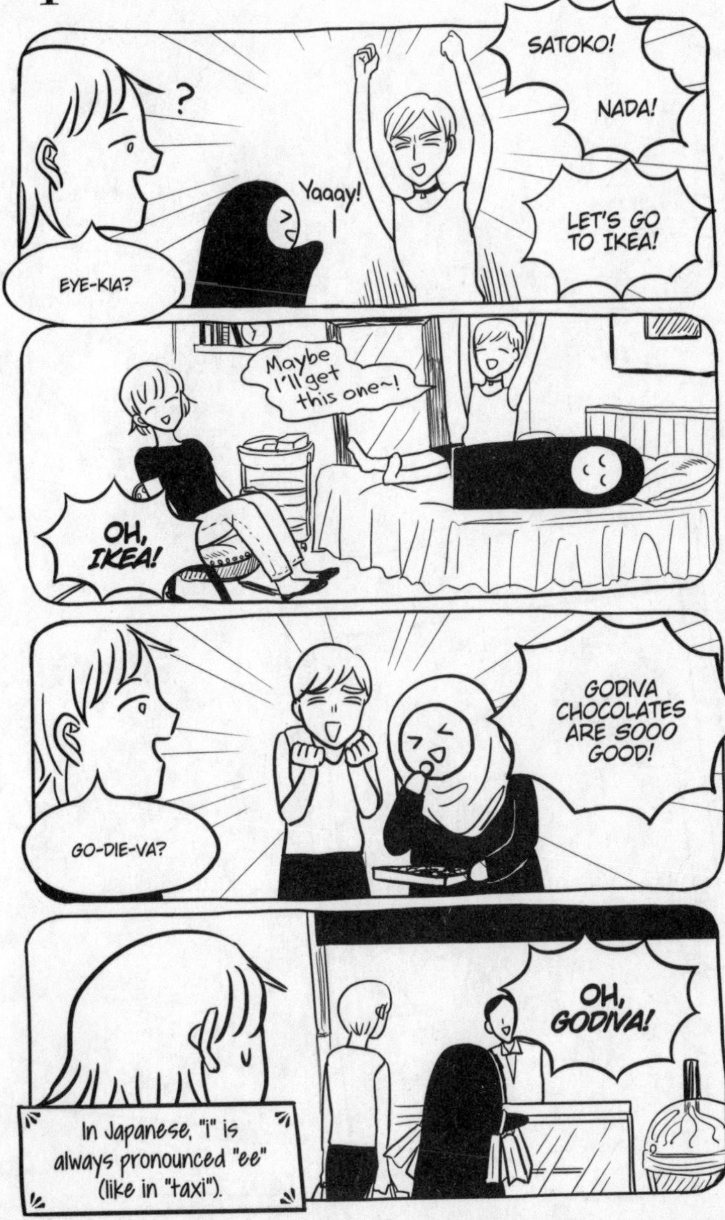
SATOKO!
NADA!
LET'S GO TO IKEA!
Yaaay!
?
EYE-KIA?
Maybe I'll get this one~!
OH, IKEA!
GODIVA CHOCOLATES ARE SOOO GOOD!
GO-DIE-VA?
OH, GODIVA!
In Japanese, "i" is always pronounced "ee" (like in "taxi").

SELFISHNESS

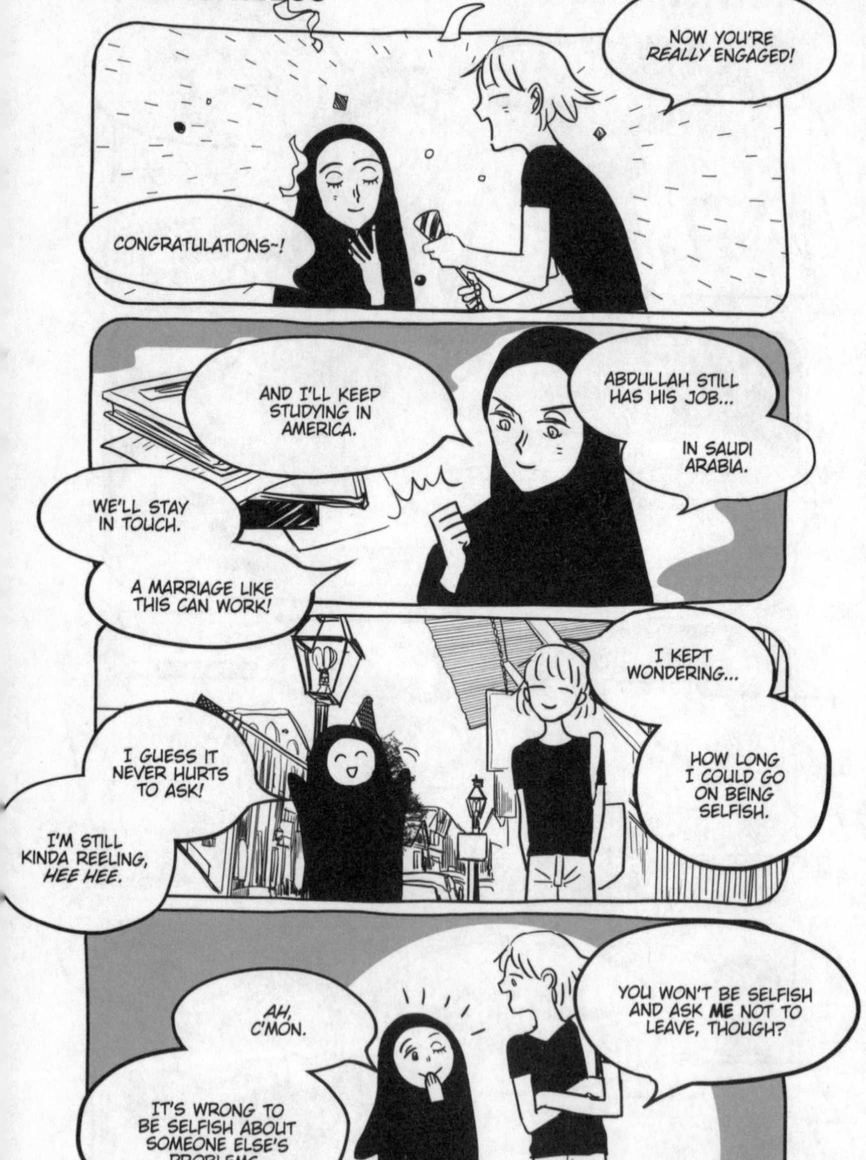
NOW YOU'RE *REALLY* ENGAGED!
CONGRATULATIONS~!
ABDULLAH STILL HAS HIS JOB...
IN SAUDI ARABIA.
AND I'LL KEEP STUDYING IN AMERICA.
WE'LL STAY IN TOUCH.
A MARRIAGE LIKE THIS CAN WORK!
I KEPT WONDERING...
HOW LONG I COULD GO ON BEING SELFISH.
I GUESS IT NEVER HURTS TO ASK!
I'M STILL KINDA REELING, *HEE HEE.*
YOU WON'T BE SELFISH AND ASK **ME** NOT TO LEAVE, THOUGH?
AH, C'MON.
IT'S WRONG TO BE SELFISH ABOUT SOMEONE ELSE'S PROBLEMS.

SELFISHNESS 2

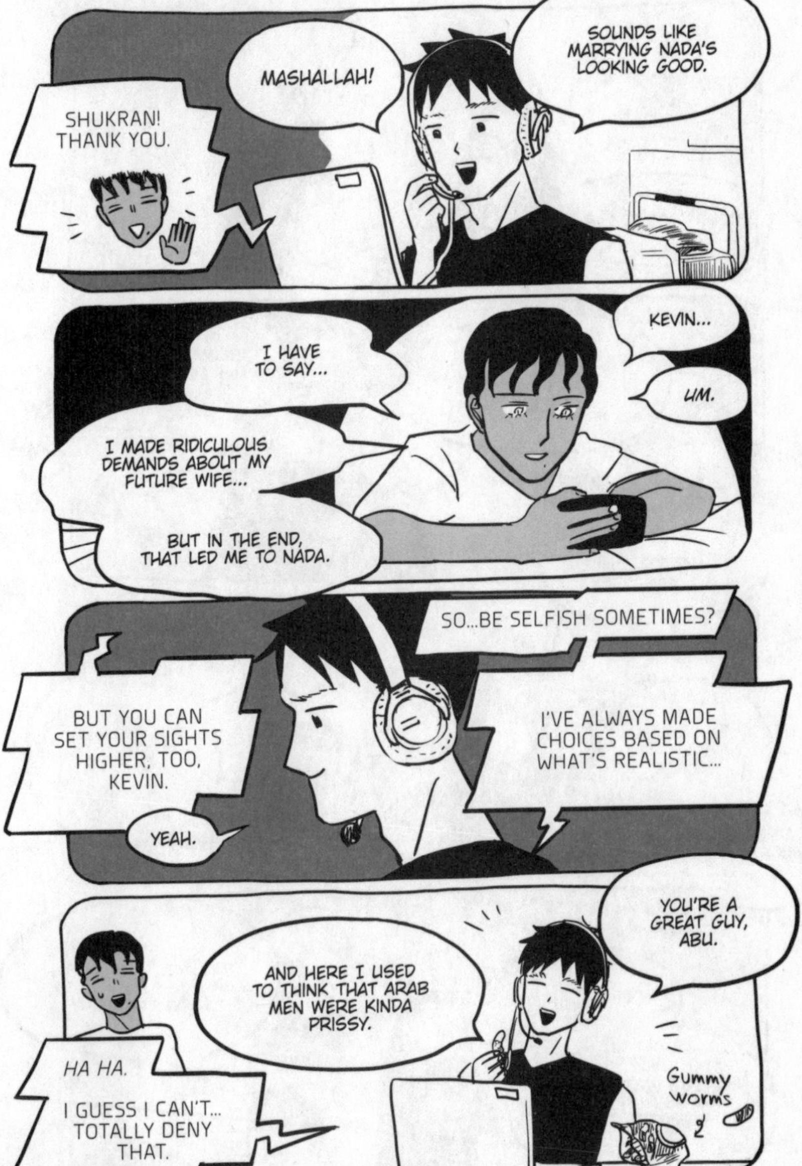
SOUNDS LIKE MARRYING NADA'S LOOKING GOOD.
MASHALLAH!
SHUKRAN! THANK YOU.
KEVIN...
UM.
I HAVE TO SAY...
I MADE RIDICULOUS DEMANDS ABOUT MY FUTURE WIFE...
BUT IN THE END, THAT LED ME TO NADA.
SO...BE SELFISH SOMETIMES?
I'VE ALWAYS MADE CHOICES BASED ON WHAT'S REALISTIC...
BUT YOU CAN SET YOUR SIGHTS HIGHER, TOO, KEVIN.
YEAH.
YOU'RE A GREAT GUY, ABU.
Gummy worms
AND HERE I USED TO THINK THAT ARAB MEN WERE KINDA PRISSY.
HA HA.
I GUESS I CAN'T... TOTALLY DENY THAT.

COLLEGE VIBES

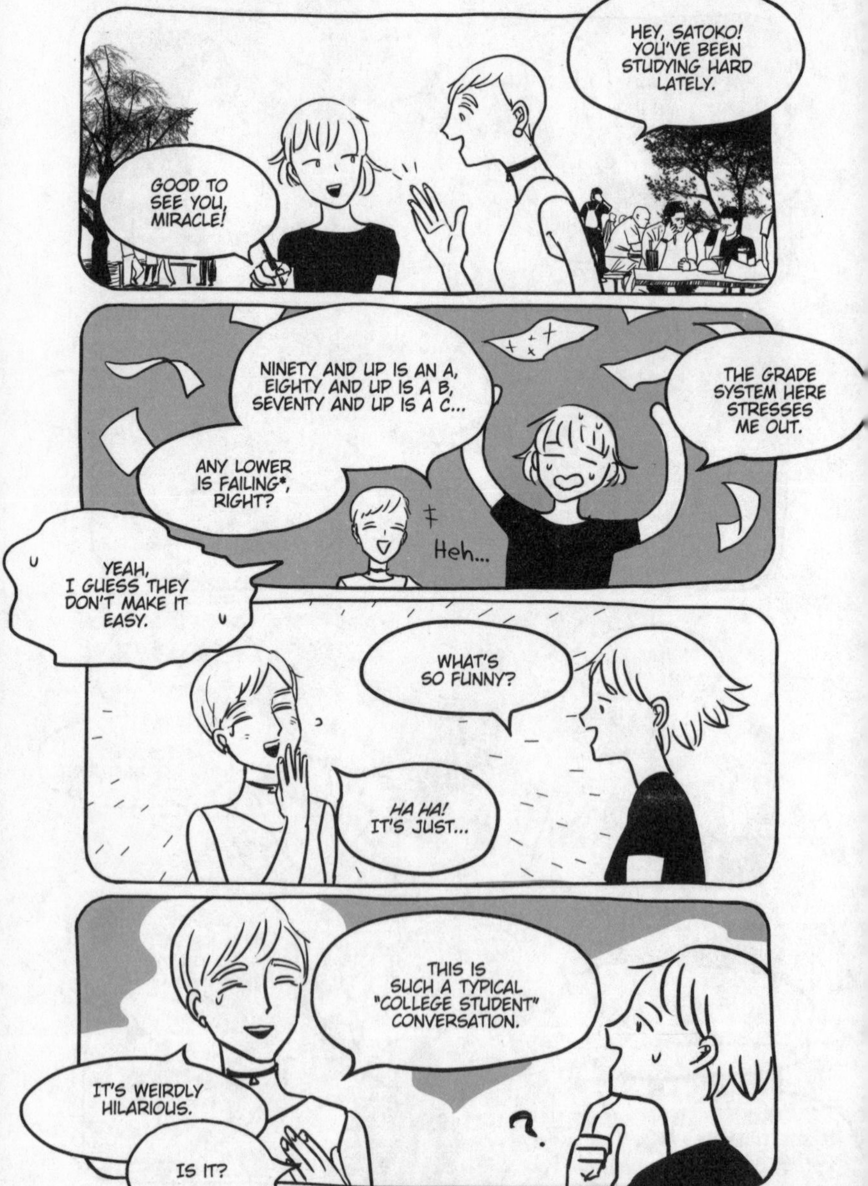
HEY, SATOKO! YOU'VE BEEN STUDYING HARD LATELY.
GOOD TO SEE YOU, MIRACLE!
THE GRADE SYSTEM HERE STRESSES ME OUT.
NINETY AND UP IS AN A, EIGHTY AND UP IS A B, SEVENTY AND UP IS A C...
ANY LOWER IS FAILING*, RIGHT?
Heh...
YEAH, I GUESS THEY DON'T MAKE IT EASY.
WHAT'S SO FUNNY?
HA HA! IT'S JUST...
THIS IS SUCH A TYPICAL "COLLEGE STUDENT" CONVERSATION.
IT'S WEIRDLY HILARIOUS.
IS IT?

**Translator's note: Grading scales vary in Japan, but generally anything above a fifty or sixty is a passing grade.*

COMPANY

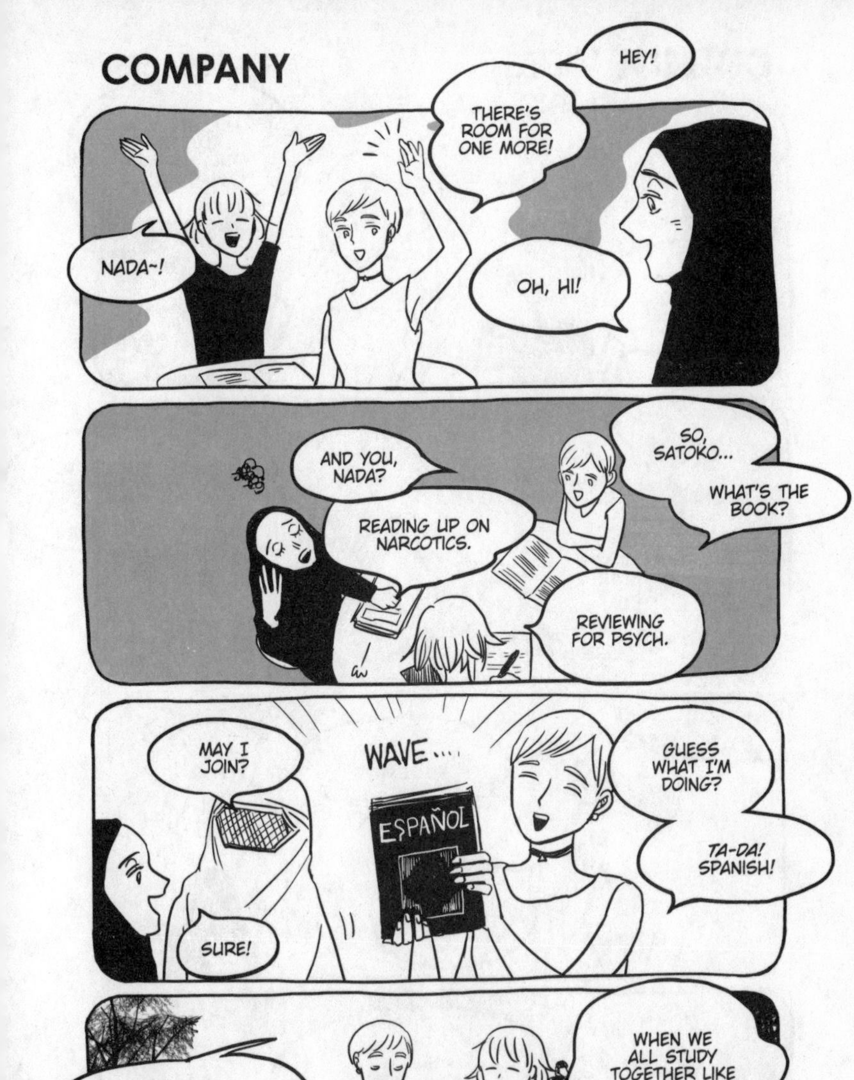
HEY!
THERE'S ROOM FOR ONE MORE!
OH, HI!
NADA~!
SO, SATOKO...
WHAT'S THE BOOK?
AND YOU, NADA?
READING UP ON NARCOTICS.
REVIEWING FOR PSYCH.
GUESS WHAT I'M DOING?
TA-DA! SPANISH!
ESPAÑOL
WAVE....
MAY I JOIN?
SURE!
WHEN WE ALL STUDY TOGETHER LIKE THIS...
IT'S NICE. LIKE WE'RE IN THE SAME BOAT.
I WAS THINKING THE SAME THING.

PACKING

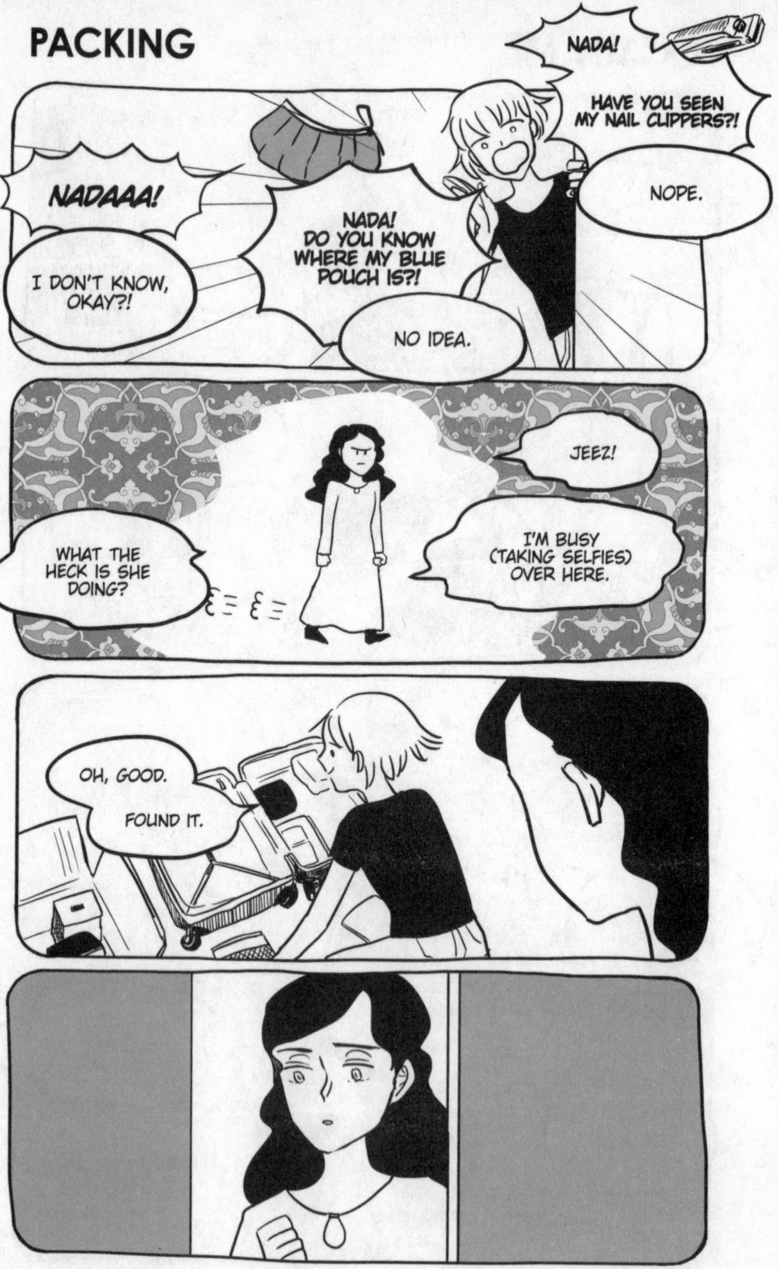
NADA!
HAVE YOU SEEN MY NAIL CLIPPERS?!
NOPE.
NADA! DO YOU KNOW WHERE MY BLUE POUCH IS?!
NO IDEA.
NADAAA!
I DON'T KNOW, OKAY?!
JEEZ!
I'M BUSY (TAKING SELFIES) OVER HERE.
WHAT THE HECK IS SHE DOING?
OH, GOOD.
FOUND IT.

EXCUSE ME

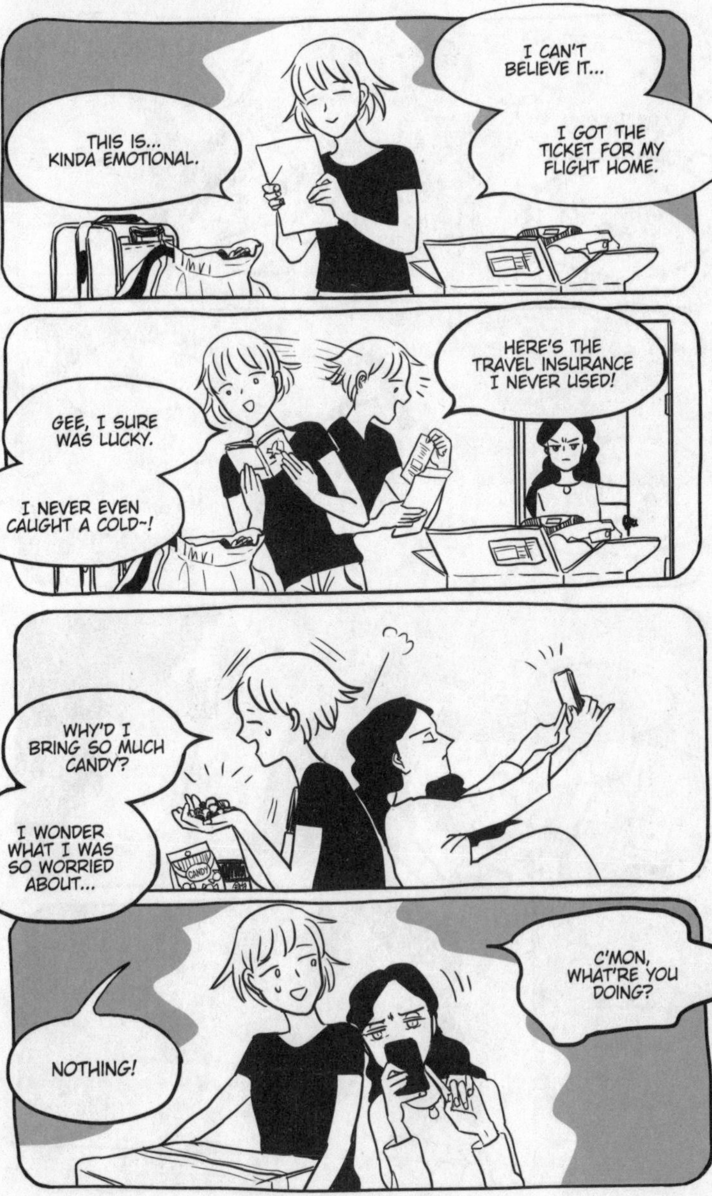
I CAN'T BELIEVE IT...
I GOT THE TICKET FOR MY FLIGHT HOME.
THIS IS... KINDA EMOTIONAL.
HERE'S THE TRAVEL INSURANCE I NEVER USED!
GEE, I SURE WAS LUCKY.
I NEVER EVEN CAUGHT A COLD~!
WHY'D I BRING SO MUCH CANDY?
I WONDER WHAT I WAS SO WORRIED ABOUT...
CANDY
C'MON, WHAT'RE YOU DOING?
NOTHING!

WHAT ABOUT YOU?

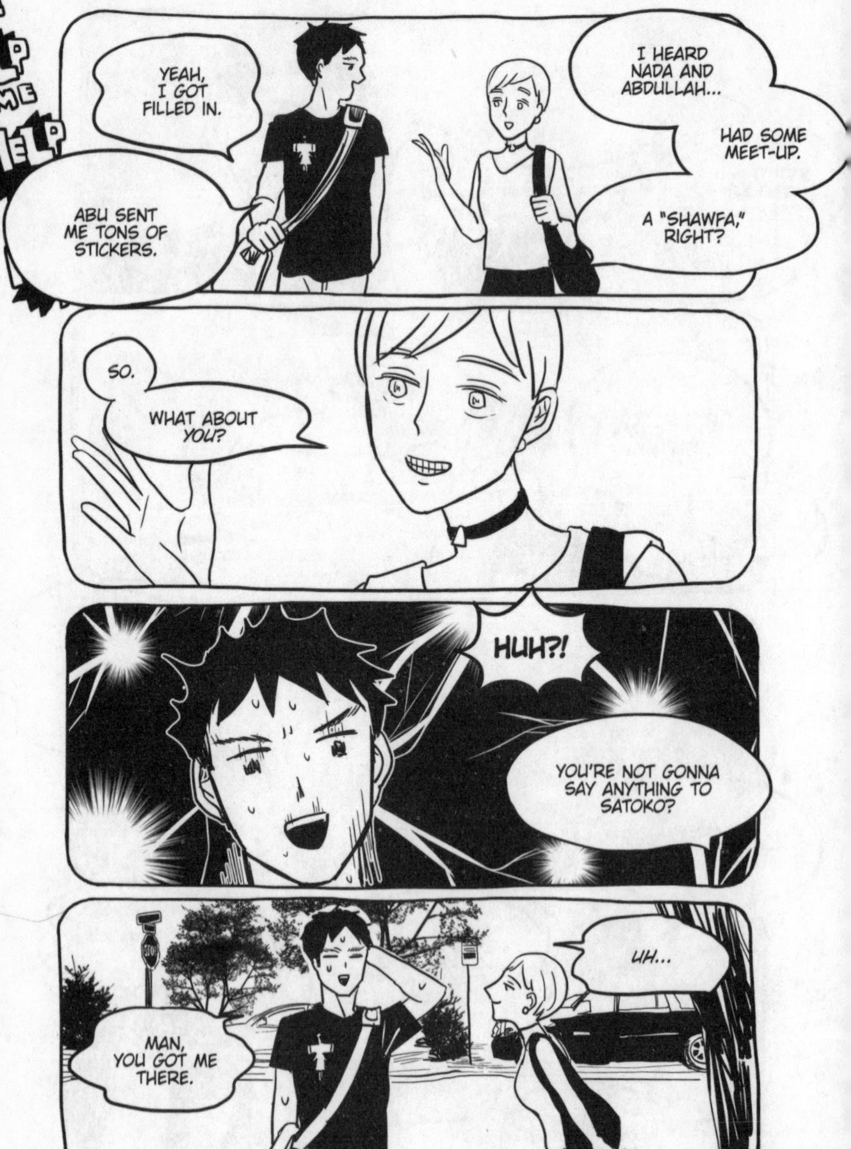
I HEARD NADA AND ABDULLAH...
HAD SOME MEET-UP.
A "SHAWFA," RIGHT?
YEAH, I GOT FILLED IN.
ABU SENT ME TONS OF STICKERS.
SO.
WHAT ABOUT *YOU?*
HUH?!
YOU'RE NOT GONNA SAY ANYTHING TO SATOKO?
UH...
MAN, YOU GOT ME THERE.

FAIR

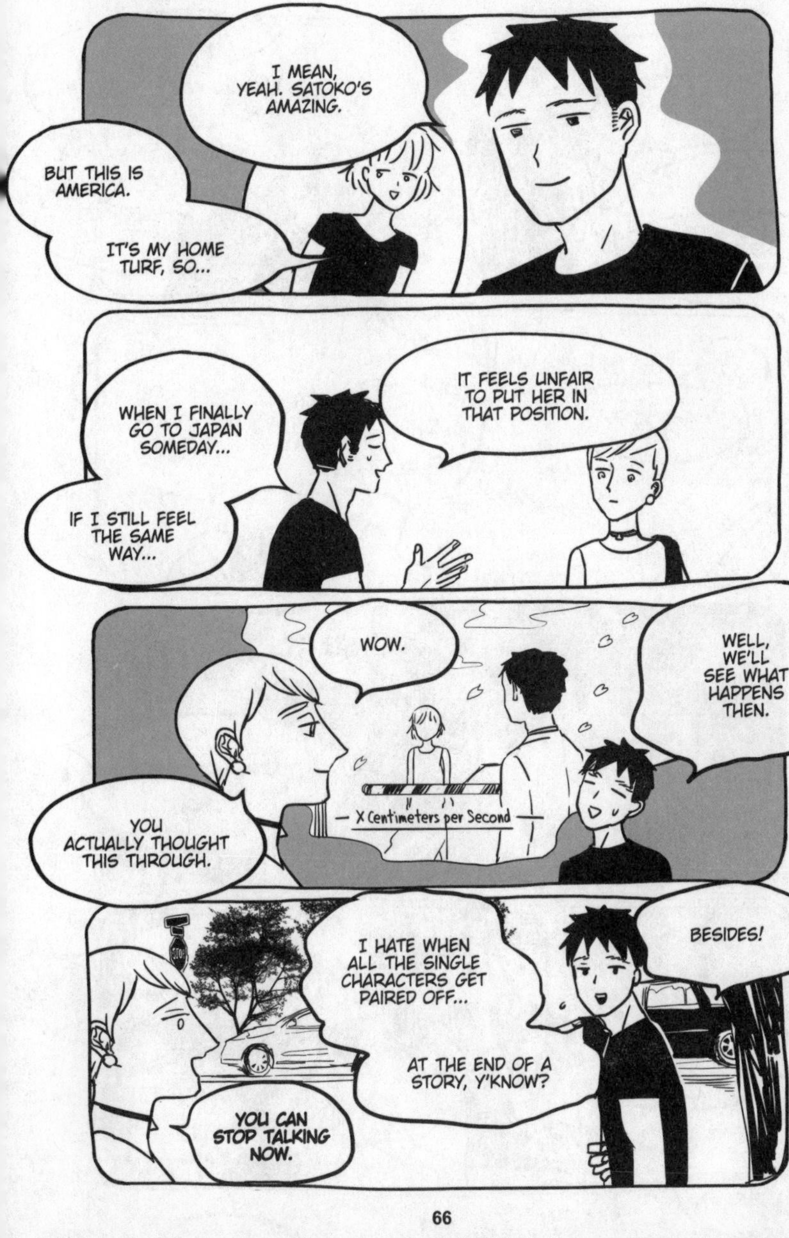
I MEAN, YEAH. SATOKO'S AMAZING.
BUT THIS IS AMERICA.
IT'S MY HOME TURF, SO...
IT FEELS UNFAIR TO PUT HER IN THAT POSITION.
WHEN I FINALLY GO TO JAPAN SOMEDAY...
IF I STILL FEEL THE SAME WAY...
WELL, WE'LL SEE WHAT HAPPENS THEN.
WOW.
X Centimeters per Second
YOU ACTUALLY THOUGHT THIS THROUGH.
BESIDES!
I HATE WHEN ALL THE SINGLE CHARACTERS GET PAIRED OFF...
AT THE END OF A STORY, Y'KNOW?
YOU CAN STOP TALKING NOW.

THANKS, BIG BROTHER

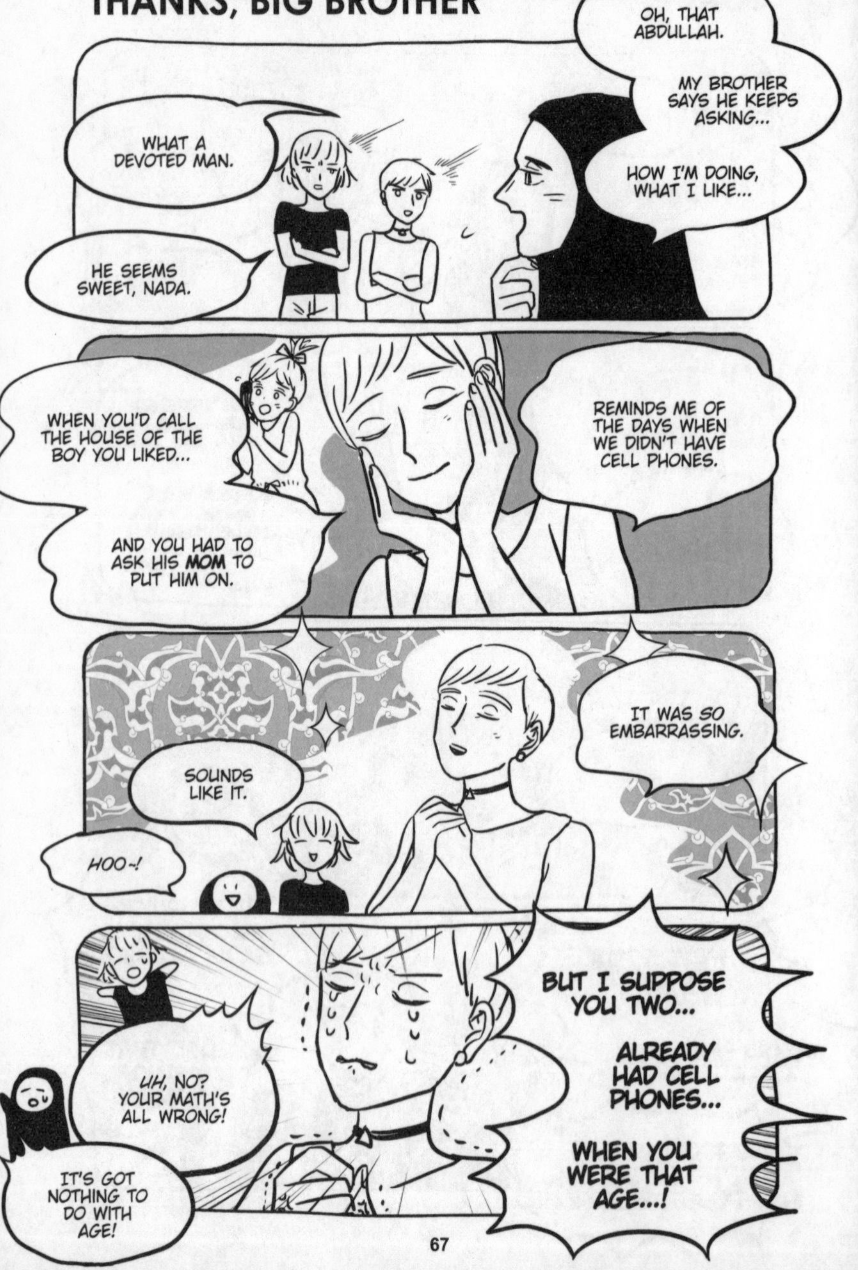
OH, THAT ABDULLAH.
MY BROTHER SAYS HE KEEPS ASKING...
HOW I'M DOING, WHAT I LIKE...
WHAT A DEVOTED MAN.
HE SEEMS SWEET, NADA.
REMINDS ME OF THE DAYS WHEN WE DIDN'T HAVE CELL PHONES.
WHEN YOU'D CALL THE HOUSE OF THE BOY YOU LIKED...
AND YOU HAD TO ASK HIS **MOM** TO PUT HIM ON.
IT WAS *SO* EMBARRASSING.
SOUNDS LIKE IT.
HOO~!
BUT I SUPPOSE YOU TWO...
ALREADY HAD CELL PHONES...
WHEN YOU WERE THAT AGE...!
UH, NO? YOUR MATH'S ALL WRONG!
IT'S GOT NOTHING TO DO WITH AGE!

LDR

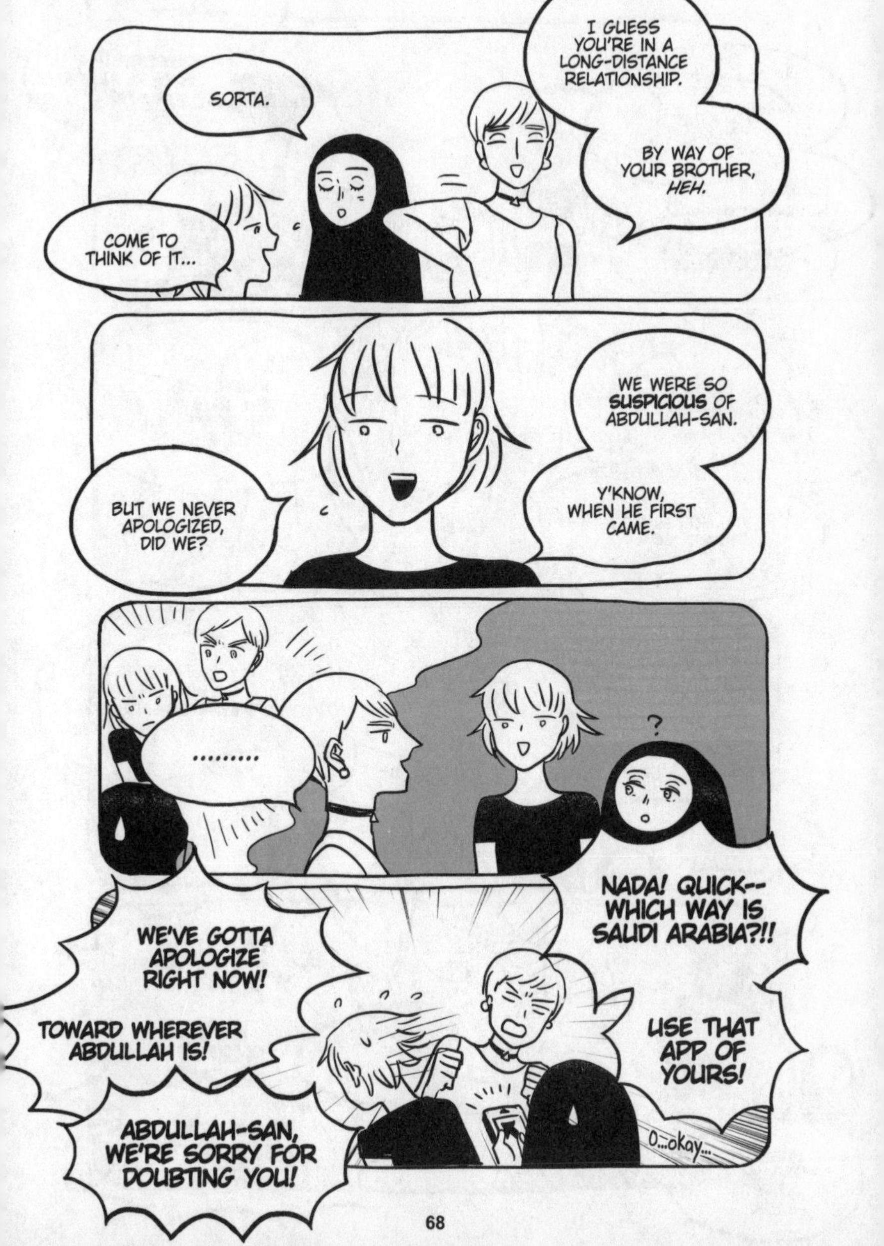
I GUESS YOU'RE IN A LONG-DISTANCE RELATIONSHIP.
BY WAY OF YOUR BROTHER, *HEH.*
SORTA.
COME TO THINK OF IT...
WE WERE SO **SUSPICIOUS** OF ABDULLAH-SAN.
Y'KNOW, WHEN HE FIRST CAME.
BUT WE NEVER APOLOGIZED, DID WE?
?
....
NADA! QUICK-- WHICH WAY IS SAUDI ARABIA?!!
USE THAT APP OF YOURS!
O...okay...
WE'VE GOTTA APOLOGIZE RIGHT NOW!
TOWARD WHEREVER ABDULLAH IS!
ABDULLAH-SAN, WE'RE SORRY FOR DOUBTING YOU!

29 YEARS OLD

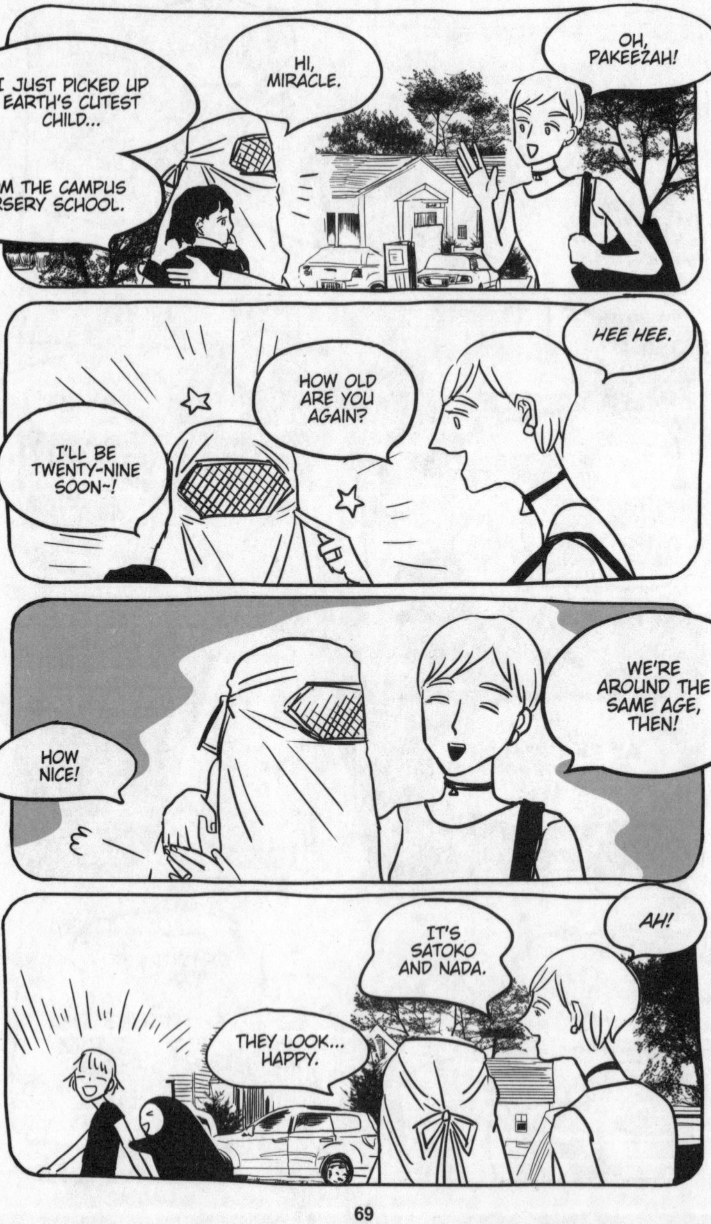
OH, PAKEEZAH!
HI, MIRACLE.
I JUST PICKED UP EARTH'S CUTEST CHILD...
FROM THE CAMPUS NURSERY SCHOOL.
HEE HEE.
HOW OLD ARE YOU AGAIN?
I'LL BE TWENTY-NINE SOON~!
WE'RE AROUND THE SAME AGE, THEN!
HOW NICE!
AH!
IT'S SATOKO AND NADA.
THEY LOOK... HAPPY.

DETOUR

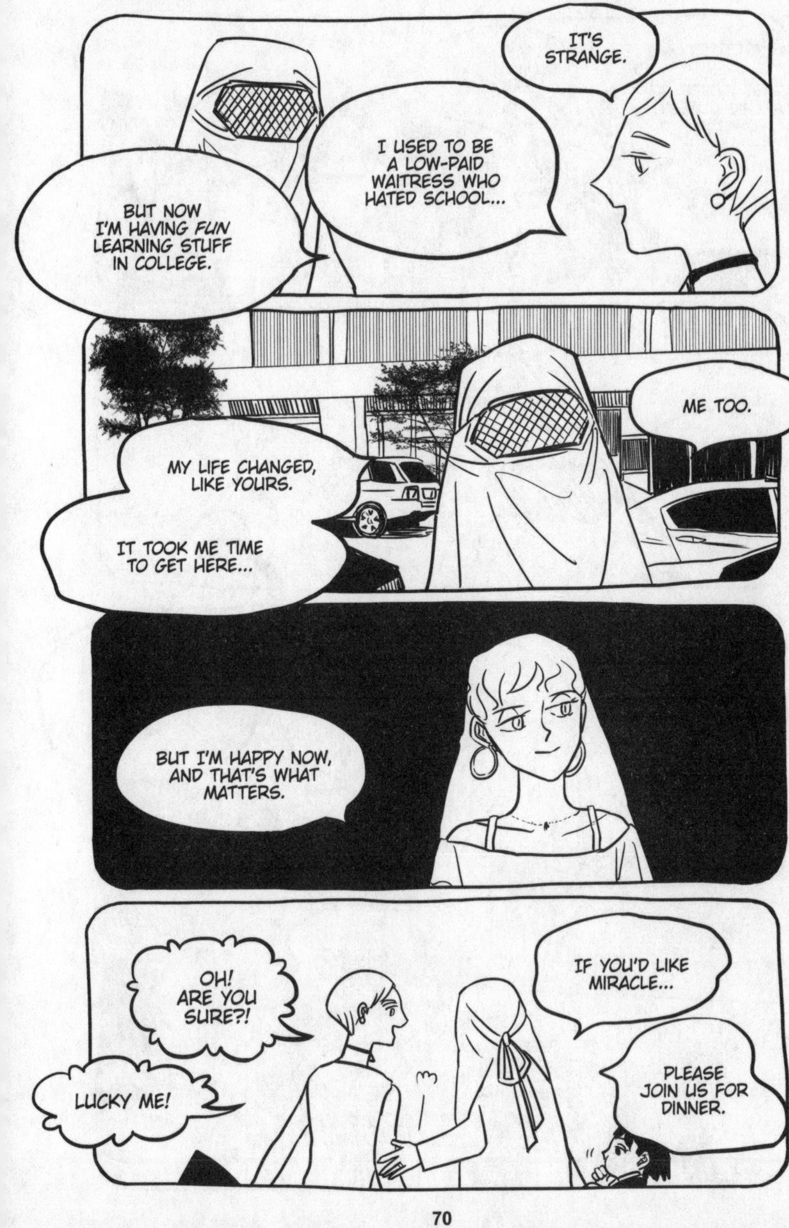
IT'S STRANGE.
I USED TO BE A LOW-PAID WAITRESS WHO HATED SCHOOL...
BUT NOW I'M HAVING *FUN* LEARNING STUFF IN COLLEGE.
ME TOO.
MY LIFE CHANGED, LIKE YOURS.
IT TOOK ME TIME TO GET HERE...
BUT I'M HAPPY NOW, AND THAT'S WHAT MATTERS.
IF YOU'D LIKE MIRACLE...
PLEASE JOIN US FOR DINNER.
OH! ARE YOU SURE?!
LUCKY ME!

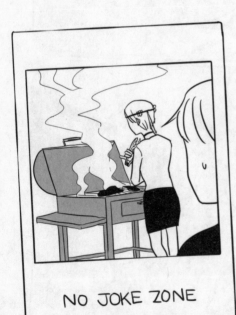

NO JOKE ZONE

COMPASSION

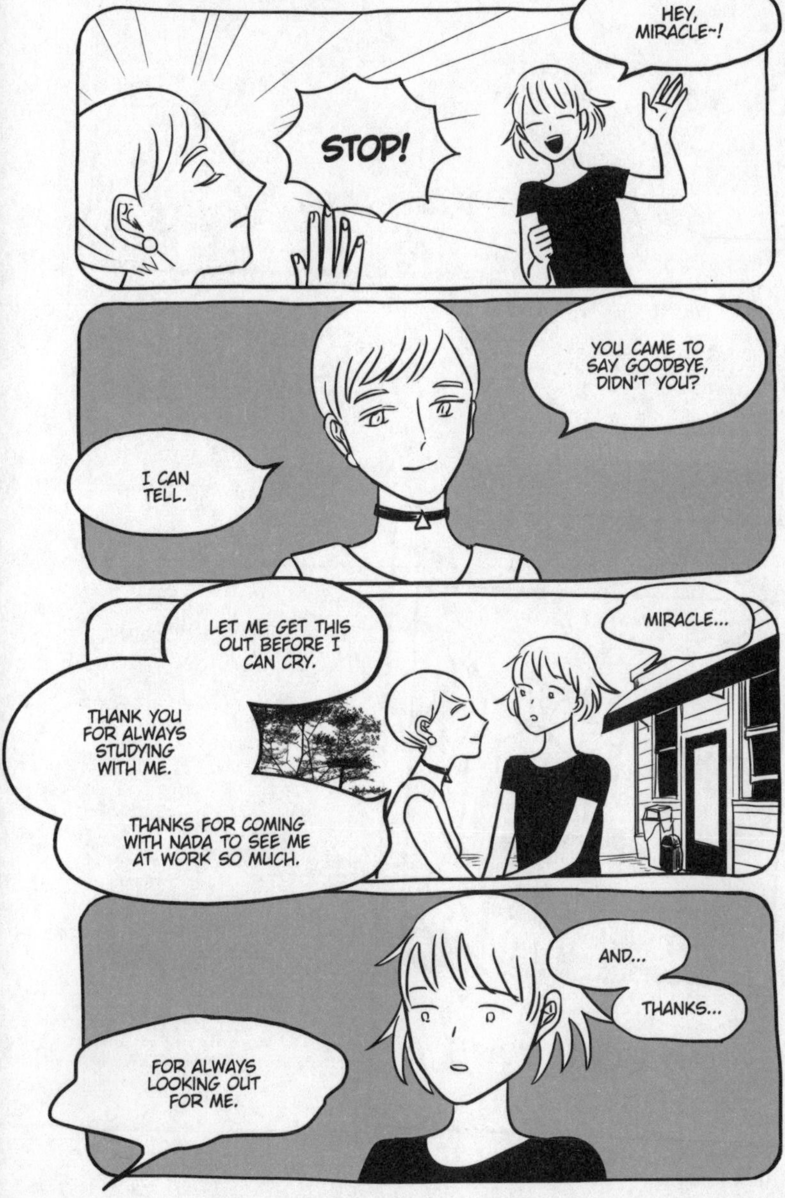
HEY, MIRACLE~!
STOP!
YOU CAME TO SAY GOODBYE, DIDN'T YOU?
I CAN TELL.
MIRACLE...
LET ME GET THIS OUT BEFORE I CAN CRY.
THANK YOU FOR ALWAYS STUDYING WITH ME.
THANKS FOR COMING WITH NADA TO SEE ME AT WORK SO MUCH.
AND...
THANKS...
FOR ALWAYS LOOKING OUT FOR ME.

I LOVE YOOOU!

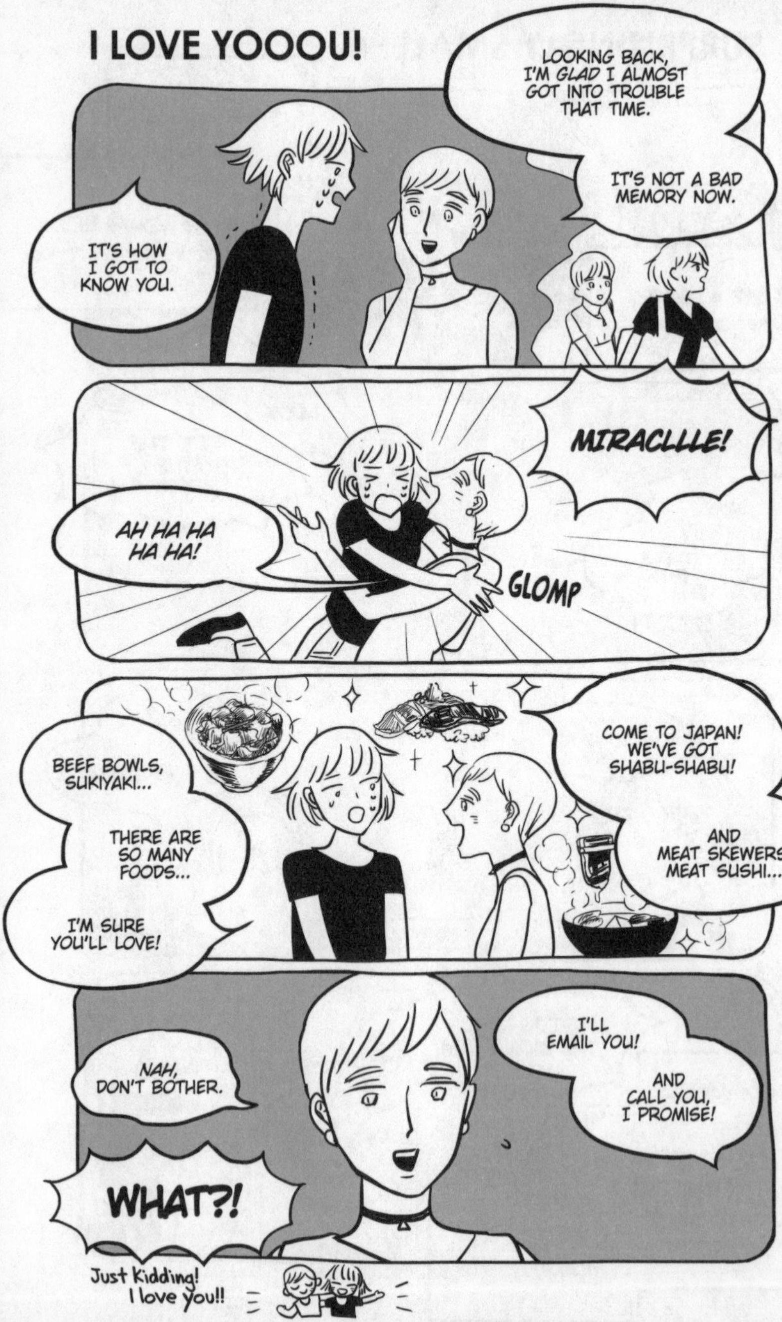

LOOKING BACK, I'M *GLAD* I ALMOST GOT INTO TROUBLE THAT TIME.
IT'S NOT A BAD MEMORY NOW.
IT'S HOW I GOT TO KNOW YOU.
MIRACLLLE!
GLOMP
AH HA HA HA HA!
COME TO JAPAN! WE'VE GOT SHABU-SHABU!
AND MEAT SKEWERS, MEAT SUSHI...
BEEF BOWLS, SUKIYAKI...
THERE ARE SO MANY FOODS...
I'M SURE YOU'LL LOVE!
I'LL EMAIL YOU!
AND CALL YOU, I PROMISE!
NAH, DON'T BOTHER.
WHAT?!
Just Kidding! I love you!!

SURPRISINGLY SMALL

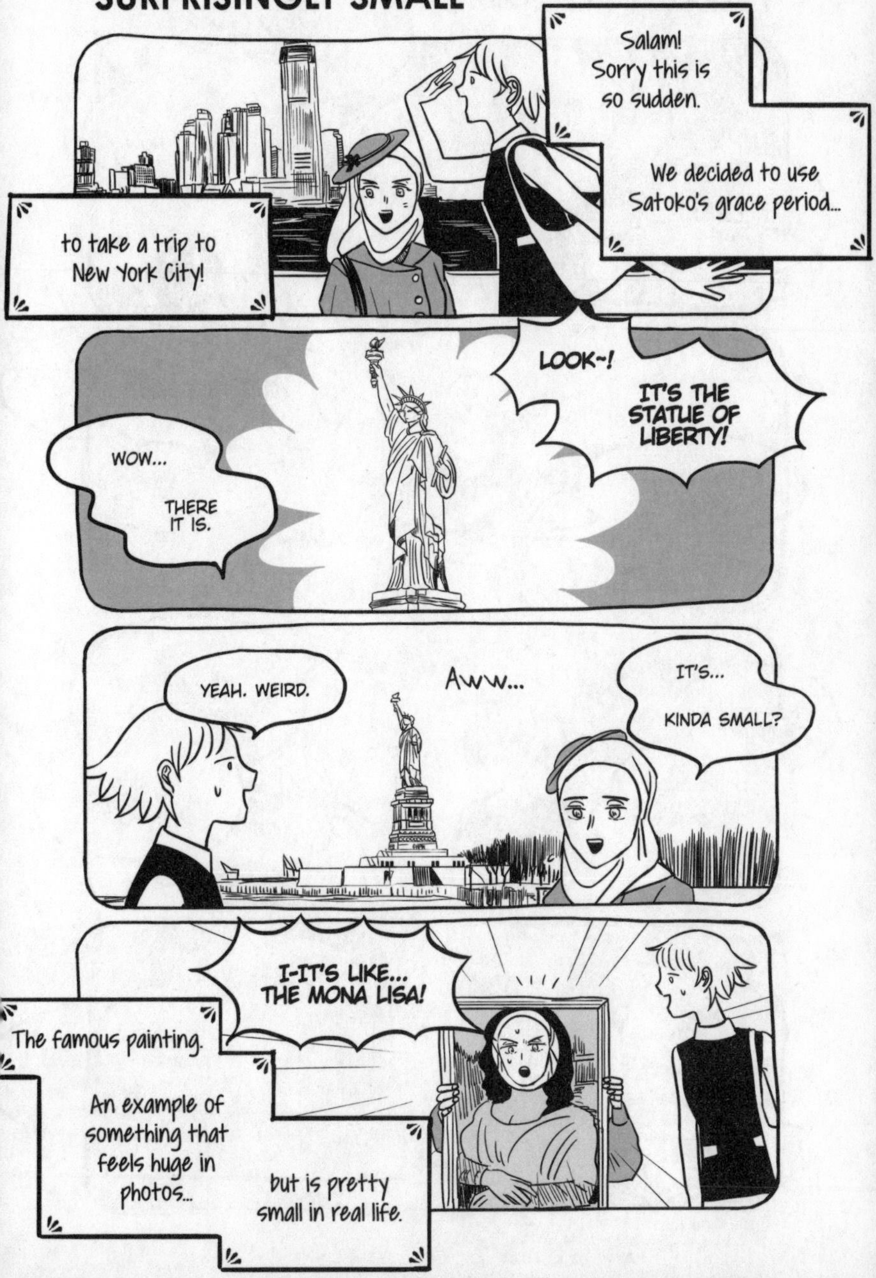
Salam! Sorry this is so sudden.
We decided to use Satoko's grace period...
to take a trip to New York City!
LOOK~!
IT'S THE STATUE OF LIBERTY!
WOW...
THERE IT IS.
IT'S...
KINDA SMALL?
Aww...
YEAH. WEIRD.
I-IT'S LIKE... THE MONA LISA!
The famous painting.
An example of something that feels huge in photos...
but is pretty small in real life.

HALAL NAIL POLISH

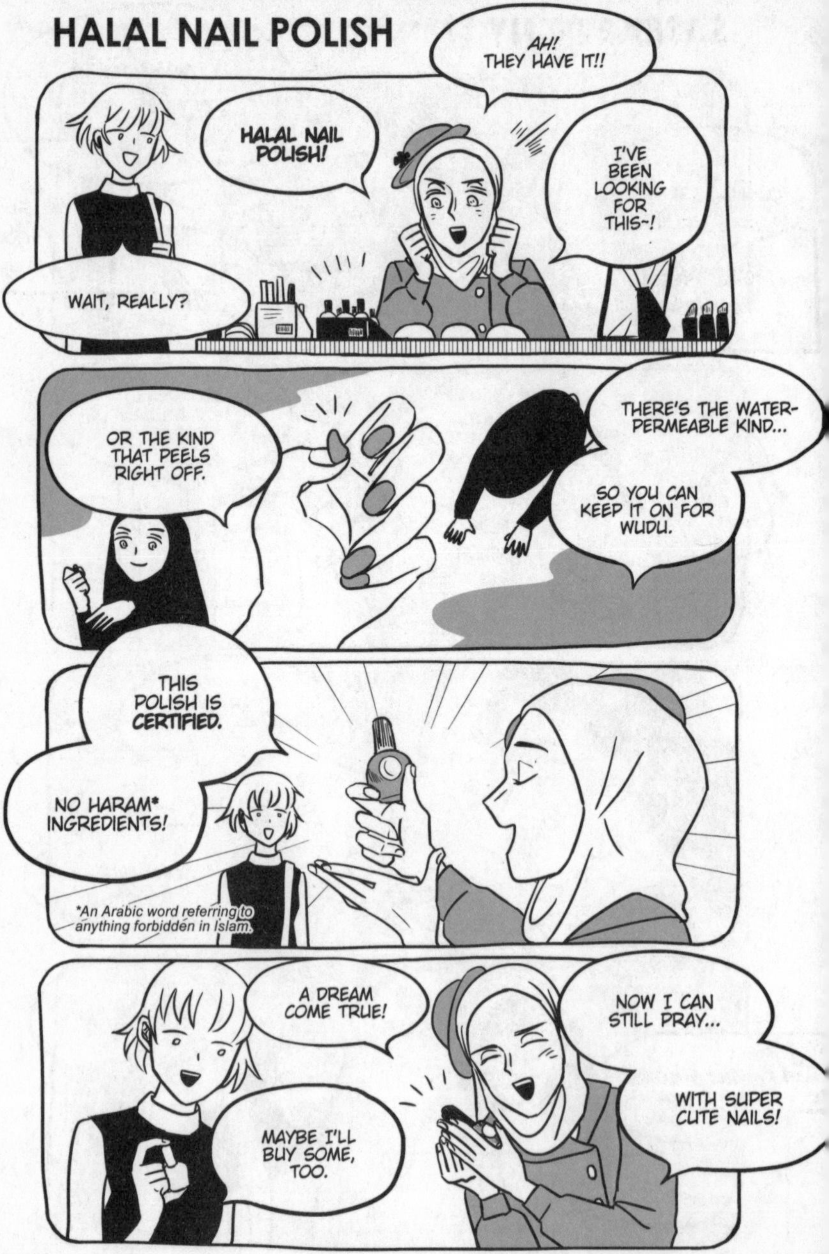
AH! THEY HAVE IT!!
I'VE BEEN LOOKING FOR THIS~!
HALAL NAIL POLISH!
WAIT, REALLY?
THERE'S THE WATER-PERMEABLE KIND...
SO YOU CAN KEEP IT ON FOR WUDU.
OR THE KIND THAT PEELS RIGHT OFF.
THIS POLISH IS **CERTIFIED.**
NO HARAM* INGREDIENTS!
*An Arabic word referring to anything forbidden in Islam.
NOW I CAN STILL PRAY...
WITH SUPER CUTE NAILS!
A DREAM COME TRUE!
MAYBE I'LL BUY SOME, TOO.

SAMAR IN NY

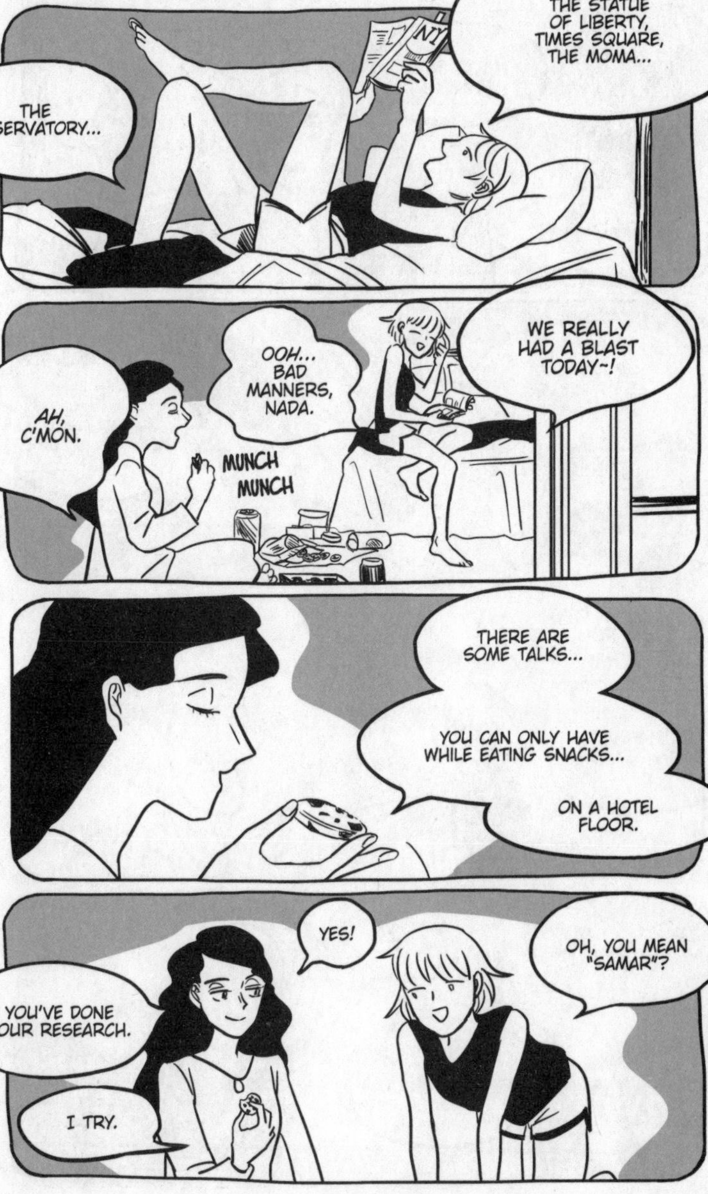
THE STATUE OF LIBERTY, TIMES SQUARE, THE MOMA...
THE OBSERVATORY...
WE REALLY HAD A BLAST TODAY~!
OOH... BAD MANNERS, NADA.
AH, C'MON.
MUNCH MUNCH
THERE ARE SOME TALKS...
YOU CAN ONLY HAVE WHILE EATING SNACKS...
ON A HOTEL FLOOR.
OH, YOU MEAN "SAMAR"?
YES!
YOU'VE DONE YOUR RESEARCH.
I TRY.

SELFIE, TAKE TWO

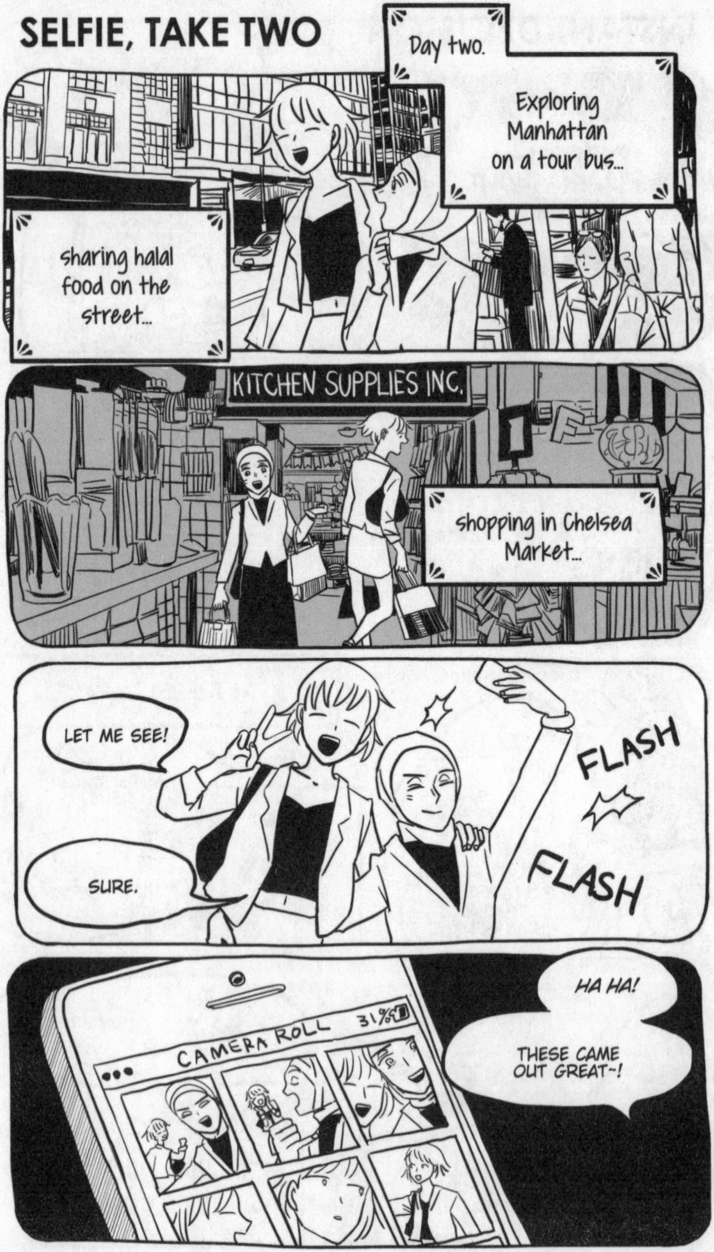

Day two.
Exploring Manhattan on a tour bus...
sharing halal food on the street...
KITCHEN SUPPLIES INC.
shopping in Chelsea Market...
LET ME SEE!
SURE.
FLASH
FLASH
CAMERA ROLL
31%
HA HA!
THESE CAME OUT GREAT~!

INSTANT DECISION

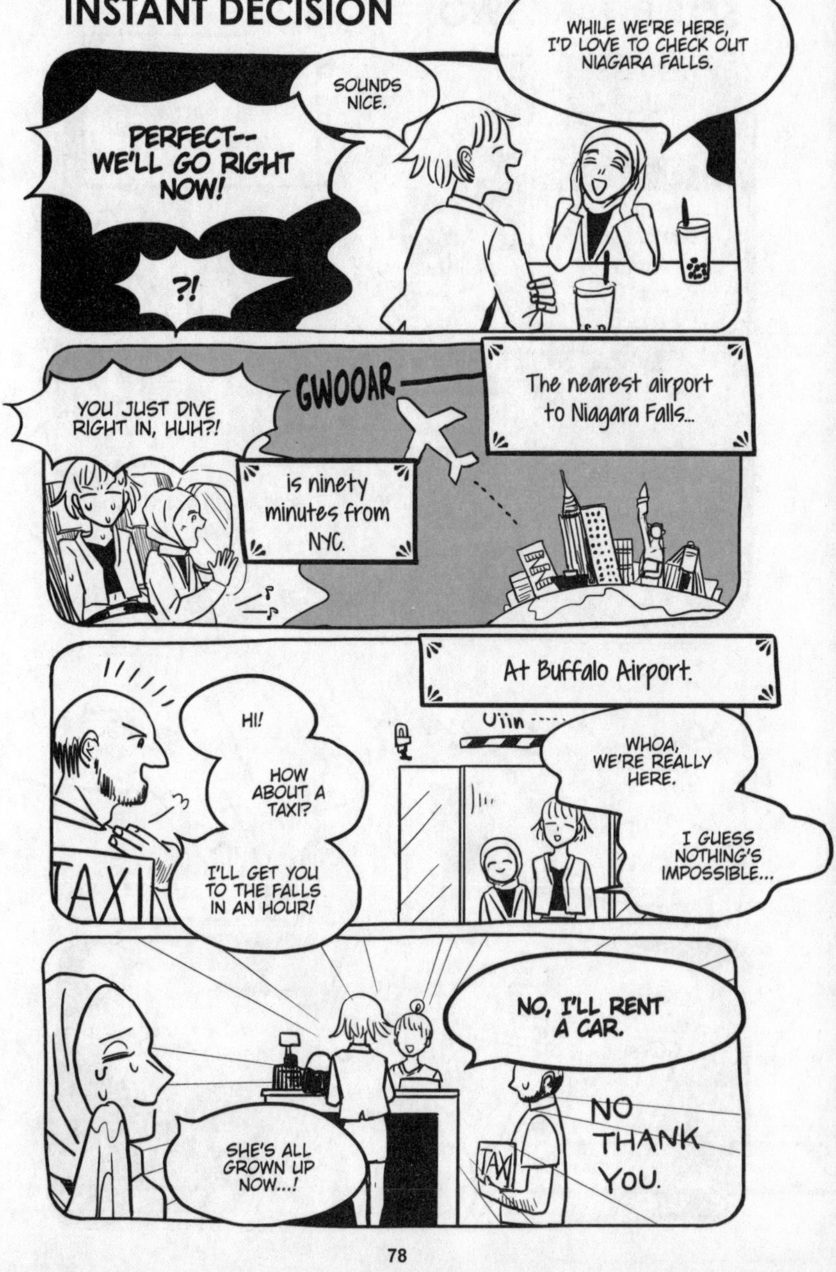

WHILE WE'RE HERE, I'D LOVE TO CHECK OUT NIAGARA FALLS.
SOUNDS NICE.
PERFECT-- WE'LL GO RIGHT NOW!
?!
The nearest airport to Niagara Falls...
GWOOAR
is ninety minutes from NYC.
YOU JUST DIVE RIGHT IN, HUH?!
At Buffalo Airport.
Uiin
WHOA, WE'RE REALLY HERE.
I GUESS NOTHING'S IMPOSSIBLE...
HI!
HOW ABOUT A TAXI?
I'LL GET YOU TO THE FALLS IN AN HOUR!
TAXI
NO, I'LL RENT A CAR.
NO THANK YOU.
TAXI
SHE'S ALL GROWN UP NOW...!

SO MUCH WATER

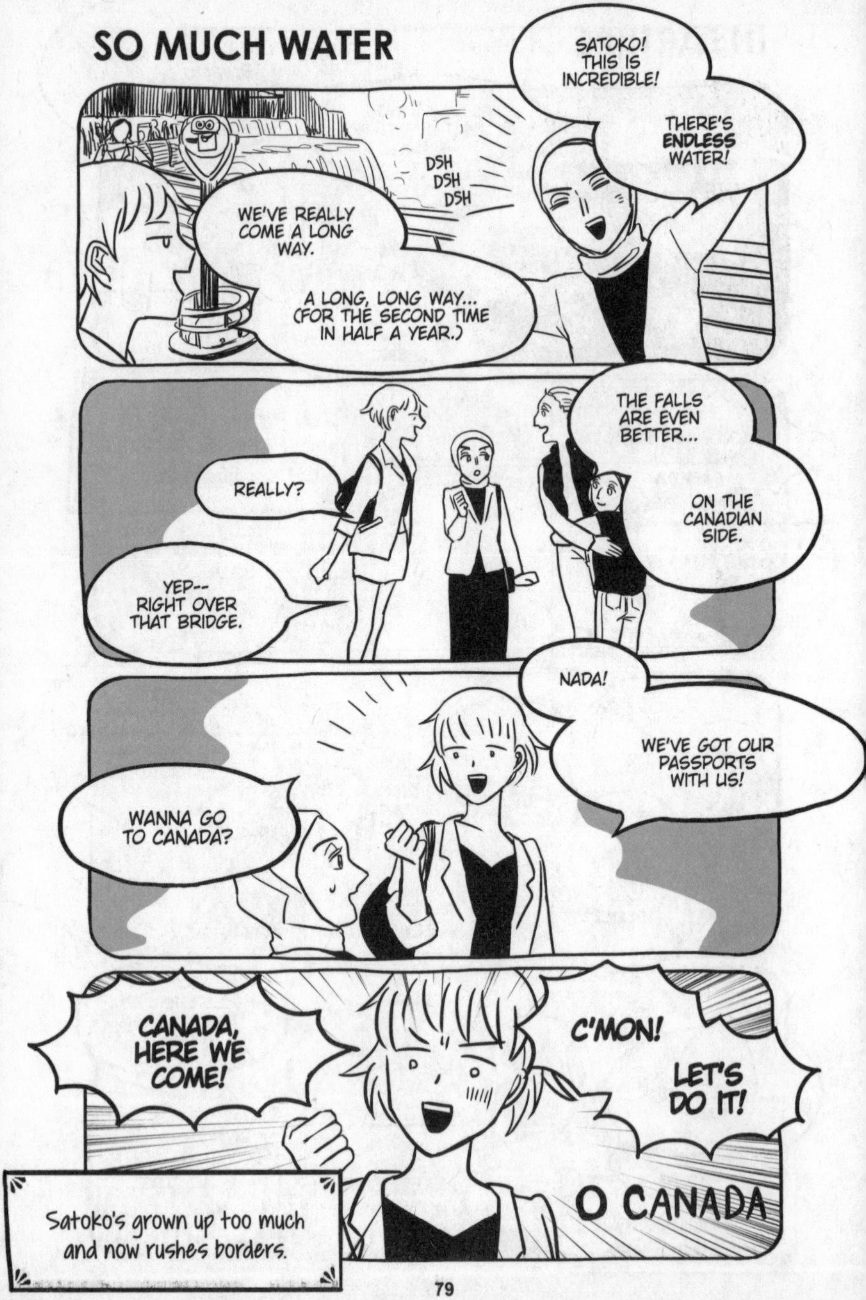

SATOKO! THIS IS INCREDIBLE!
THERE'S **ENDLESS** WATER!
DSH DSH DSH
WE'VE REALLY COME A LONG WAY.
A LONG, LONG WAY... (FOR THE SECOND TIME IN HALF A YEAR.)
THE FALLS ARE EVEN BETTER...
ON THE CANADIAN SIDE.
REALLY?
YEP-- RIGHT OVER THAT BRIDGE.
NADA!
WE'VE GOT OUR PASSPORTS WITH US!
WANNA GO TO CANADA?
C'MON!
LET'S DO IT!
CANADA, HERE WE COME!
O CANADA
Satoko's grown up too much and now rushes borders.

DEPARTURE

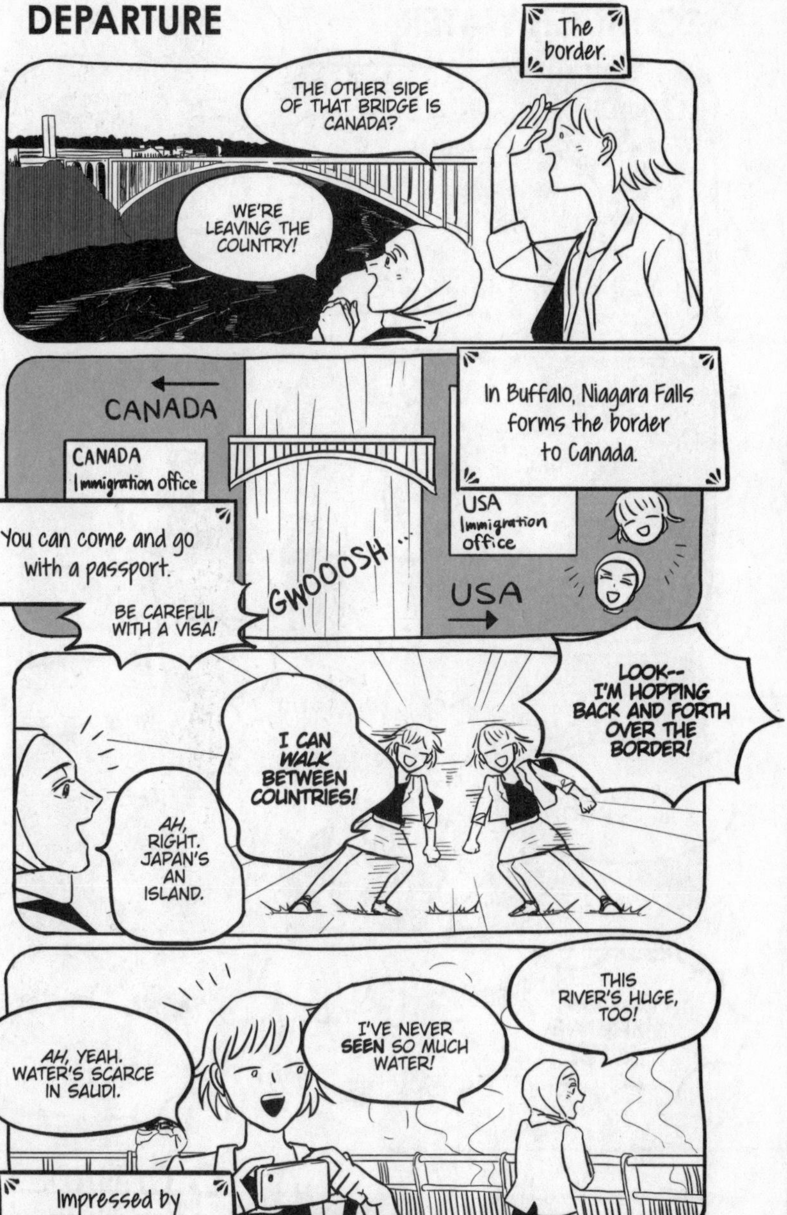
The border.
THE OTHER SIDE OF THAT BRIDGE IS CANADA?
WE'RE LEAVING THE COUNTRY!
In Buffalo, Niagara Falls forms the border to Canada.
USA Immigration office
USA
GWOOOSH ..
CANADA
CANADA Immigration office
You can come and go with a passport.
BE CAREFUL WITH A VISA!
LOOK-- I'M HOPPING BACK AND FORTH OVER THE BORDER!
I CAN *WALK* BETWEEN COUNTRIES!
AH, RIGHT. JAPAN'S AN ISLAND.
THIS RIVER'S HUGE, TOO!
I'VE NEVER **SEEN** SO MUCH WATER!
AH, YEAH. WATER'S SCARCE IN SAUDI.
Impressed by different things.

THE VIEW

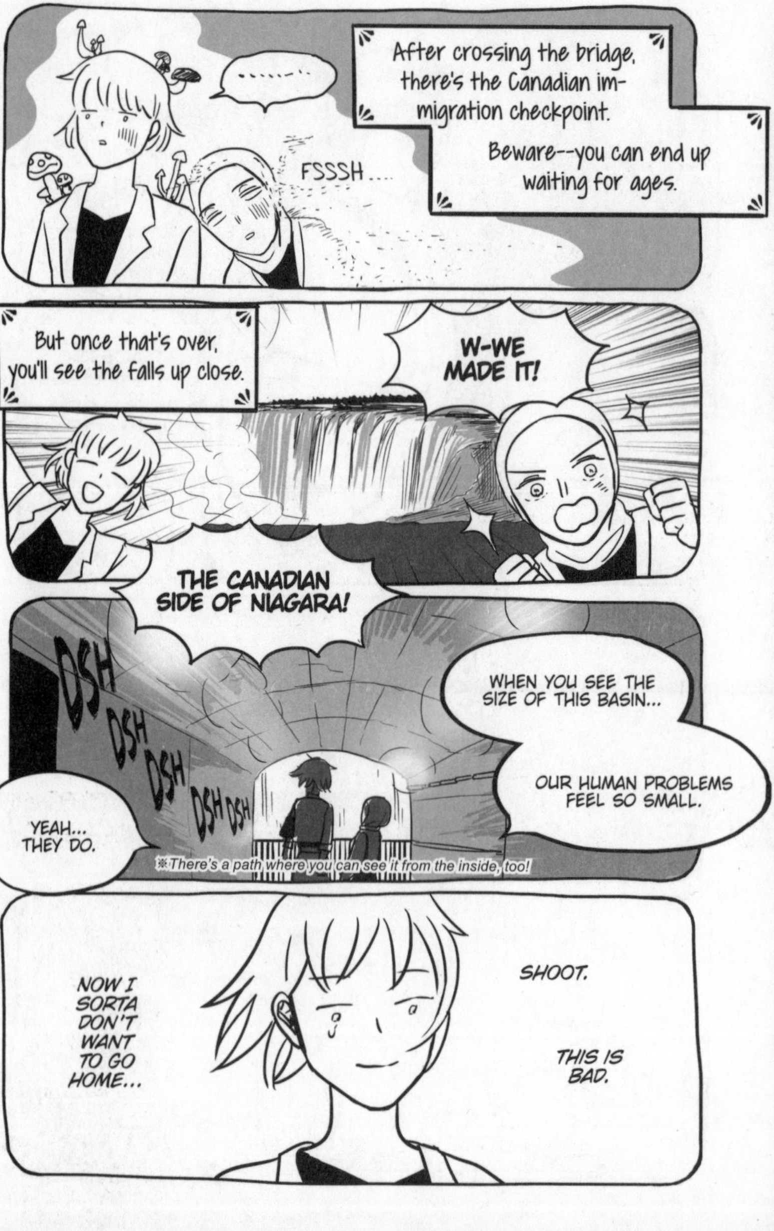
After crossing the bridge, there's the Canadian im-migration checkpoint.
......
Beware--you can end up waiting for ages.
FSSSH....
W-WE MADE IT!
But once that's over, you'll see the falls up close.
THE CANADIAN SIDE OF NIAGARA!
WHEN YOU SEE THE SIZE OF THIS BASIN...
OUR HUMAN PROBLEMS FEEL SO SMALL.
DSH DSH DSH DSH DSH
YEAH... THEY DO.
※There's a path where you can see it from the inside, too!
SHOOT.
THIS IS BAD.
NOW I SORTA DON'T WANT TO GO HOME...

BORDER

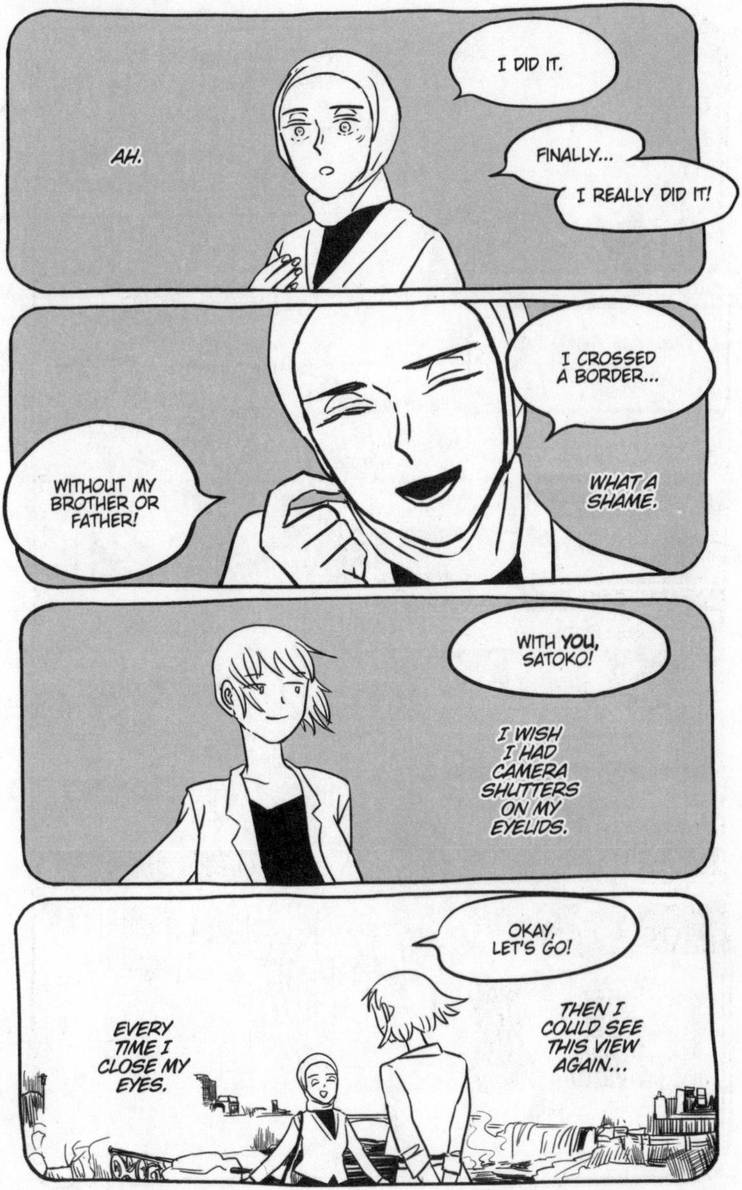
I DID IT.
FINALLY...
I REALLY DID IT!
AH.
I CROSSED A BORDER...
WHAT A SHAME.
WITHOUT MY BROTHER OR FATHER!
WITH YOU, SATOKO!
I WISH I HAD CAMERA SHUTTERS ON MY EYELIDS.
OKAY, LET'S GO!
THEN I COULD SEE THIS VIEW AGAIN...
EVERY TIME I CLOSE MY EYES.

COMMEMORATIVE PHOTO

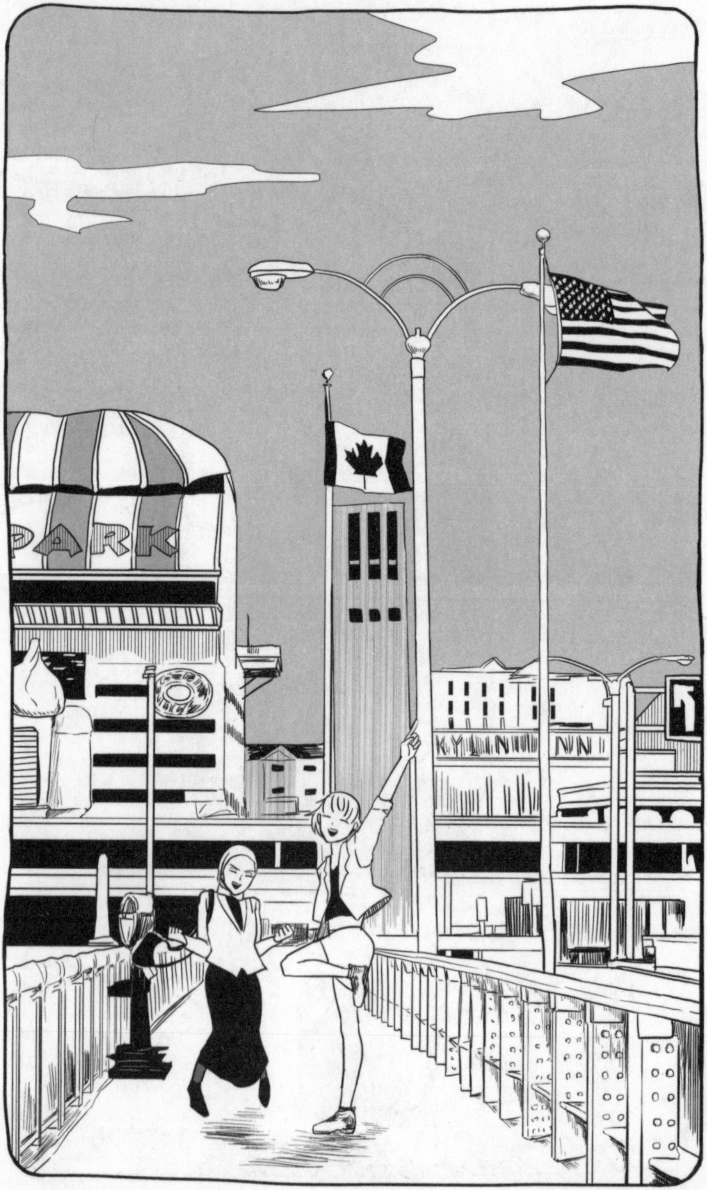
PARK

RELAXATION

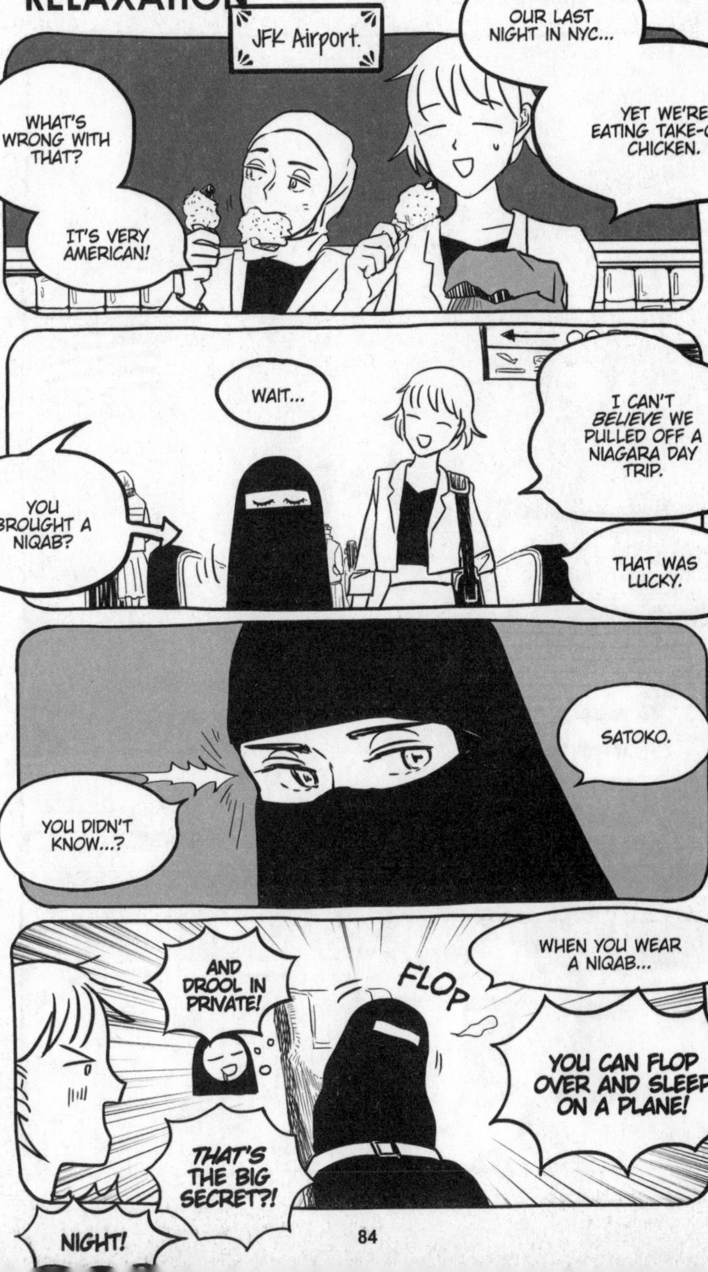

JFK Airport.
OUR LAST NIGHT IN NYC...
YET WE'RE EATING TAKE-OUT CHICKEN.
WHAT'S WRONG WITH THAT?
IT'S VERY AMERICAN!
I CAN'T *BELIEVE* WE PULLED OFF A NIAGARA DAY TRIP.
THAT WAS LUCKY.
WAIT...
YOU BROUGHT A NIQAB?
SATOKO.
YOU DIDN'T KNOW...?
WHEN YOU WEAR A NIQAB...
YOU CAN FLOP OVER AND SLEEP ON A PLANE!
FLOP
AND DROOL IN PRIVATE!
THAT'S THE BIG SECRET?!
NIGHT!

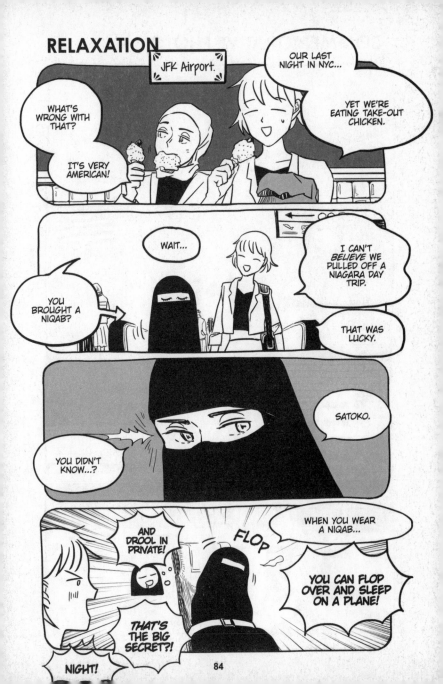

WELL?

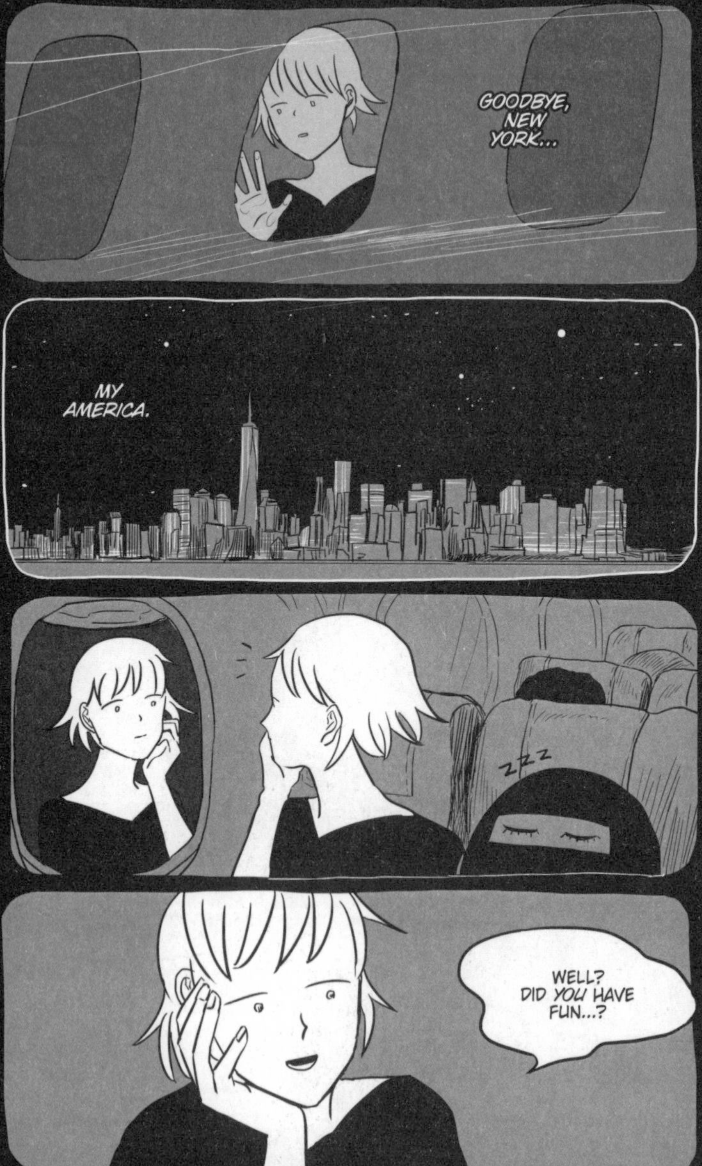
GOODBYE, NEW YORK...
MY AMERICA.
ZZZ
WELL? DID *YOU* HAVE FUN...?

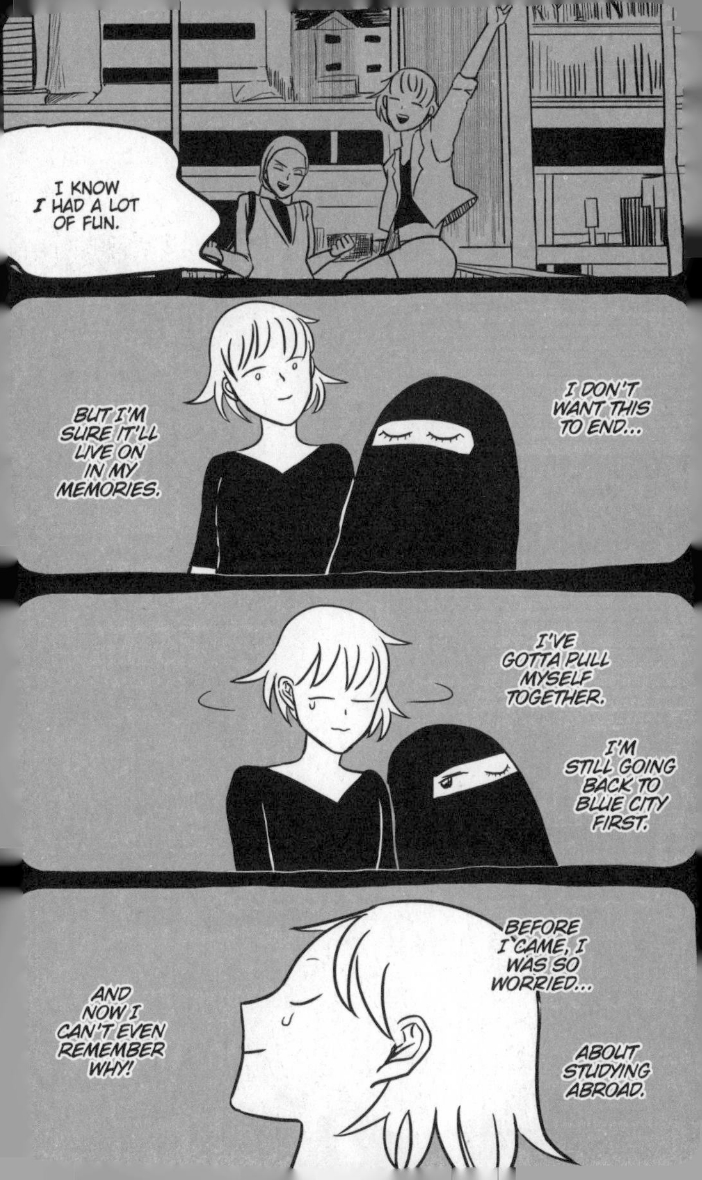
I KNOW I HAD A LOT OF FUN.
I DON'T WANT THIS TO END...
BUT I'M SURE IT'LL LIVE ON IN MY MEMORIES.
I'VE GOTTA PULL MYSELF TOGETHER.
I'M STILL GOING BACK TO BLUE CITY FIRST.
BEFORE I CAME, I WAS SO WORRIED...
ABOUT STUDYING ABROAD.
AND NOW I CAN'T EVEN REMEMBER WHY!

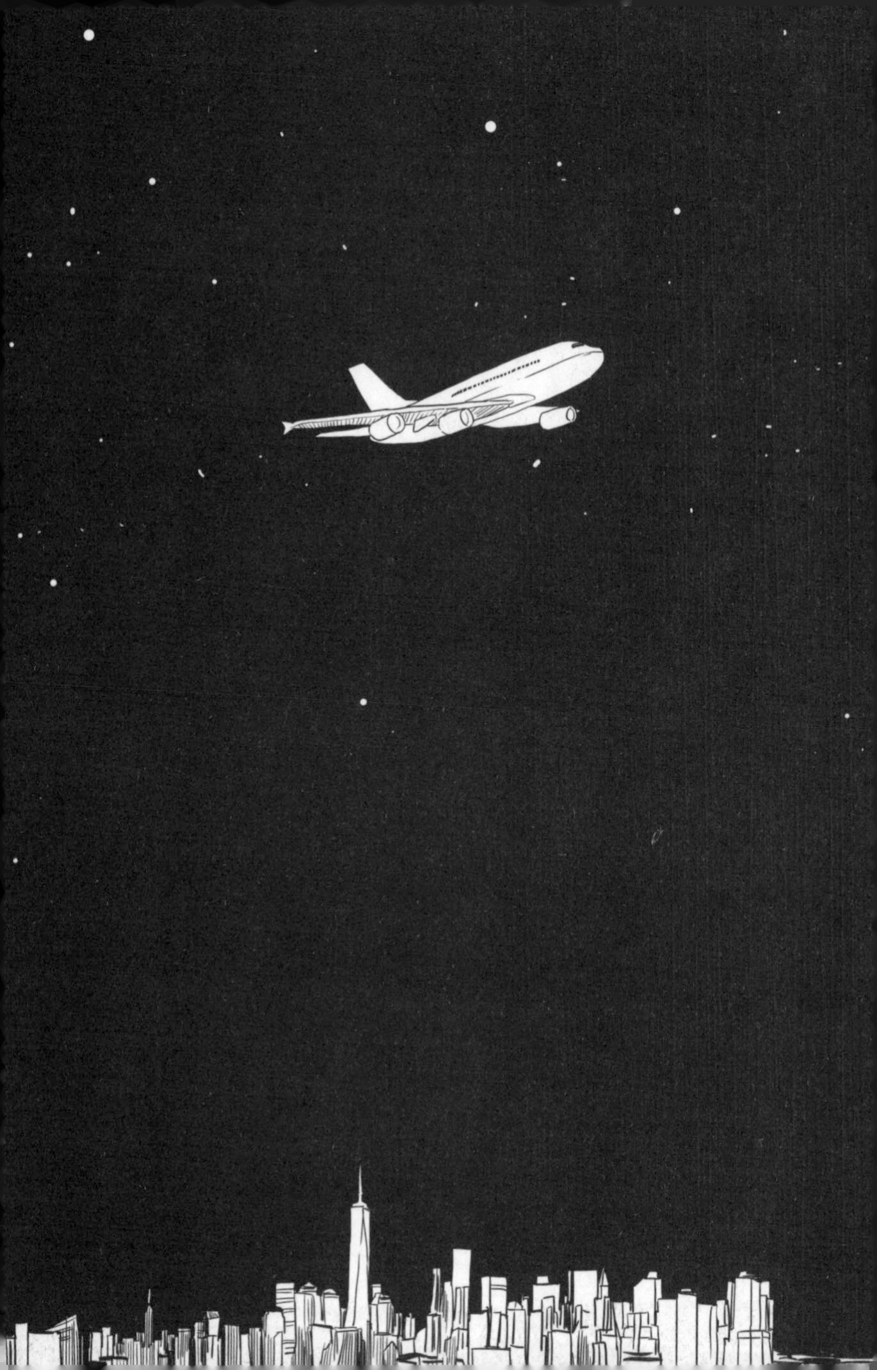

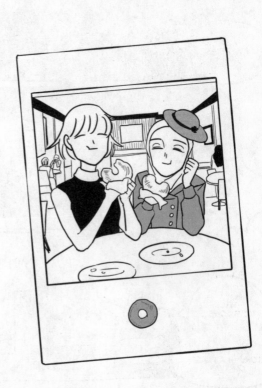

FOOTWORK

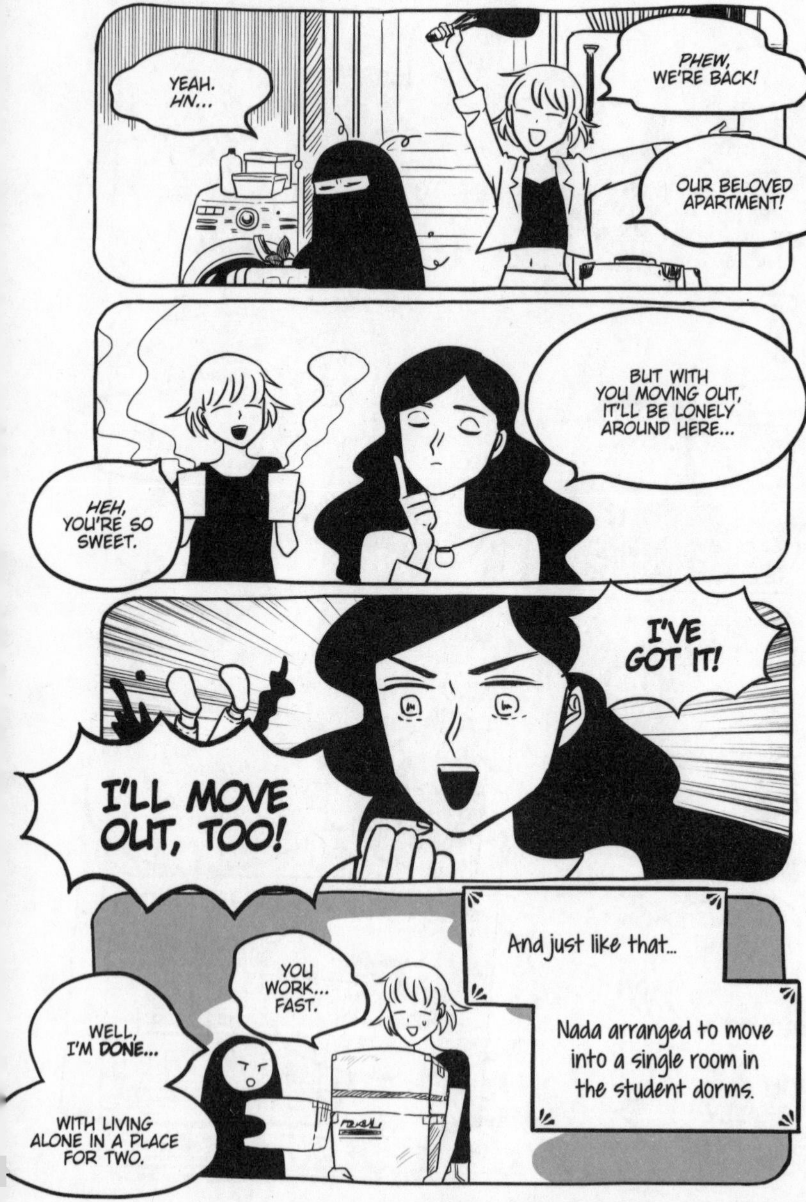
PHEW, WE'RE BACK!
OUR BELOVED APARTMENT!
YEAH. HN...
BUT WITH YOU MOVING OUT, IT'LL BE LONELY AROUND HERE...
HEH, YOU'RE SO SWEET.
I'VE GOT IT!
I'LL MOVE OUT, TOO!
And just like that...
Nada arranged to move into a single room in the student dorms.
YOU WORK... FAST.
WELL, I'M DONE...
WITH LIVING ALONE IN A PLACE FOR TWO.

PACKING TOGETHER

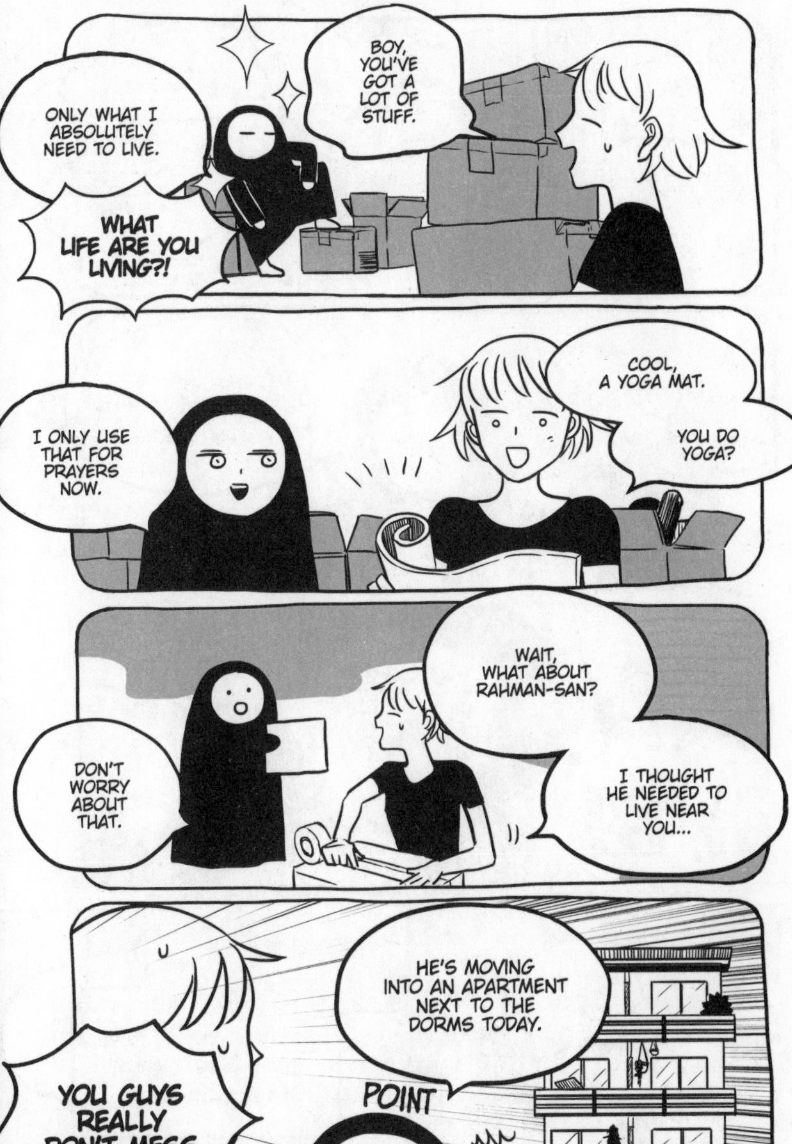
BOY, YOU'VE GOT A LOT OF STUFF.
ONLY WHAT I ABSOLUTELY NEED TO LIVE.
WHAT LIFE ARE YOU LIVING?!
COOL, A YOGA MAT.
YOU DO YOGA?
I ONLY USE THAT FOR PRAYERS NOW.
WAIT, WHAT ABOUT RAHMAN-SAN?
I THOUGHT HE NEEDED TO LIVE NEAR YOU...
DON'T WORRY ABOUT THAT.
HE'S MOVING INTO AN APARTMENT NEXT TO THE DORMS TODAY.
POINT
YOU GUYS REALLY DON'T MESS AROUND!

FIRST DAY

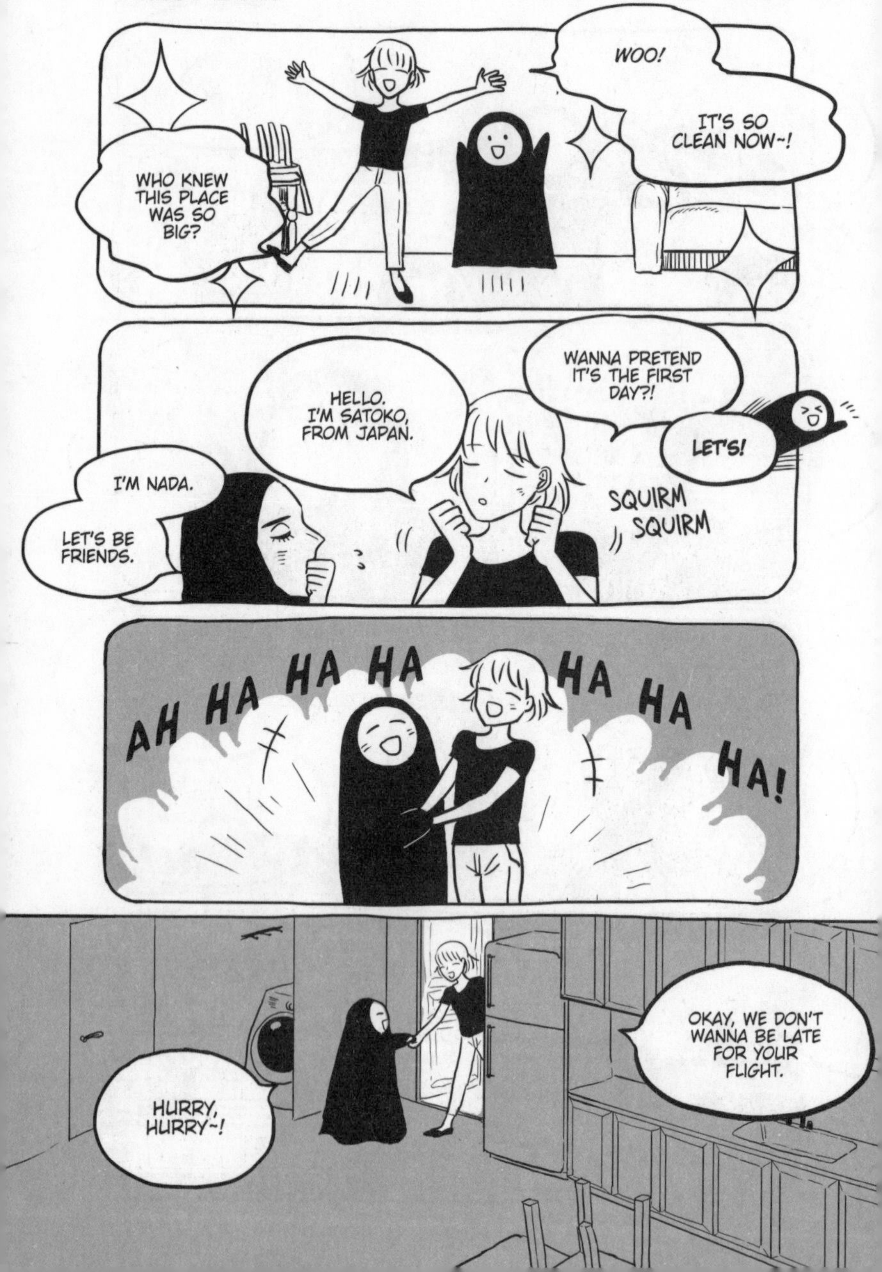
WOO!
IT'S SO CLEAN NOW~!
WHO KNEW THIS PLACE WAS SO BIG?
WANNA PRETEND IT'S THE FIRST DAY?!
LET'S!
SQUIRM SQUIRM
HELLO. I'M SATOKO, FROM JAPAN.
I'M NADA.
LET'S BE FRIENDS.
AH HA HA HA HA HA HA!
OKAY, WE DON'T WANNA BE LATE FOR YOUR FLIGHT.
HURRY, HURRY~!

TO THE AIRPORT

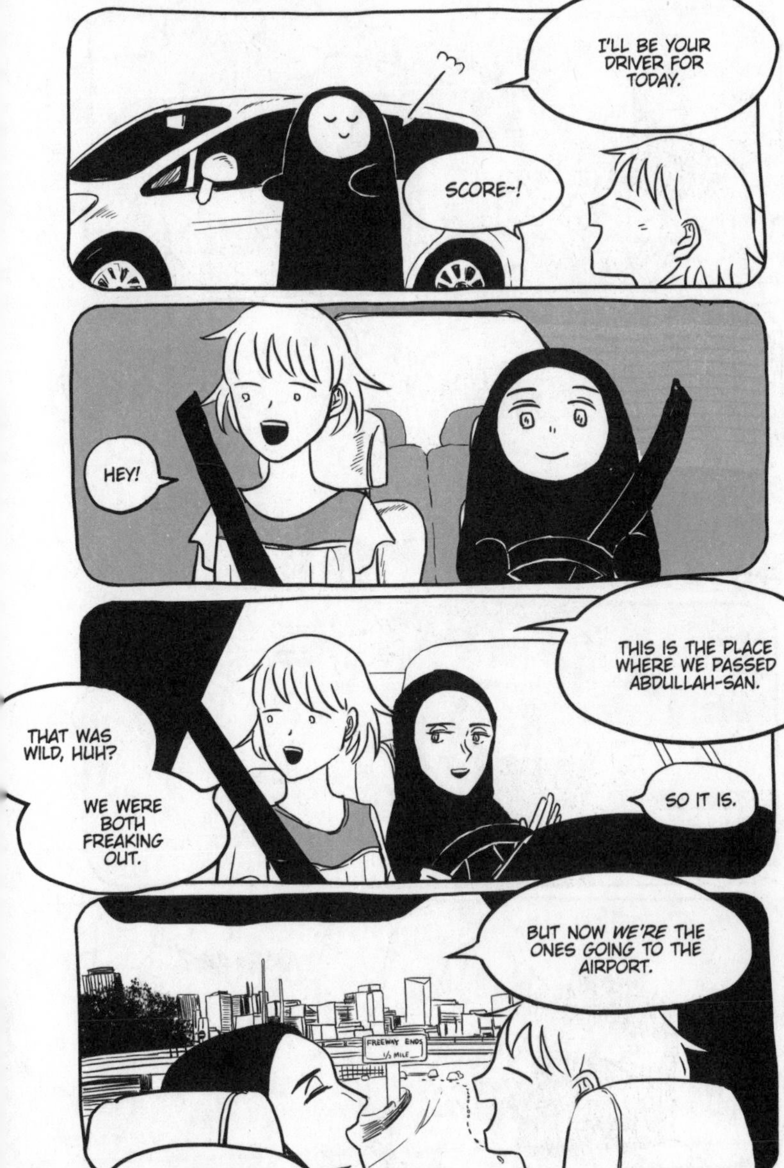
I'LL BE YOUR DRIVER FOR TODAY.
SCORE~!
HEY!
THIS IS THE PLACE WHERE WE PASSED ABDULLAH-SAN.
THAT WAS WILD, HUH?
SO IT IS.
WE WERE BOTH FREAKING OUT.
BUT NOW *WE'RE* THE ONES GOING TO THE AIRPORT.
FREEWAY ENDS
1/2 MILE
IT FEELS WEIRD, *HEH.*

SURPRISE

*Sign: Have a safe trip.

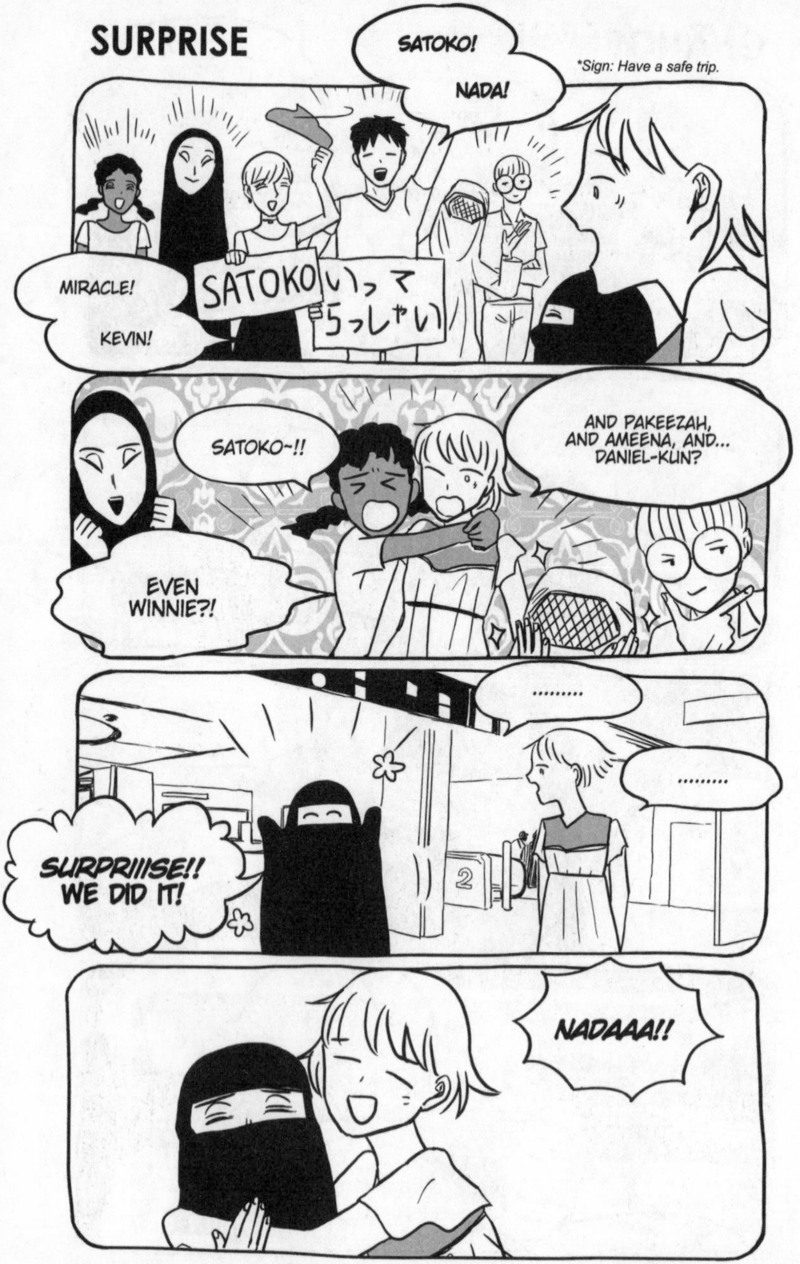
SATOKO!
NADA!
SATOKO いってらっしゃい
MIRACLE!
KEVIN!
AND PAKEEZAH, AND AMEENA, AND... DANIEL-KUN?
SATOKO~!!
EVEN WINNIE?!
....
....
SURPRIIISE!! WE DID IT!
NADAAA!!

CHANGE

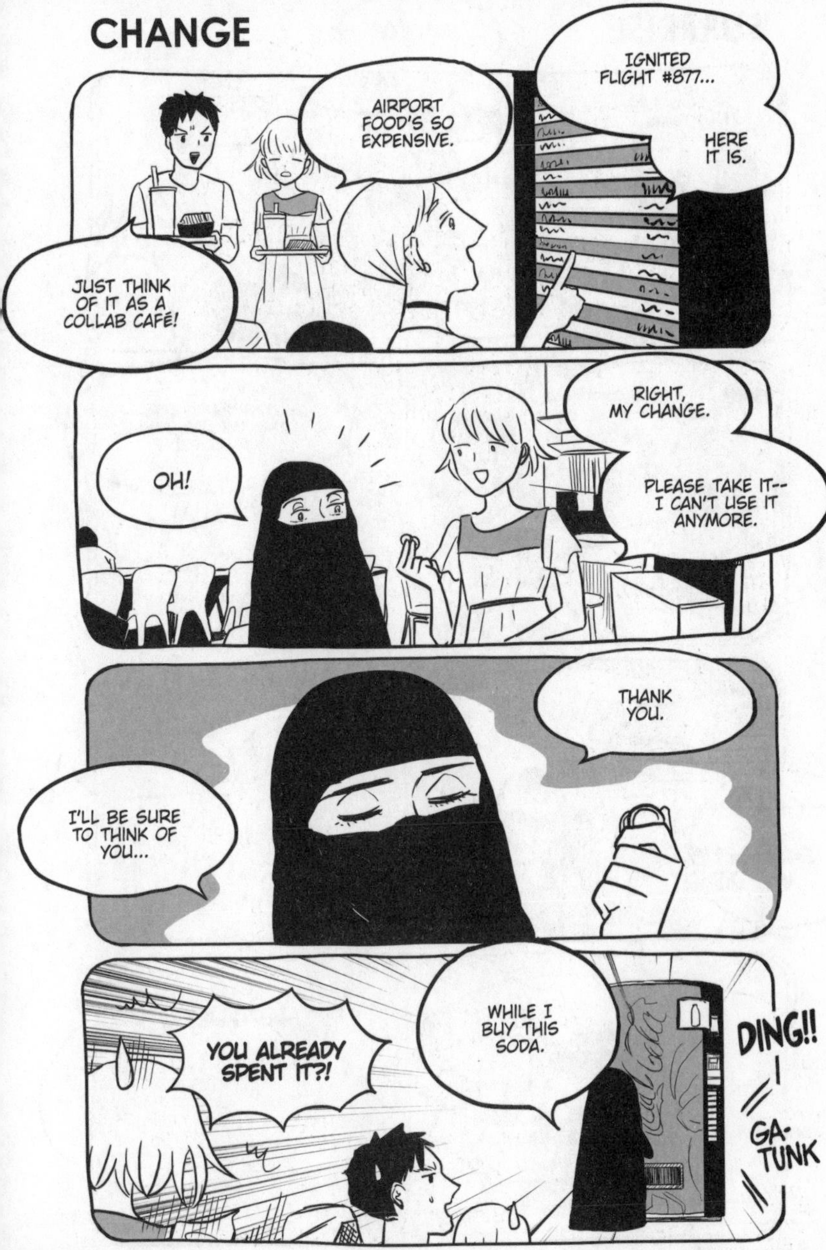
IGNITED FLIGHT #877...
HERE IT IS.
AIRPORT FOOD'S SO EXPENSIVE.
JUST THINK OF IT AS A COLLAB CAFÉ!
RIGHT, MY CHANGE.
PLEASE TAKE IT-- I CAN'T USE IT ANYMORE.
OH!
THANK YOU.
I'LL BE SURE TO THINK OF YOU...
WHILE I BUY THIS SODA.
DING!!
GA-TUNK
YOU ALREADY SPENT IT?!

BELIEF

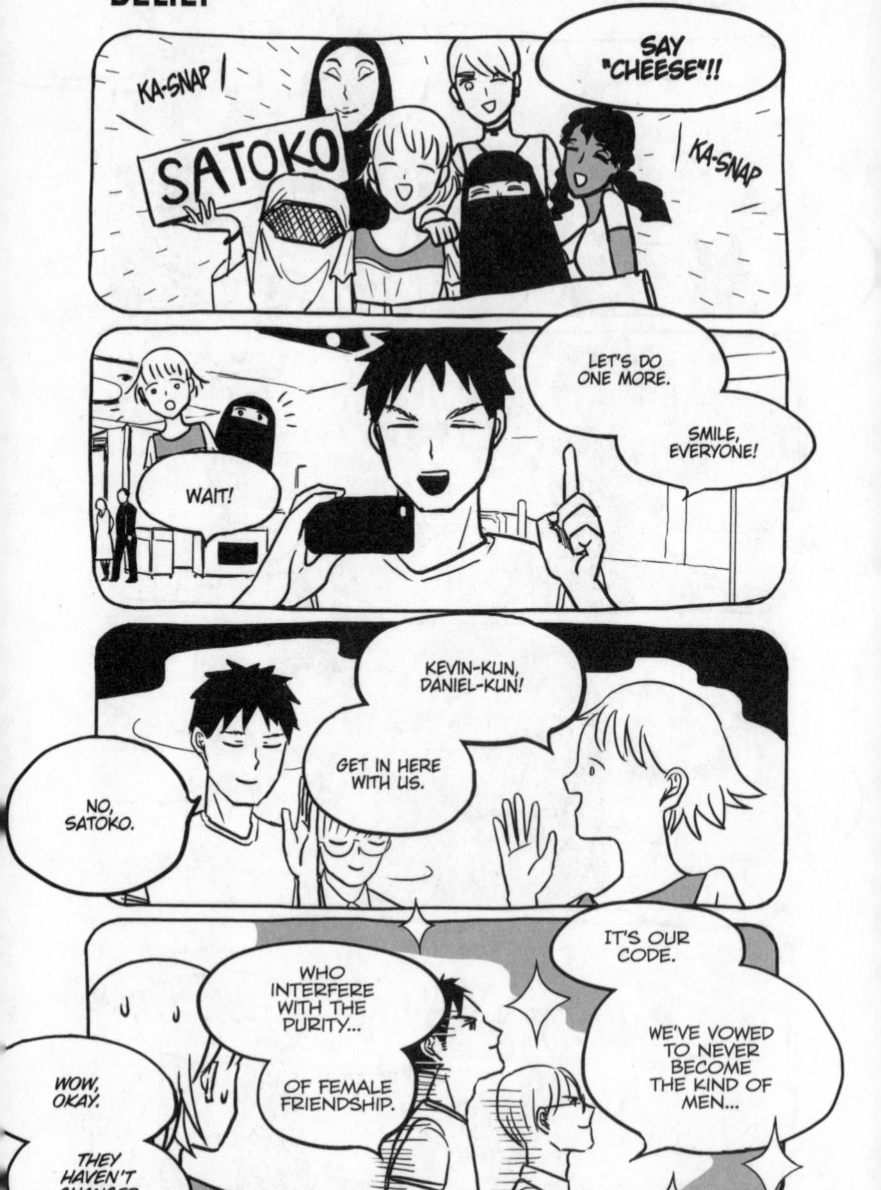
SAY "CHEESE"!!
KA-SNAP
KA-SNAP
SATOKO
LET'S DO ONE MORE.
SMILE, EVERYONE!
WAIT!
KEVIN-KUN, DANIEL-KUN!
GET IN HERE WITH US.
NO, SATOKO.
IT'S OUR CODE.
WE'VE VOWED TO NEVER BECOME THE KIND OF MEN...
WHO INTERFERE WITH THE PURITY...
OF FEMALE FRIENDSHIP.
WOW, OKAY.
THEY HAVEN'T CHANGED A BIT.

YOU GUYS

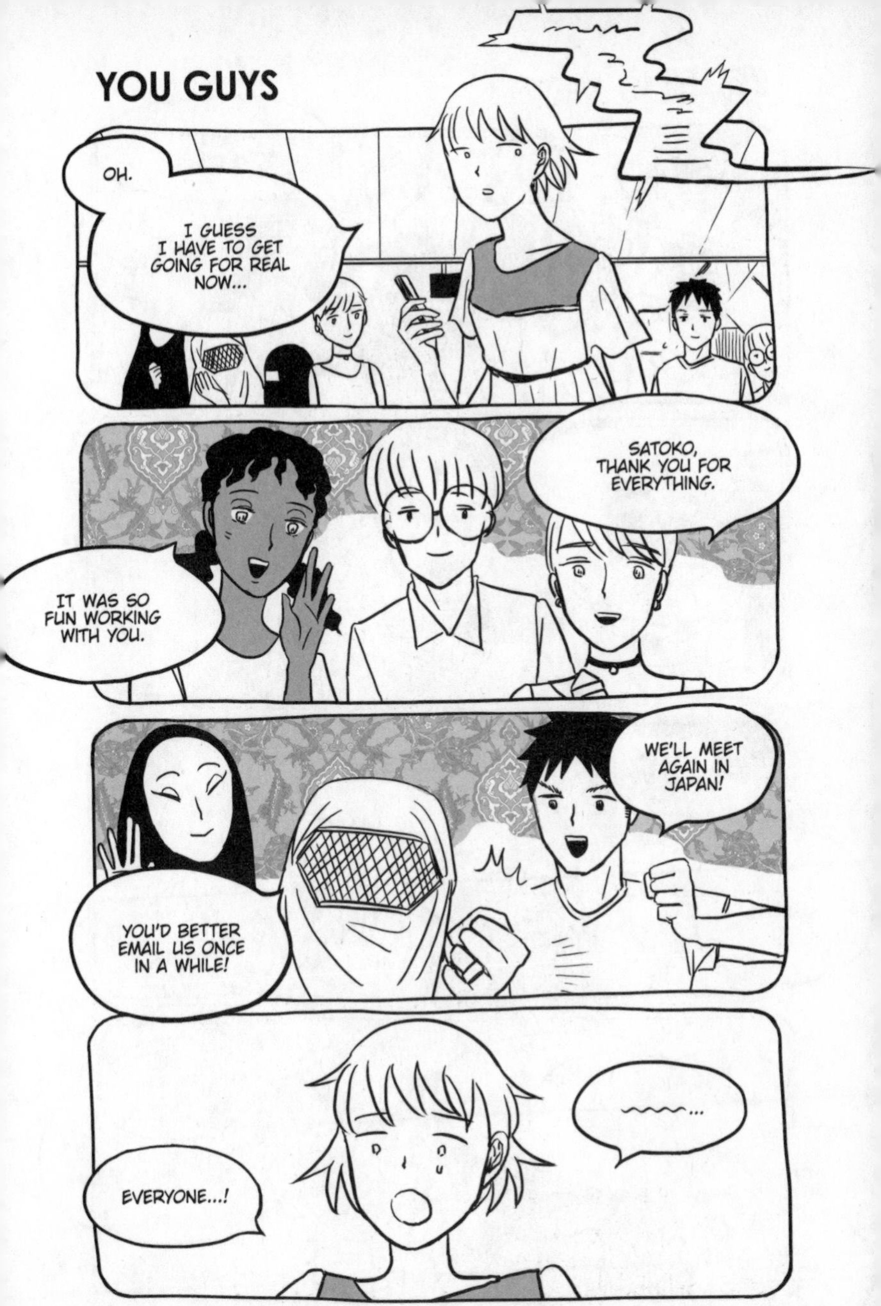
OH.
I GUESS I HAVE TO GET GOING FOR REAL NOW...
SATOKO, THANK YOU FOR EVERYTHING.
IT WAS SO FUN WORKING WITH YOU.
WE'LL MEET AGAIN IN JAPAN!
YOU'D BETTER EMAIL US ONCE IN A WHILE!
EVERYONE...!

DO YOU MIND?

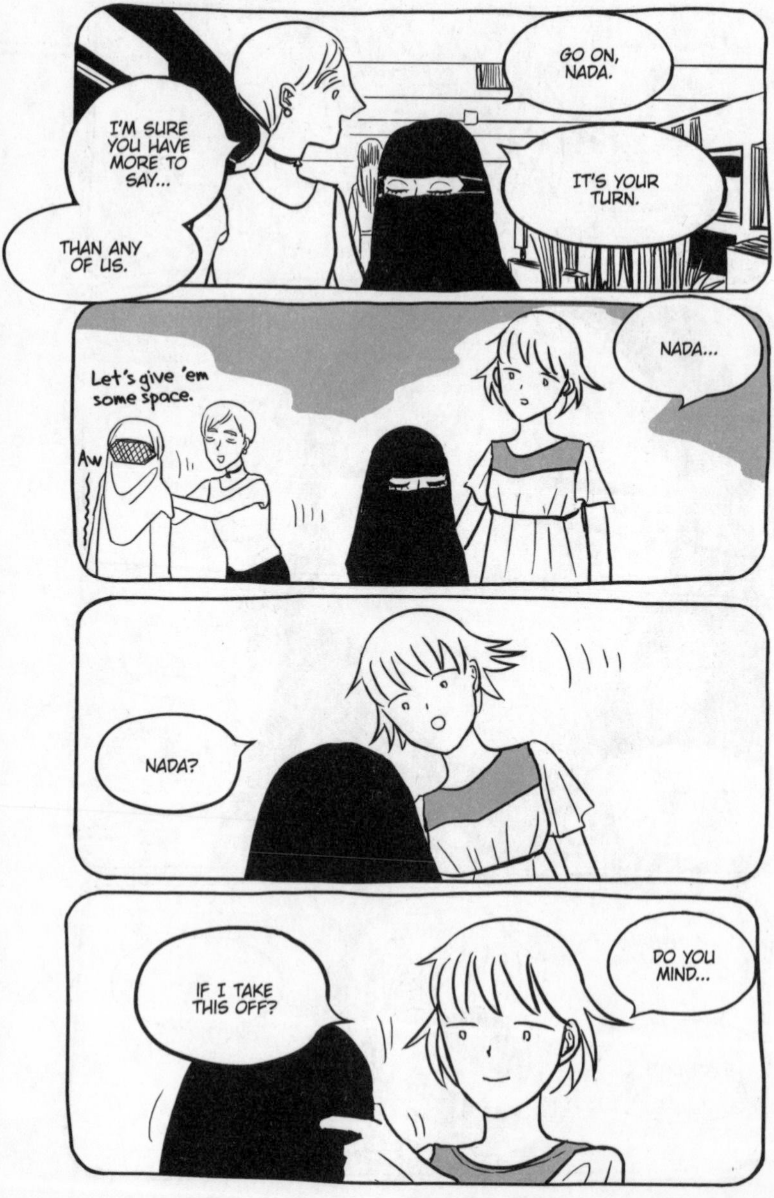
GO ON, NADA.
IT'S YOUR TURN.
I'M SURE YOU HAVE MORE TO SAY...
THAN ANY OF US.
NADA...
Let's give 'em some space.
Aw
NADA?
DO YOU MIND...
IF I TAKE THIS OFF?

JERK

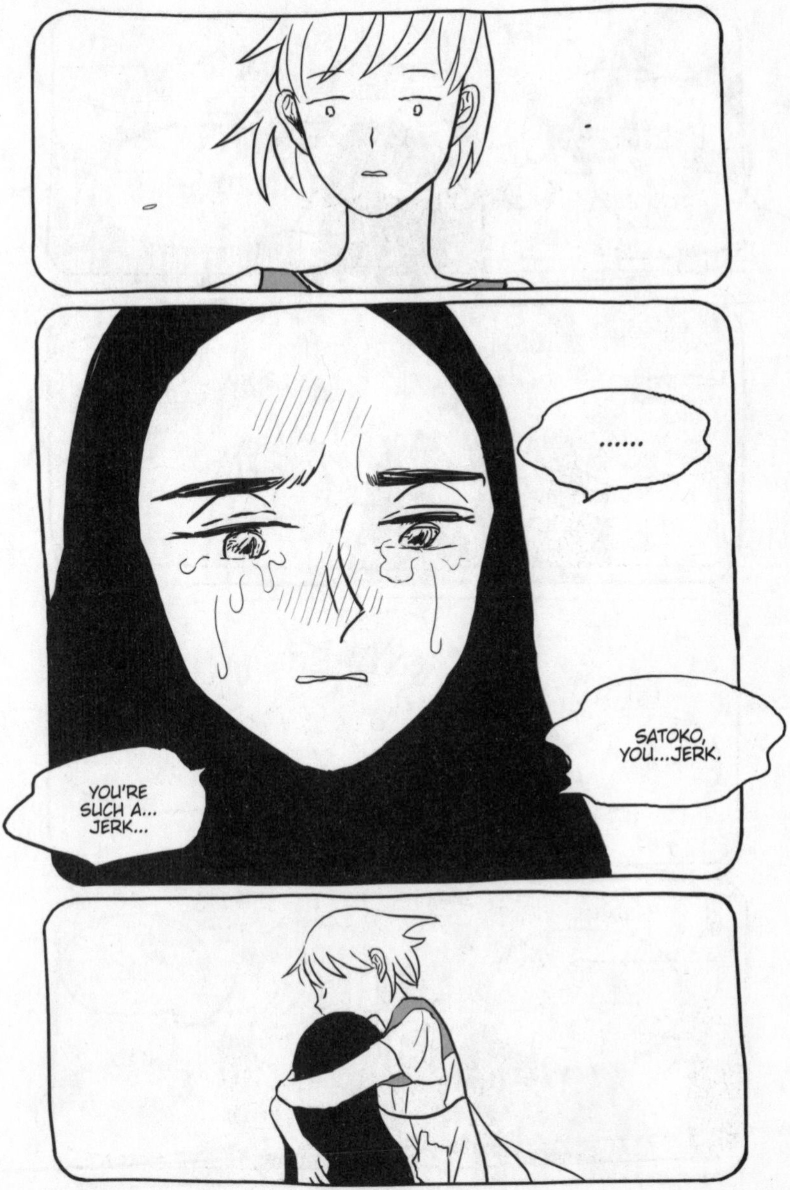
......
SATOKO, YOU...JERK.
YOU'RE SUCH A... JERK...

THANK YOU

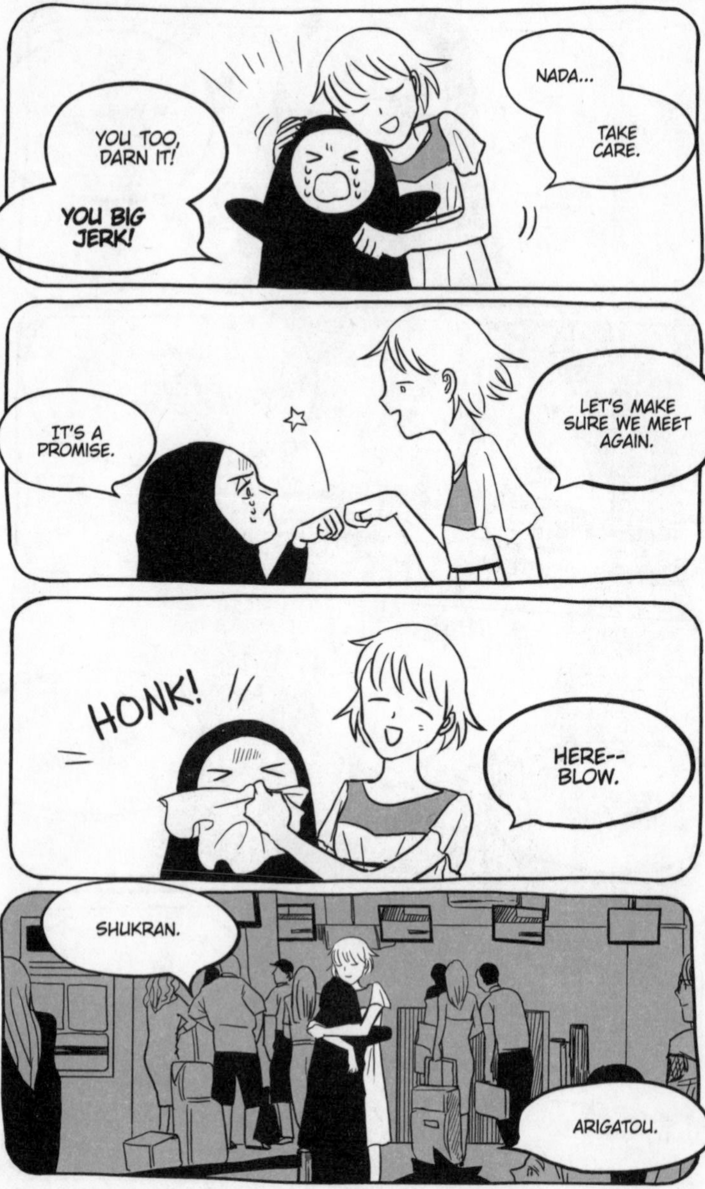

NADA...
TAKE CARE.
YOU TOO, DARN IT!
YOU BIG JERK!
LET'S MAKE SURE WE MEET AGAIN.
IT'S A PROMISE.
HERE-- BLOW.
HONK!
SHUKRAN.
ARIGATOU.

WHY?

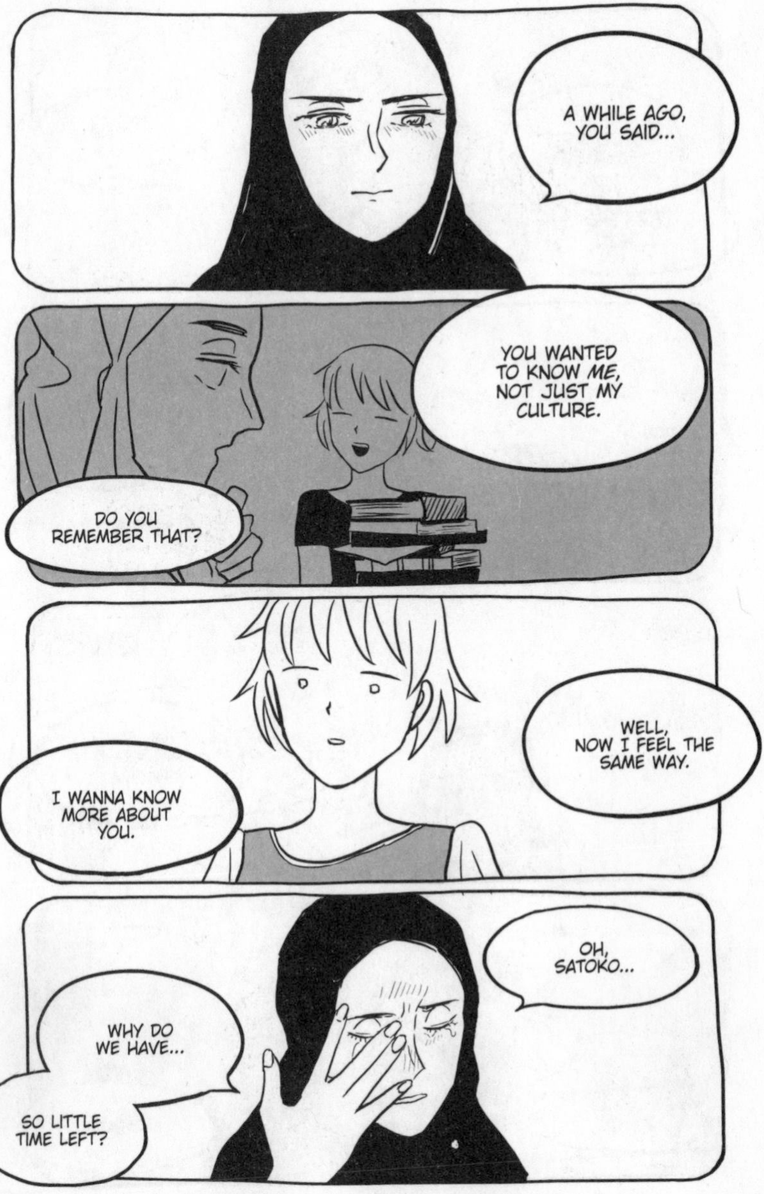
A WHILE AGO, YOU SAID...
YOU WANTED TO KNOW *ME*, NOT JUST MY CULTURE.
DO YOU REMEMBER THAT?
WELL, NOW I FEEL THE SAME WAY.
I WANNA KNOW MORE ABOUT YOU.
OH, SATOKO...
WHY DO WE HAVE...
SO LITTLE TIME LEFT?

I LOVE YOU

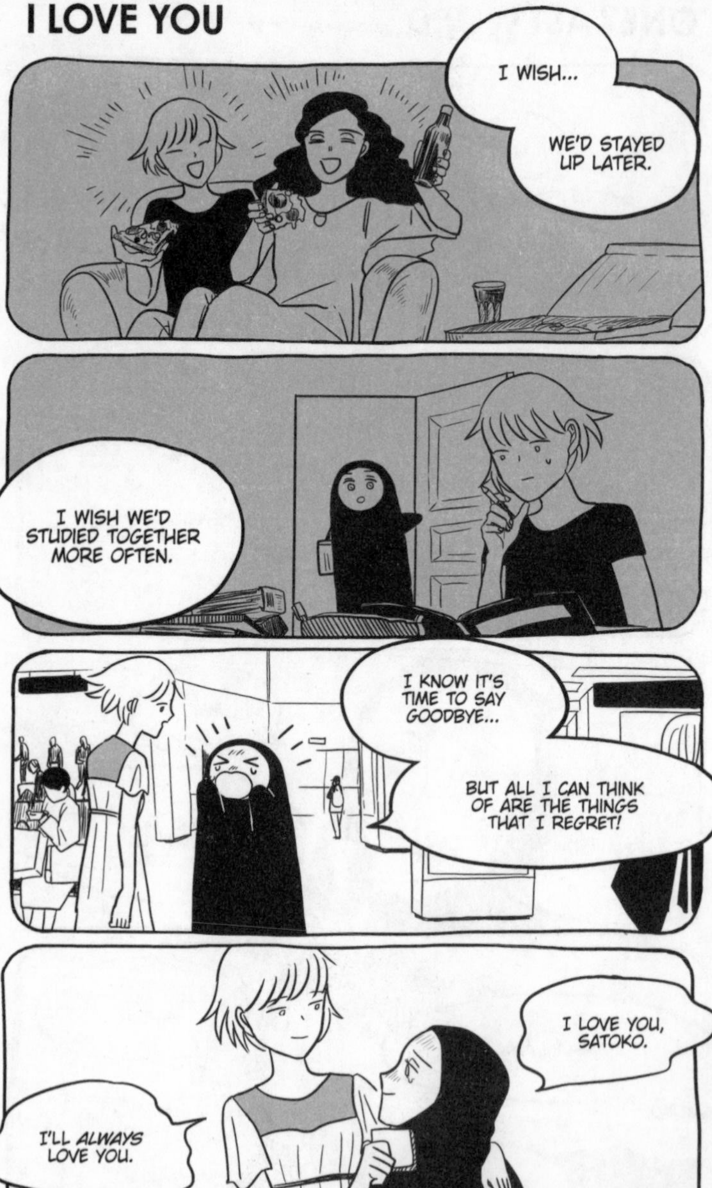
I WISH...
WE'D STAYED UP LATER.
I WISH WE'D STUDIED TOGETHER MORE OFTEN.
I KNOW IT'S TIME TO SAY GOODBYE...
BUT ALL I CAN THINK OF ARE THE THINGS THAT I REGRET!
I LOVE YOU, SATOKO.
I'LL *ALWAYS* LOVE YOU.

ONE LAST WORD

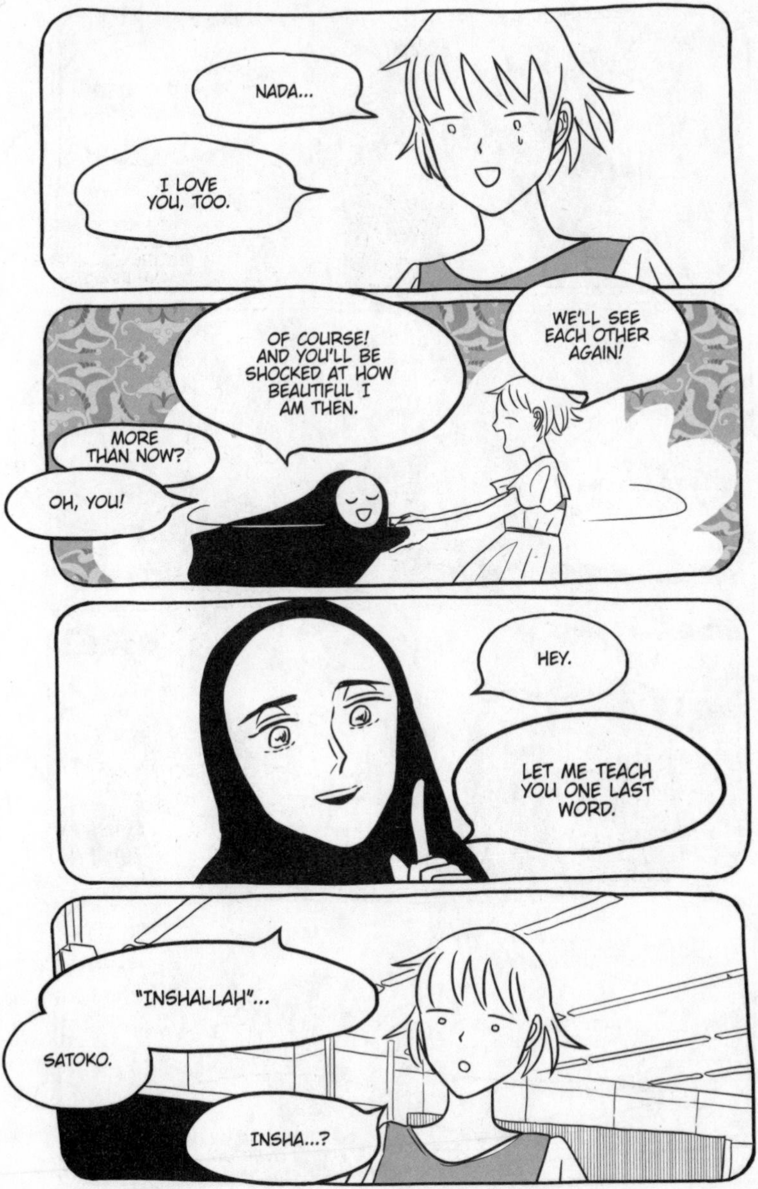
NADA...
I LOVE YOU, TOO.
WE'LL SEE EACH OTHER AGAIN!
OF COURSE! AND YOU'LL BE SHOCKED AT HOW BEAUTIFUL I AM THEN.
MORE THAN NOW?
OH, YOU!
HEY.
LET ME TEACH YOU ONE LAST WORD.
"INSHALLAH"...
SATOKO.
INSHA...?

INSHALLAH

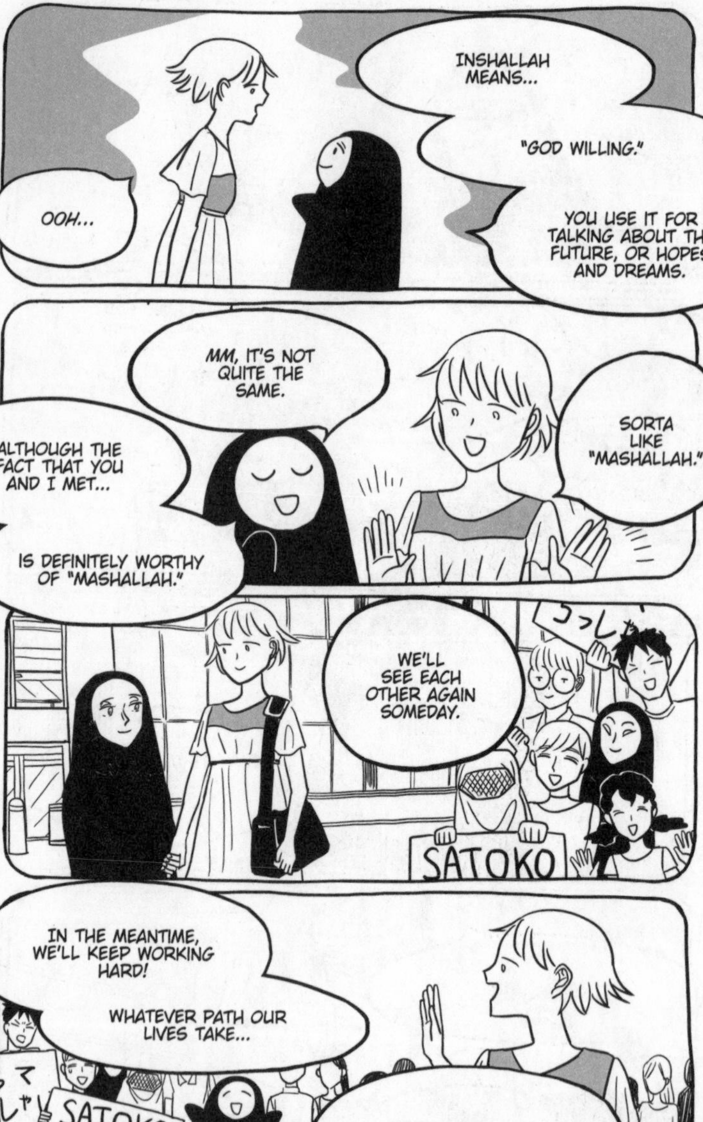
INSHALLAH MEANS...
"GOD WILLING."
YOU USE IT FOR TALKING ABOUT THE FUTURE, OR HOPES AND DREAMS.
OOH...
SORTA LIKE "MASHALLAH."
MM, IT'S NOT QUITE THE SAME.
ALTHOUGH THE FACT THAT YOU AND I MET...
IS DEFINITELY WORTHY OF "MASHALLAH."
WE'LL SEE EACH OTHER AGAIN SOMEDAY.
SATOKO
IN THE MEANTIME, WE'LL KEEP WORKING HARD!
WHATEVER PATH OUR LIVES TAKE...
SATOKO
I'M SURE GOD WILL WATCH OVER US.

BYE

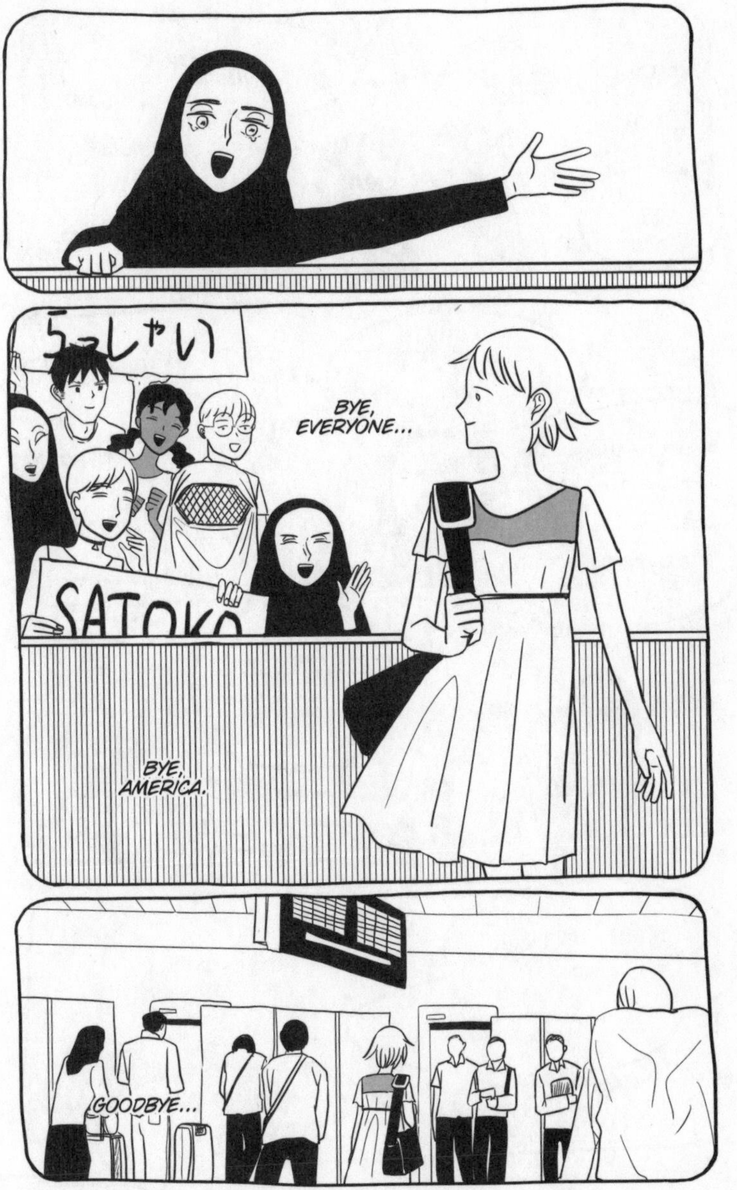
らっしゃい
SATOKO
BYE, EVERYONE...
BYE, AMERICA.
GOODBYE...

JAPAN

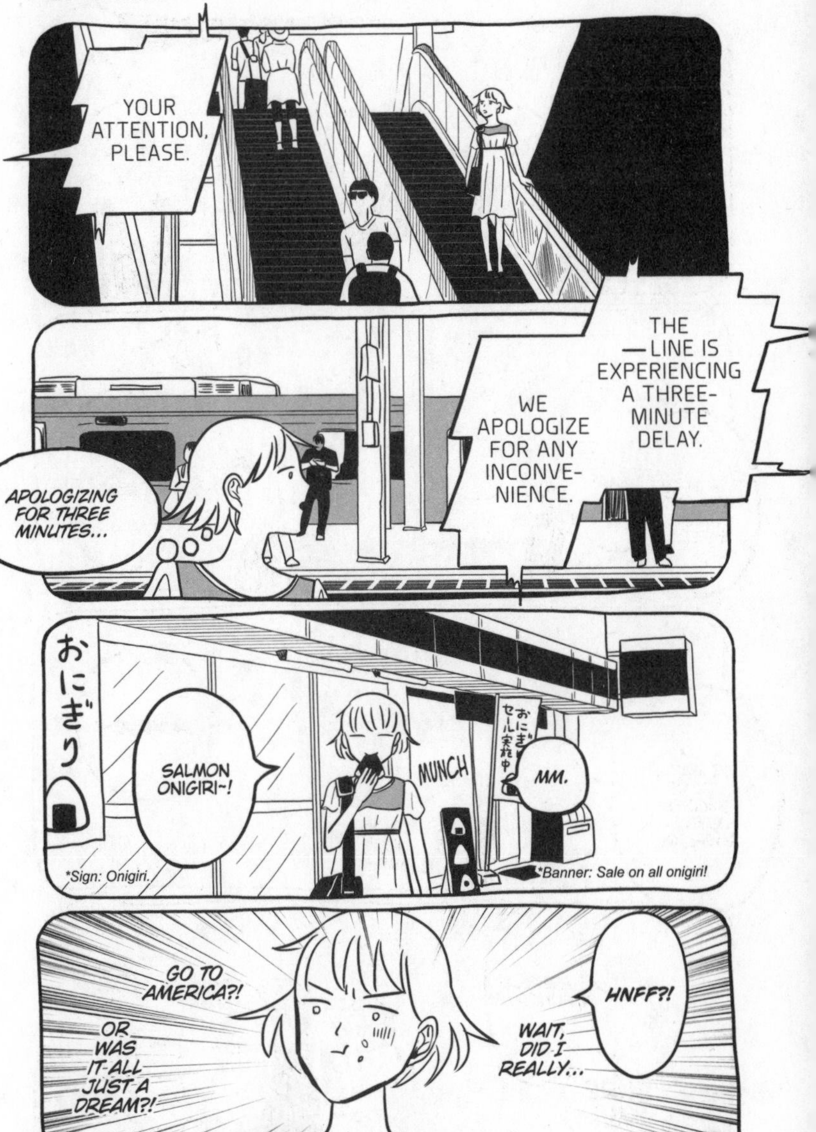
YOUR ATTENTION, PLEASE.
THE —LINE IS EXPERIENCING A THREE-MINUTE DELAY.
WE APOLOGIZE FOR ANY INCONVENIENCE.
APOLOGIZING FOR THREE MINUTES...
MM.
おにぎ
セール実施中
MUNCH
SALMON ONIGIRI~!
おにぎり
*Banner: Sale on all onigiri!
*Sign: Onigiri.
HNFF?!
WAIT, DID I REALLY...
GO TO AMERICA?!
OR WAS IT ALL JUST A DREAM?!

MOM

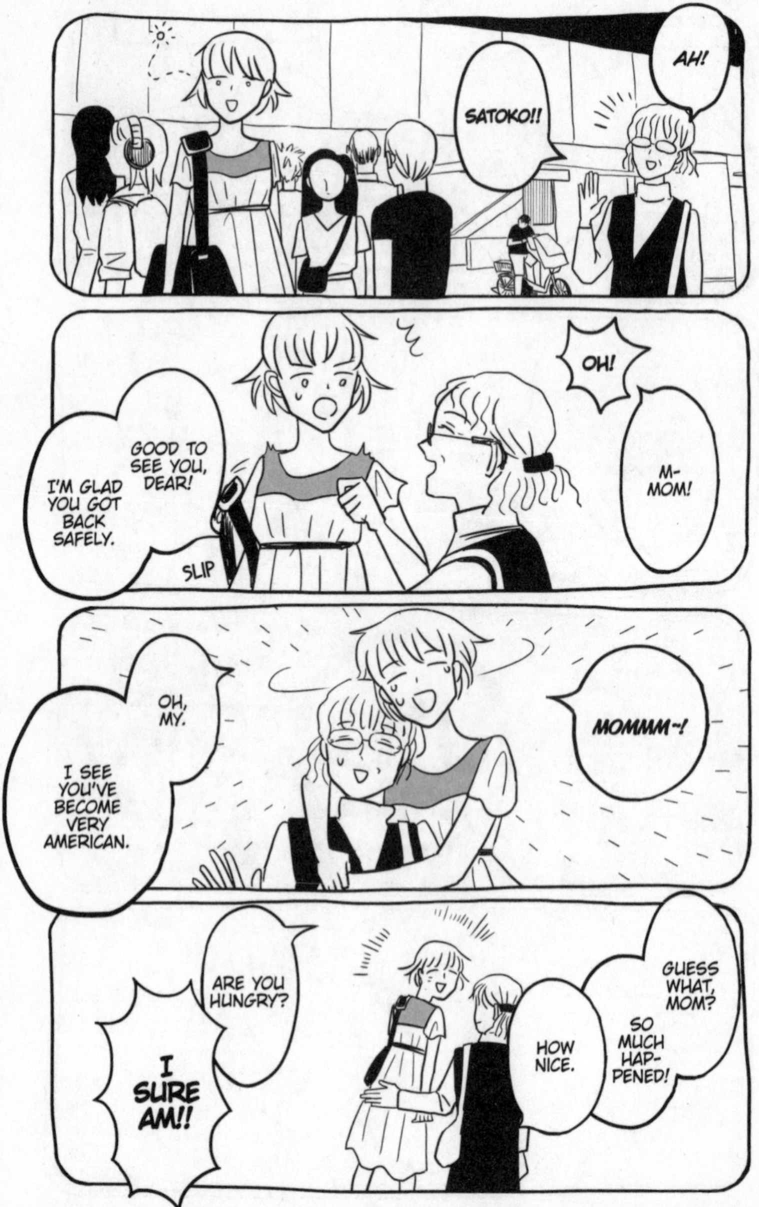
AH!
SATOKO!!
OH!
M-MOM!
GOOD TO SEE YOU, DEAR!
I'M GLAD YOU GOT BACK SAFELY.
SLIP
MOMMM~!
OH, MY.
I SEE YOU'VE BECOME VERY AMERICAN.
GUESS WHAT, MOM?
SO MUCH HAP-PENED!
HOW NICE.
ARE YOU HUNGRY?
I SURE AM!!

RESTAURANT TIME

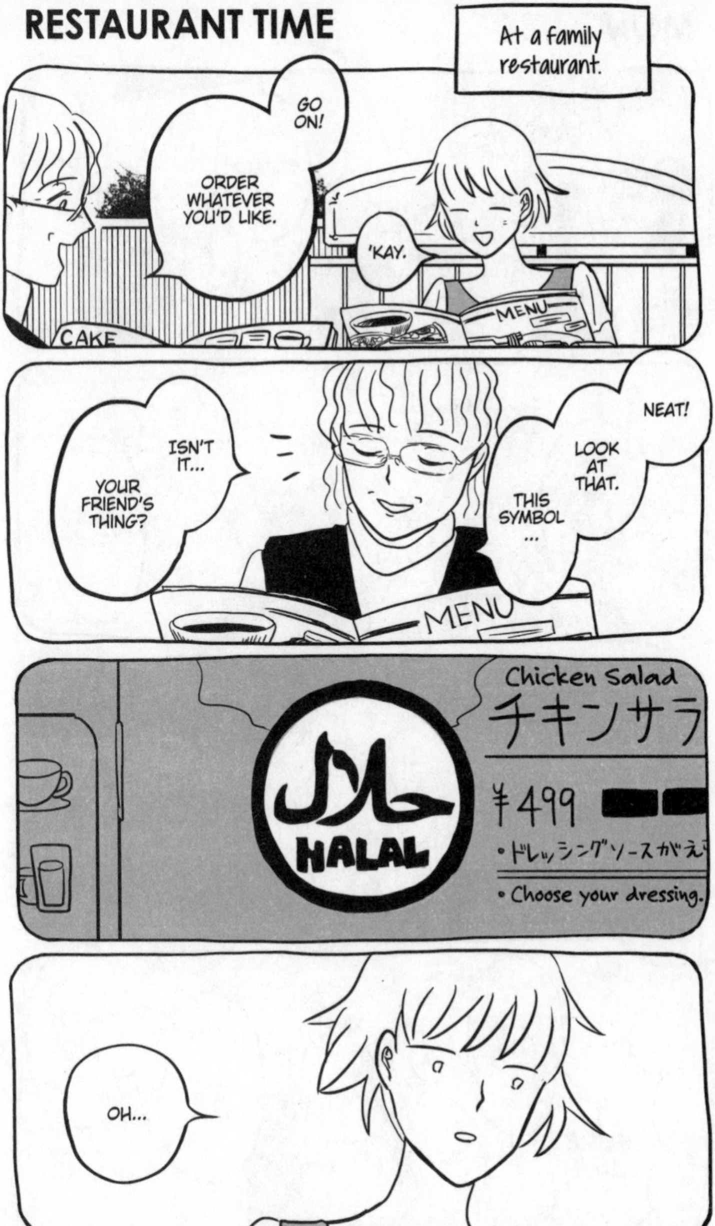
At a family restaurant.
GO ON!
ORDER WHATEVER YOU'D LIKE.
'KAY.
CAKE
MENU
NEAT!
LOOK AT THAT.
THIS SYMBOL ...
ISN'T IT...
YOUR FRIEND'S THING?
MENU
Chicken Salad
チキンサラ
HALAL
¥499
・ドレッシングソースがえ
・Choose your dressing.
OH...

MEMORIES

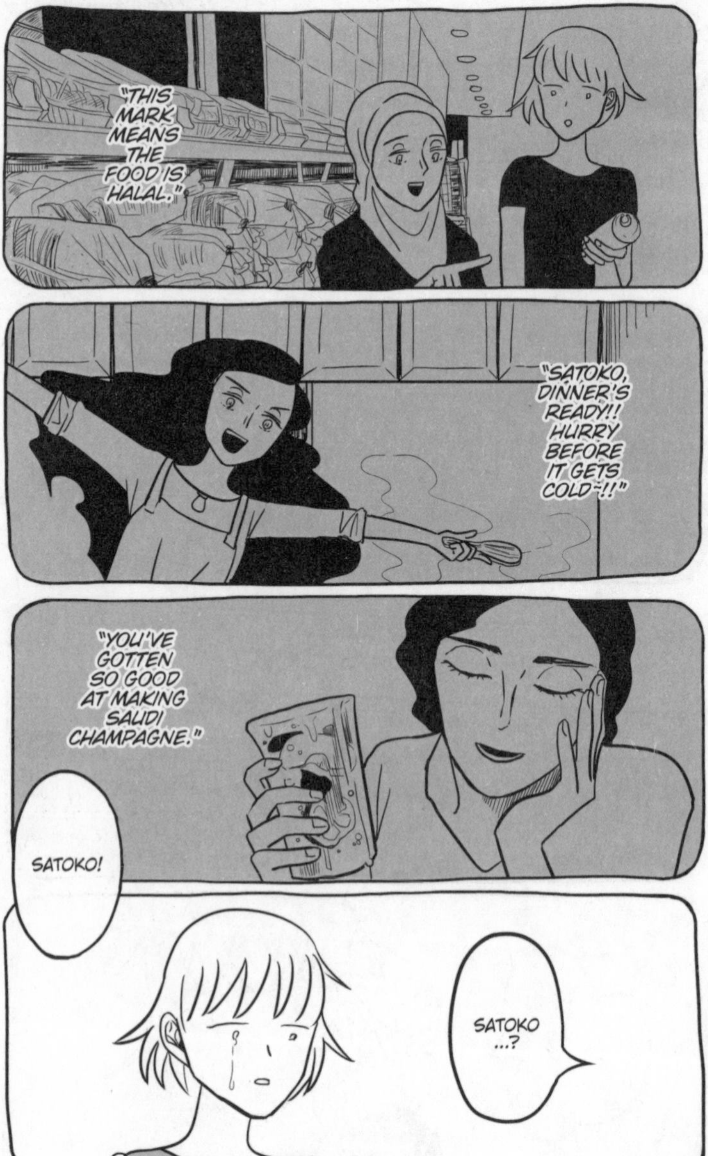
"THIS MARK MEANS THE FOOD IS HALAL."
"SATOKO, DINNER'S READY!! HURRY BEFORE IT GETS COLD~!!"
"YOU'VE GOTTEN SO GOOD AT MAKING SAUDI CHAMPAGNE."
SATOKO!
SATOKO ...?

REMINISCE

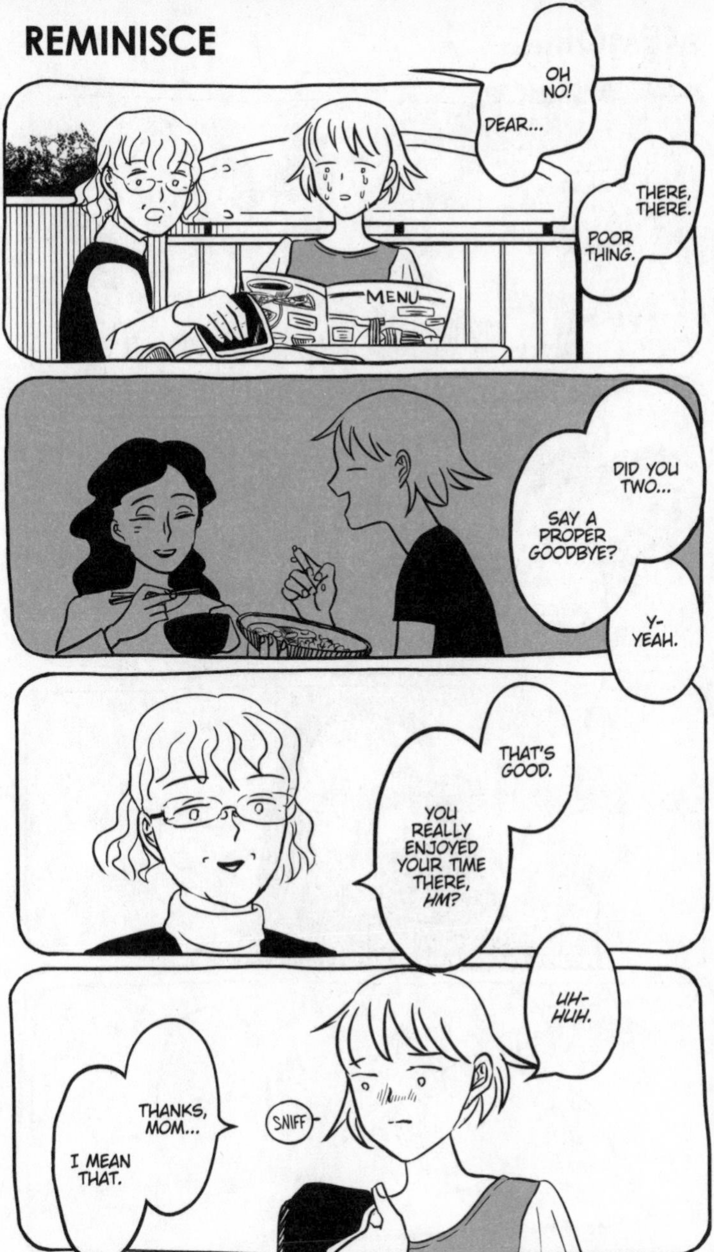
OH NO! DEAR...
THERE, THERE. POOR THING.
MENU
DID YOU TWO... SAY A PROPER GOODBYE?
Y- YEAH.
THAT'S GOOD. YOU REALLY ENJOYED YOUR TIME THERE, *HM?*
UH-HUH.
SNIFF
THANKS, MOM... I MEAN THAT.

THANK YOU

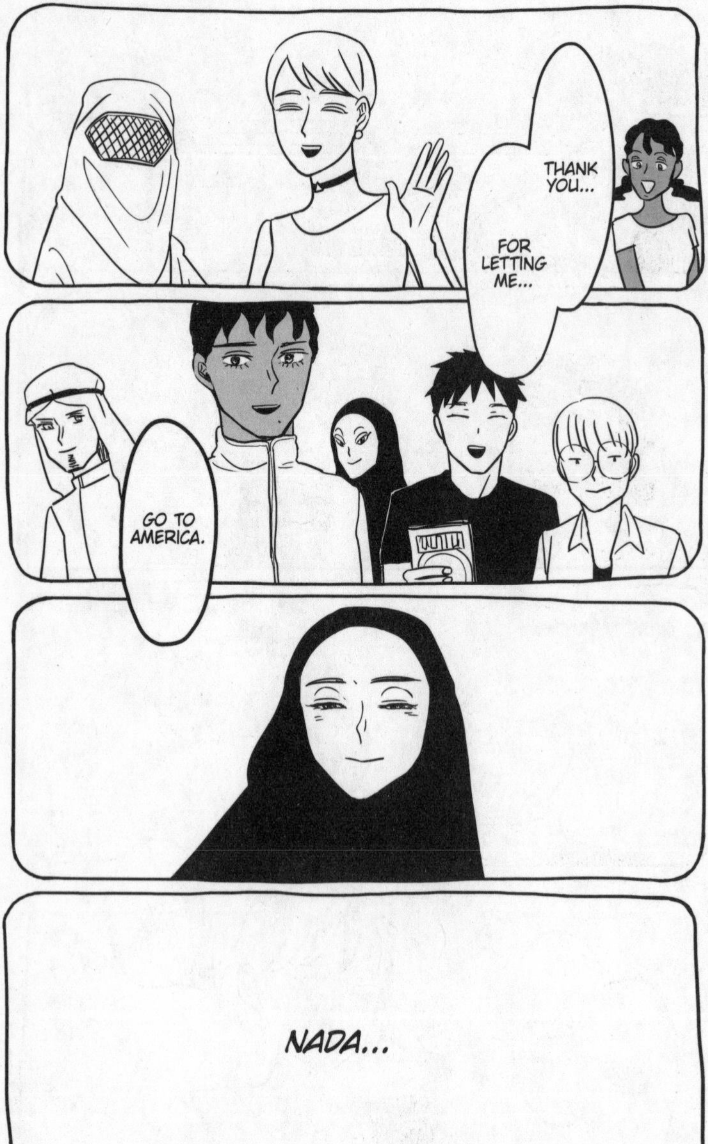
THANK YOU...
FOR LETTING ME...
GO TO AMERICA.
NADA...

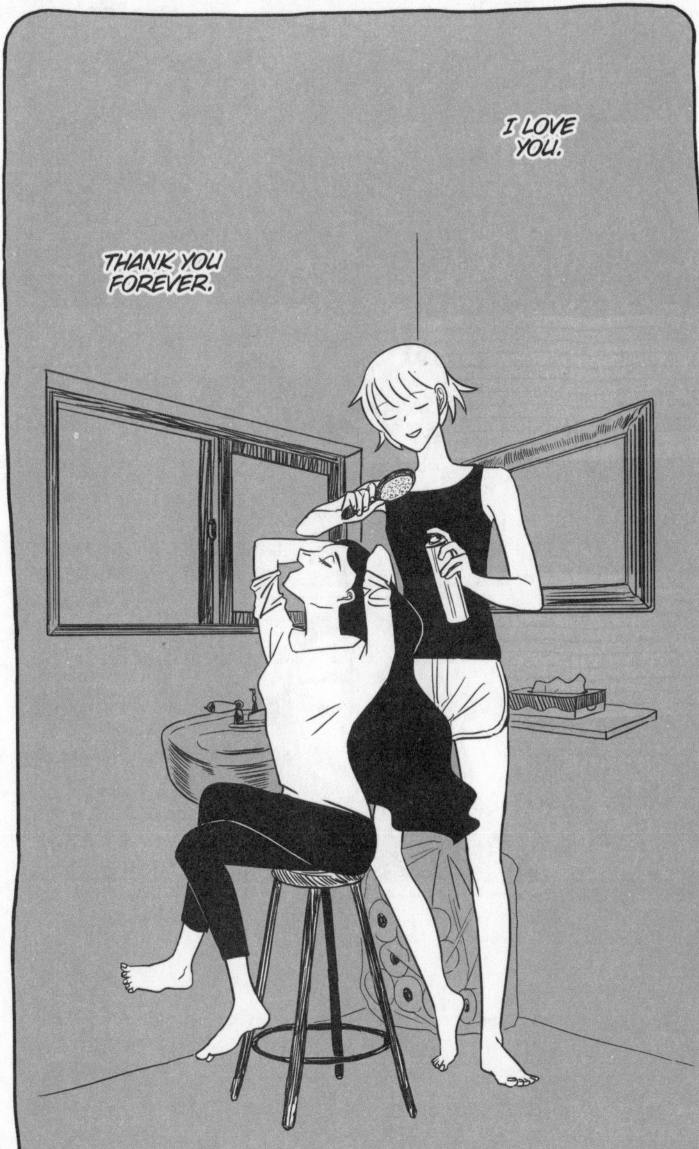
I LOVE YOU.
THANK YOU FOREVER.

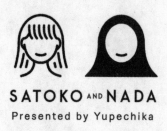

SATOKO AND NADA

Presented by Yupechika

END

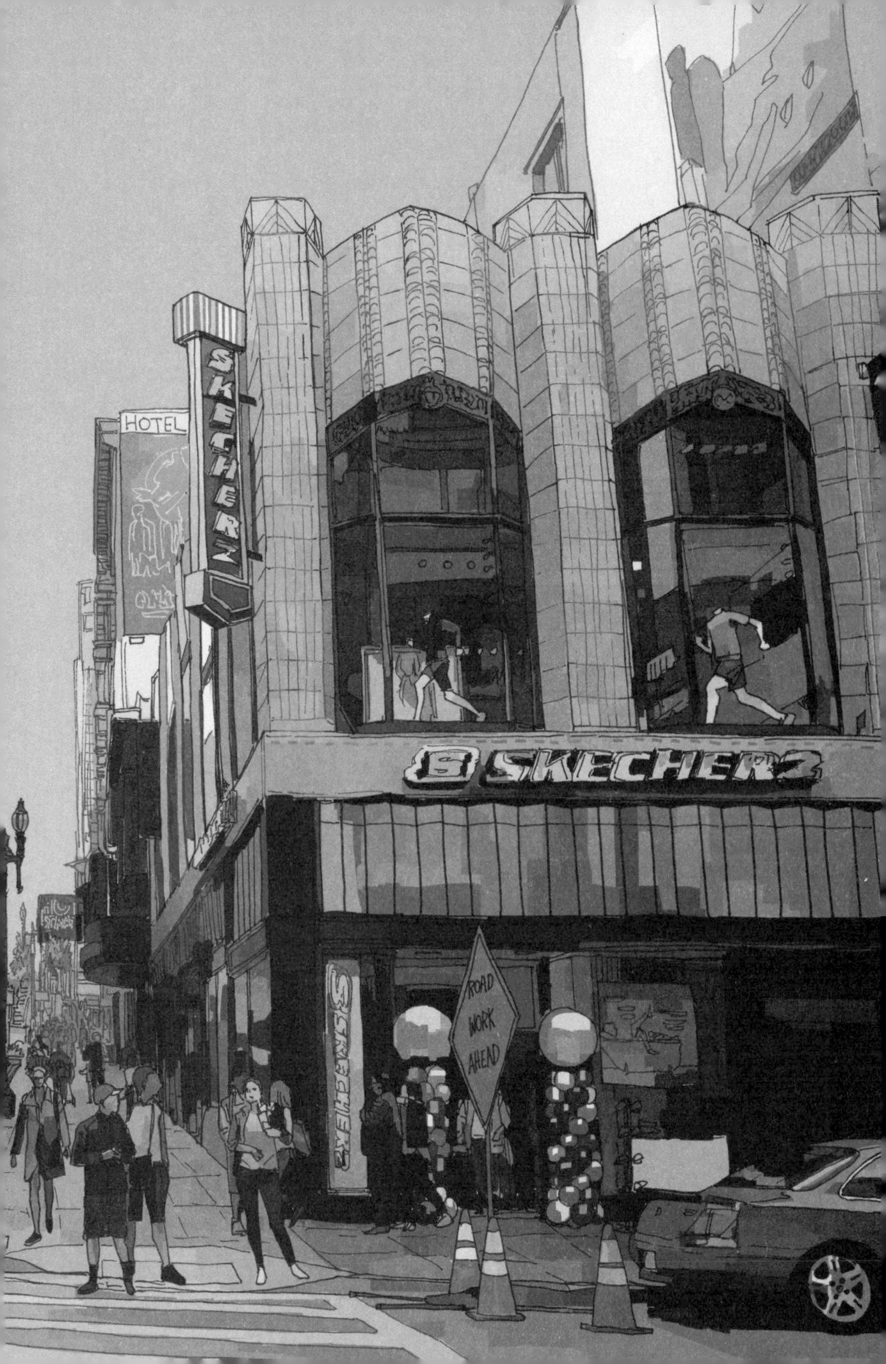
HOTEL
SKECHERS
SKECHERS
ROAD WORK AHEAD
SKECHERS

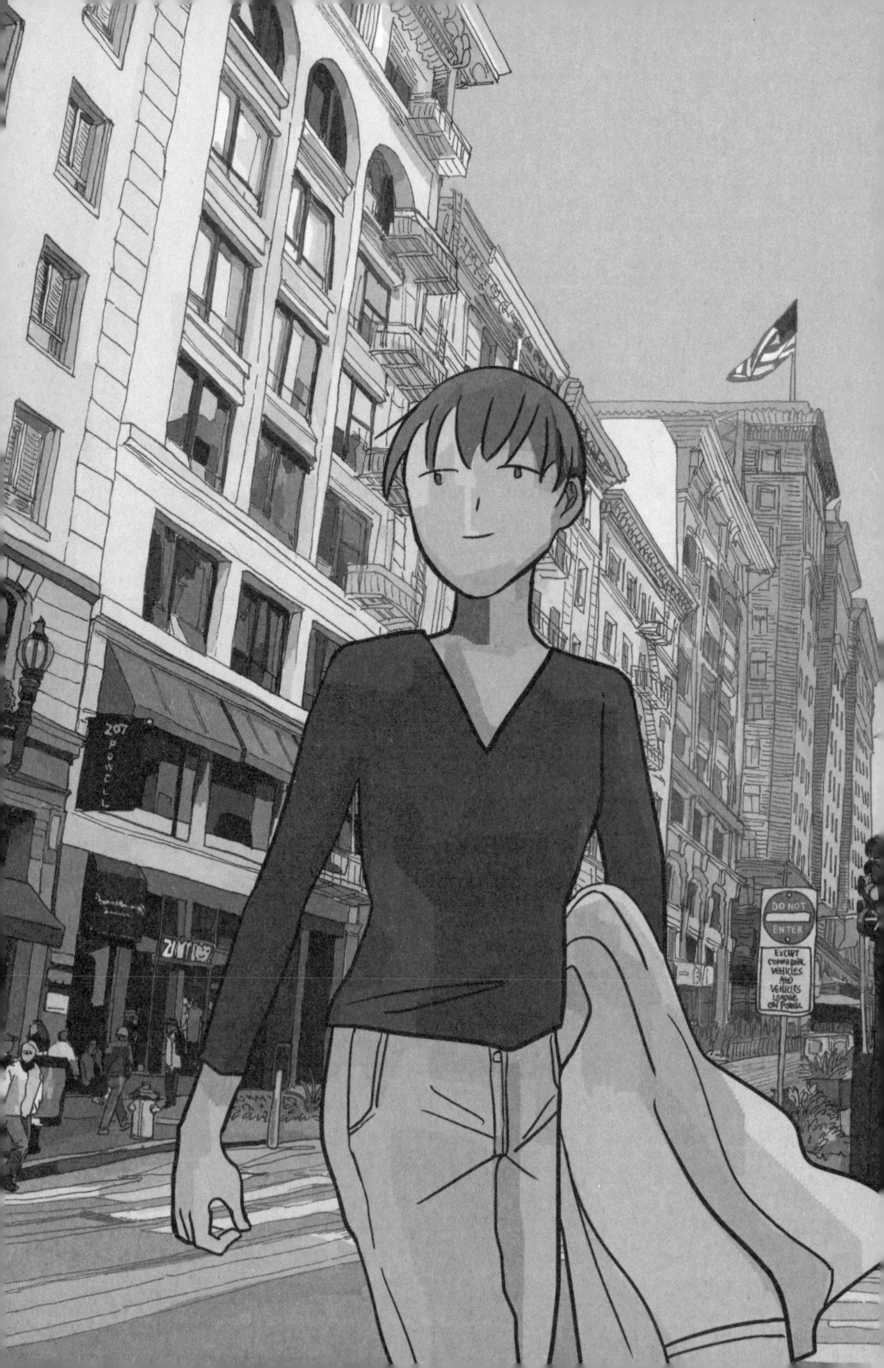
207 POWELL
DO NOT ENTER
EXCEPT COMMERCIAL VEHICLES AND VEHICLES LOADING ON POWELL

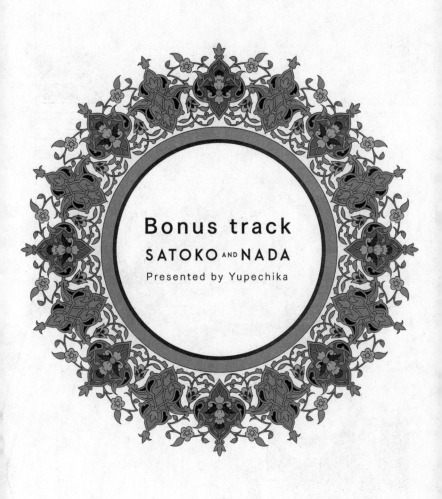

Bonus track

SATOKO AND NADA

Presented by Yupechika

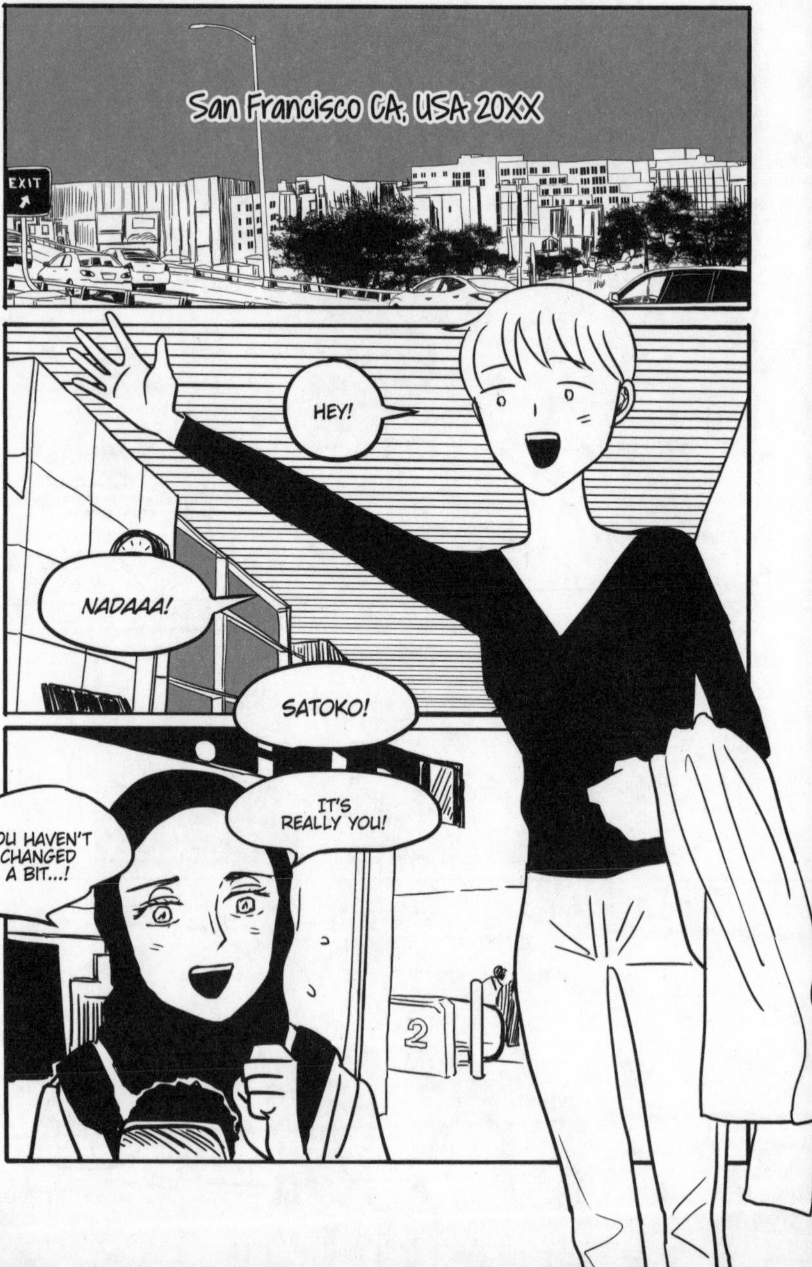
San Francisco CA, USA 20XX
EXIT
HEY!
NADAAA!
SATOKO!
IT'S REALLY YOU!
YOU HAVEN'T CHANGED A BIT...!
2

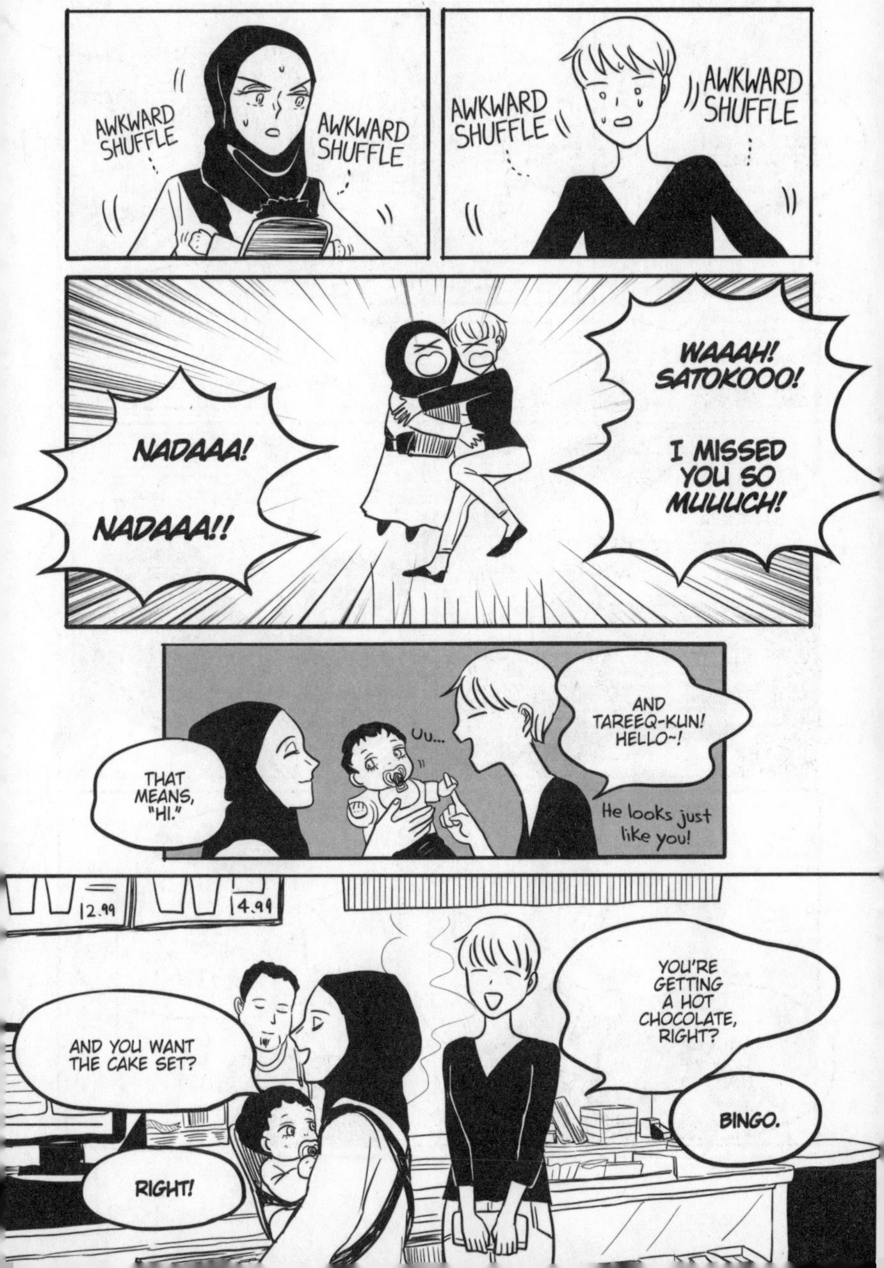
AWKWARD SHUFFLE
AWKWARD SHUFFLE
AWKWARD SHUFFLE
AWKWARD SHUFFLE
WAAAH! SATOKOOO!
I MISSED YOU SO MUUUCH!
NADAAA!
NADAAA!!
AND TAREEQ-KUN! HELLO~!
Uu...
He looks just like you!
THAT MEANS, "HI."
12.99
14.99
YOU'RE GETTING A HOT CHOCOLATE, RIGHT?
BINGO.
AND YOU WANT THE CAKE SET?
RIGHT!

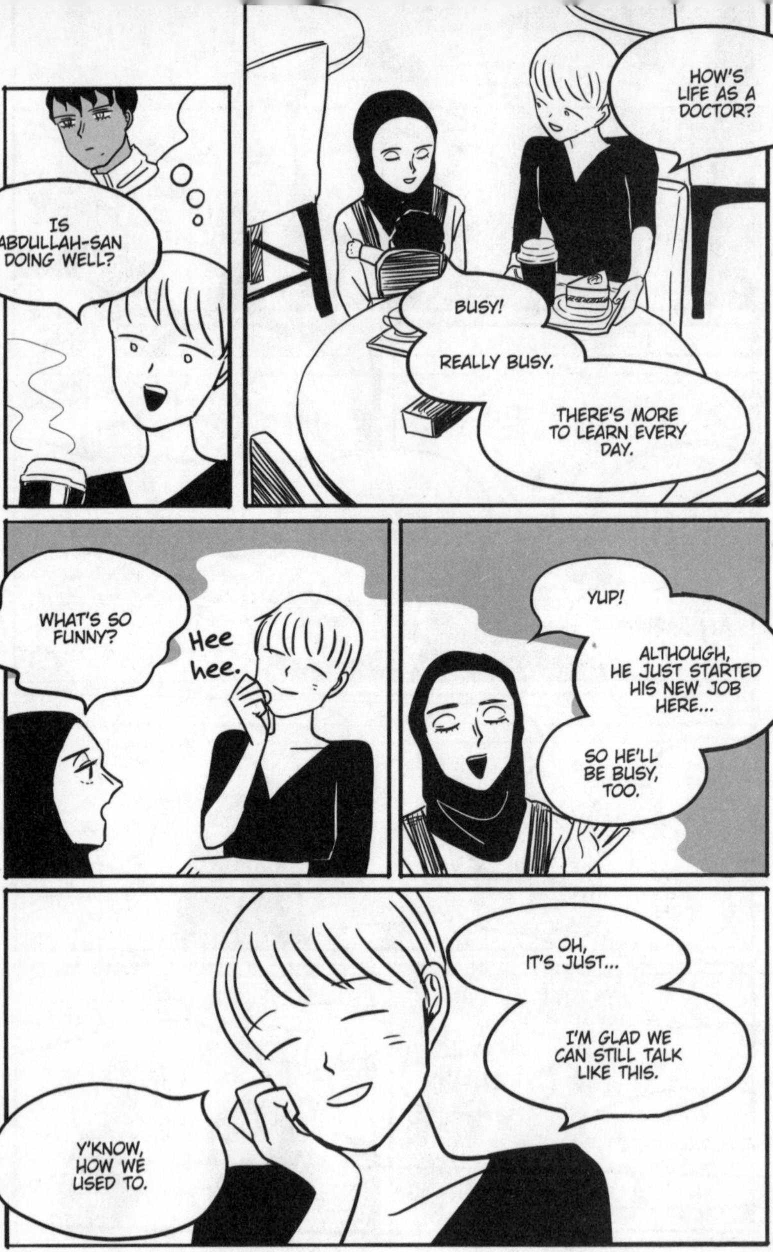
HOW'S LIFE AS A DOCTOR?
BUSY!
REALLY BUSY.
THERE'S MORE TO LEARN EVERY DAY.
IS ABDULLAH-SAN DOING WELL?
YUP!
ALTHOUGH, HE JUST STARTED HIS NEW JOB HERE...
SO HE'LL BE BUSY, TOO.
Hee hee.
WHAT'S SO FUNNY?
OH, IT'S JUST...
I'M GLAD WE CAN STILL TALK LIKE THIS.
Y'KNOW, HOW WE USED TO.

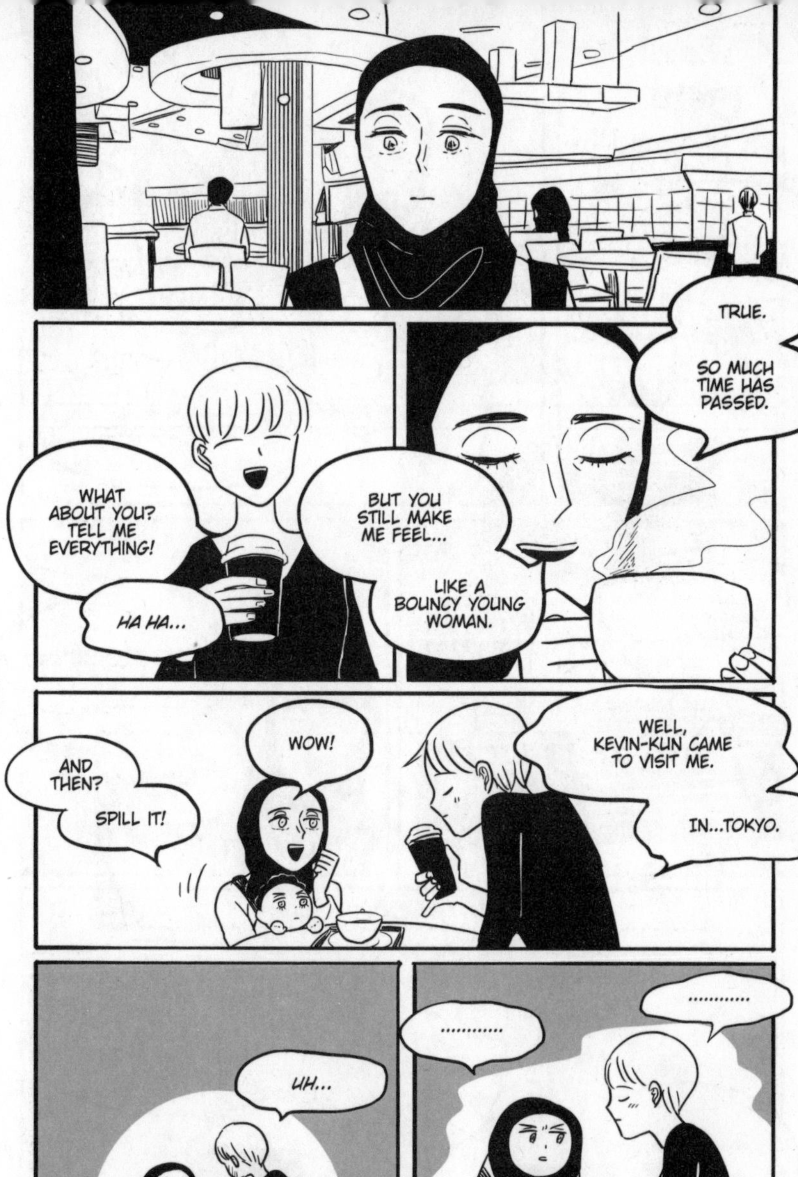
TRUE.
SO MUCH TIME HAS PASSED.
BUT YOU STILL MAKE ME FEEL...
LIKE A BOUNCY YOUNG WOMAN.
WHAT ABOUT YOU? TELL ME EVERYTHING!
HA HA...
WELL, KEVIN-KUN CAME TO VISIT ME.
IN...TOKYO.
WOW!
AND THEN?
SPILL IT!
....
....
UH...

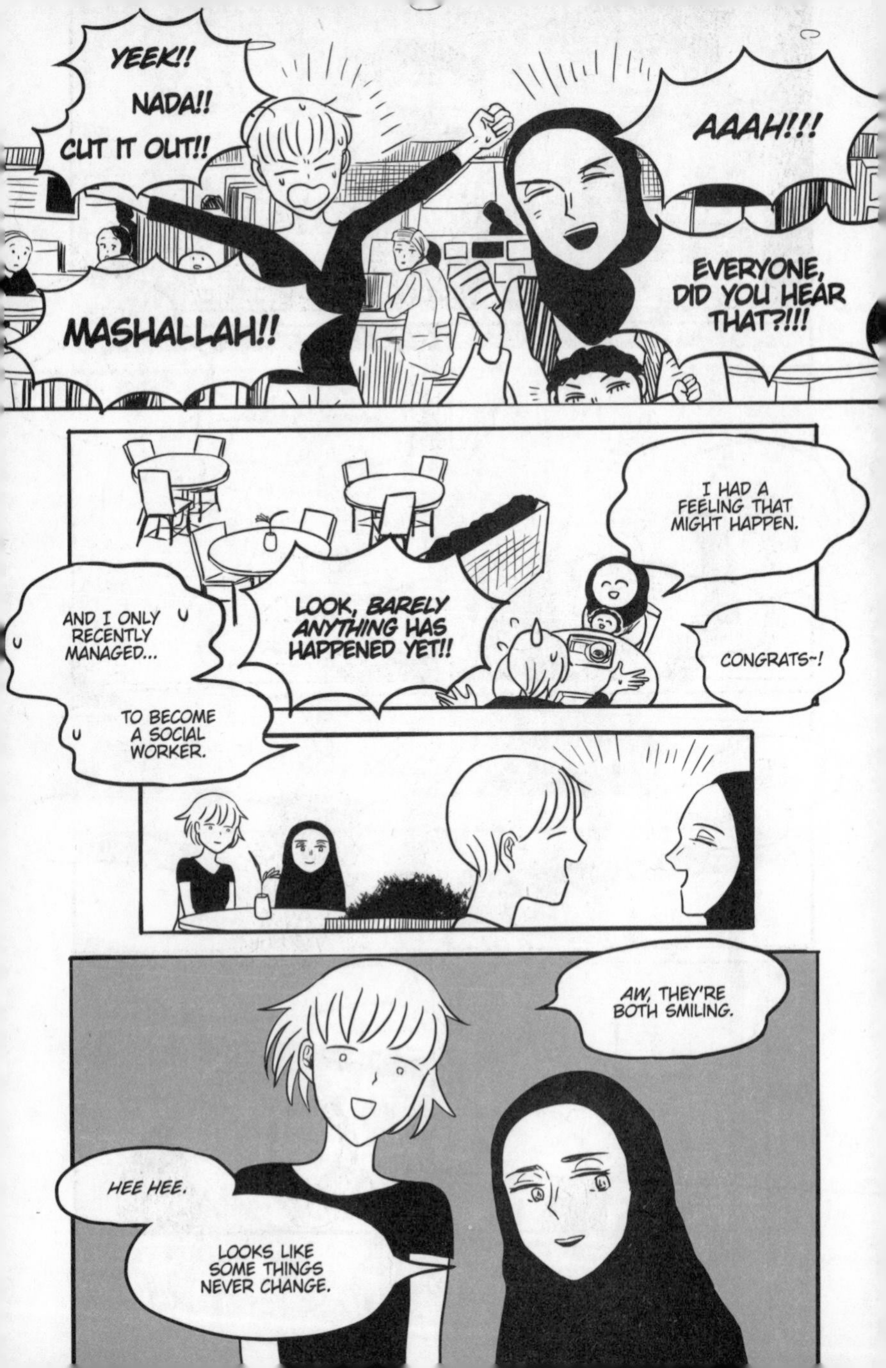
AAAH!!!
EVERYONE, DID YOU HEAR THAT?!!!
YEEK!! NADA!! CUT IT OUT!!
MASHALLAH!!
I HAD A FEELING THAT MIGHT HAPPEN.
CONGRATS~!
LOOK, BARELY ANYTHING HAS HAPPENED YET!!
AND I ONLY RECENTLY MANAGED...
TO BECOME A SOCIAL WORKER.
AW, THEY'RE BOTH SMILING.
HEE HEE.
LOOKS LIKE SOME THINGS NEVER CHANGE.

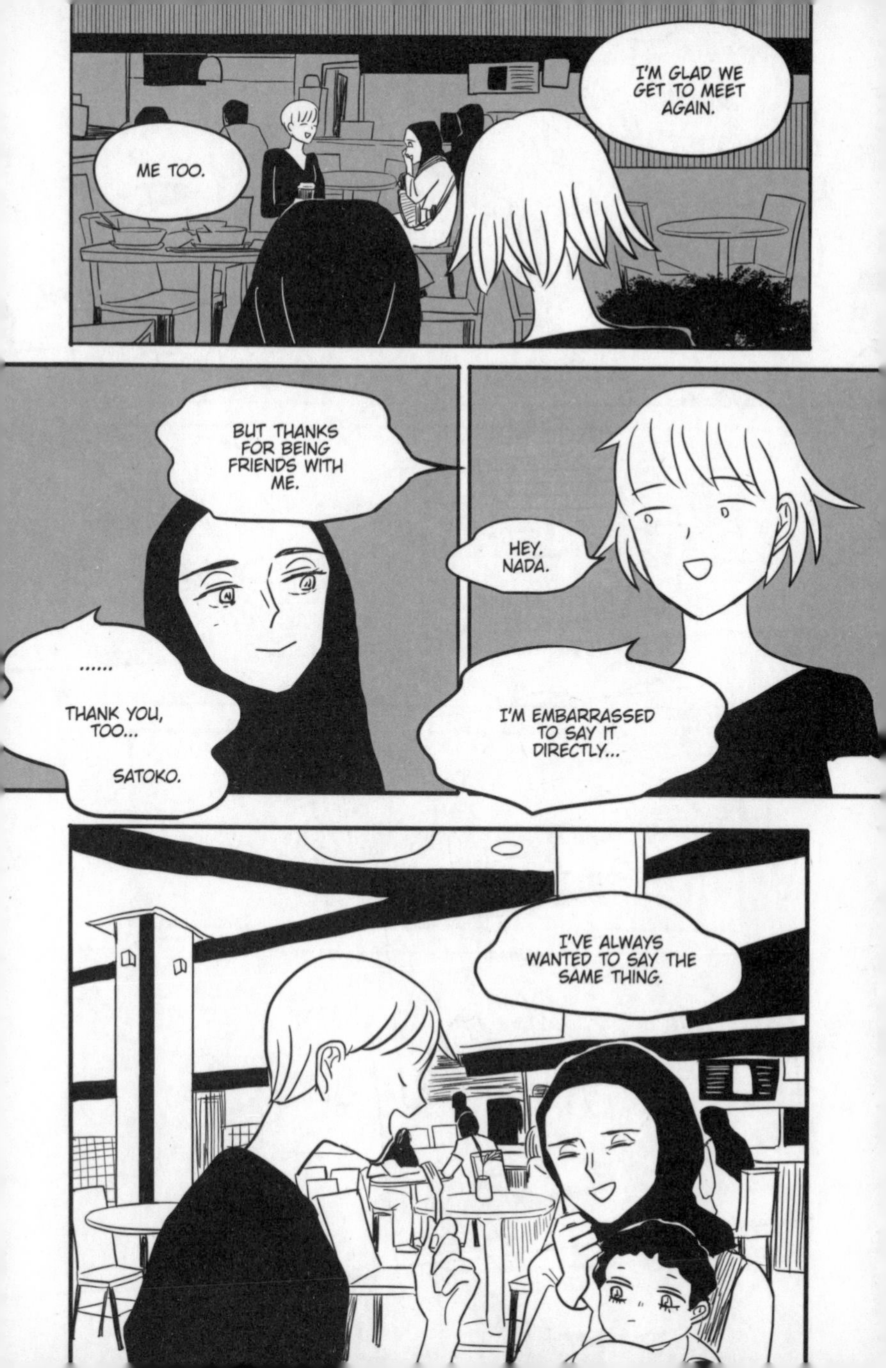
I'M GLAD WE GET TO MEET AGAIN.
ME TOO.
HEY. NADA.
I'M EMBARRASSED TO SAY IT DIRECTLY...
BUT THANKS FOR BEING FRIENDS WITH ME.
...... THANK YOU, TOO... SATOKO.
I'VE ALWAYS WANTED TO SAY THE SAME THING.

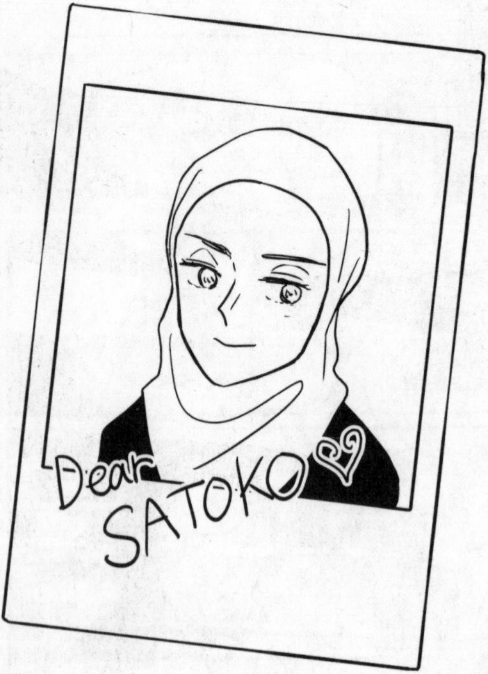
Dear
SATOKO

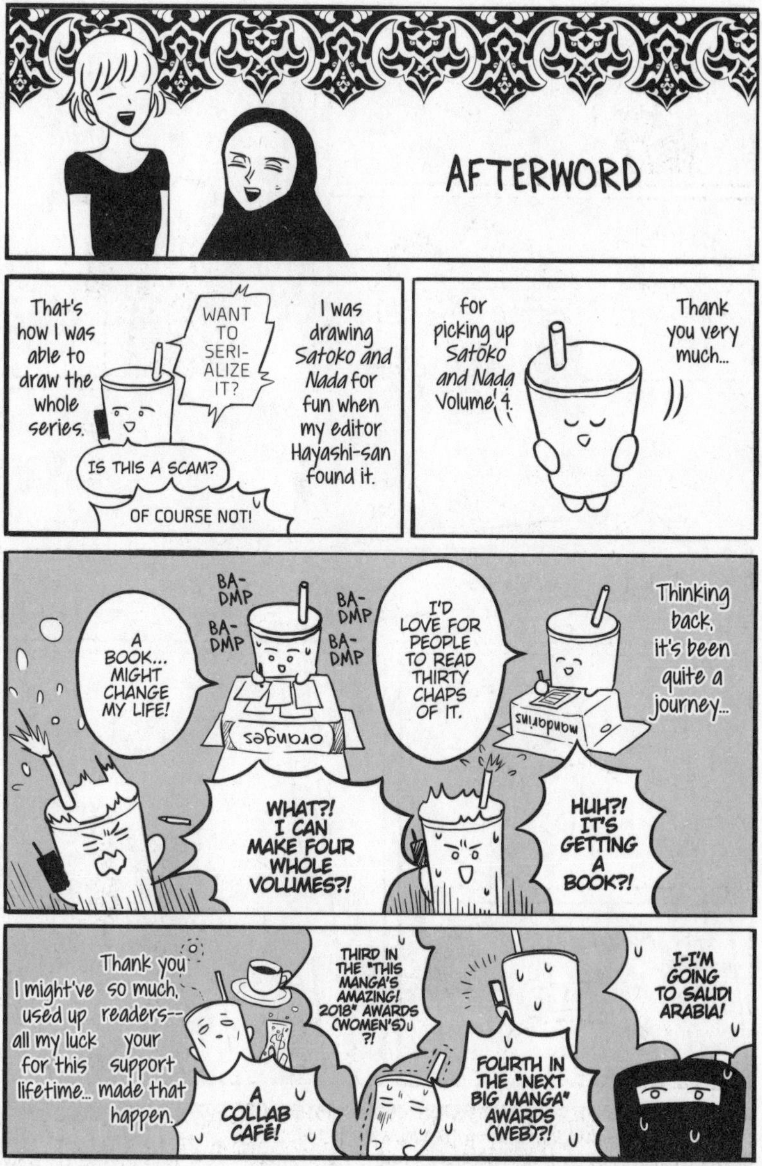
AFTERWORD
Thank you very much...
for picking up Satoko and Nada Volume 4.
I was drawing Satoko and Nada for fun when my editor Hayashi-san found it.
WANT TO SERIALIZE IT?
IS THIS A SCAM?
OF COURSE NOT!
That's how I was able to draw the whole series.
Thinking back, it's been quite a journey...
mandarins
I'D LOVE FOR PEOPLE TO READ THIRTY CHAPS OF IT.
HUH?! IT'S GETTING A BOOK?!
BA-DMP
BA-DMP
BA-DMP
BA-DMP
oranges
A BOOK... MIGHT CHANGE MY LIFE!
WHAT?! I CAN MAKE FOUR WHOLE VOLUMES?!
I-I'M GOING TO SAUDI ARABIA!
FOURTH IN THE "NEXT BIG MANGA" AWARDS (WEB)?!
THIRD IN THE "THIS MANGA'S AMAZING! 2018" AWARDS (WOMEN'S)?!
A COLLAB CAFÉ!
Thank you so much, readers--your support made that happen.
I might've used up all my luck for this lifetime...

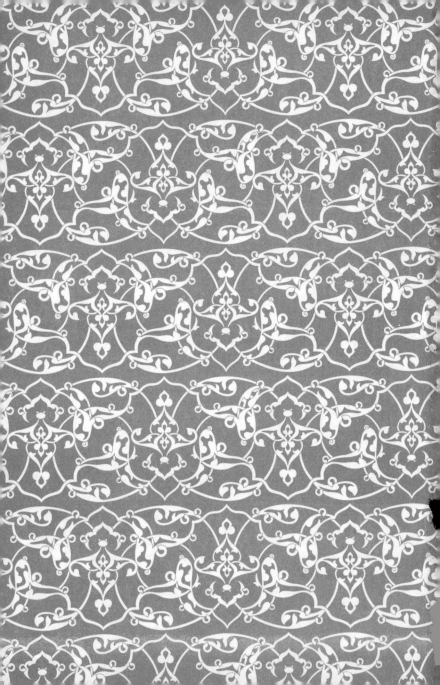

SEVEN SEAS ENTERTAINMENT PRESENTS

SATOKO AND NADA VOL. 4

story and art by **YUPECHIKA** script advisor: **MARIE NISHIMORI**

TRANSLATION
Jenny McKeon

ADAPTATION
Lianne Sentar

LETTERING AND RETOUCH
Karis Page

COVER DESIGN
Kris Aubin

PROOFREADER
Dawn Davis

EDITOR
Jenn Grunigen

PREPRESS TECHNICIAN
Rhiannon Rasmussen-Silverstein

PRODUCTION MANAGER
Lissa Pattillo

MANAGING EDITOR
Julie Davis

ASSOCIATE PUBLISHER
Adam Arnold

PUBLISHER
Jason DeAngelis

SATOKO TO NADA VOLUME 4

First published in Japan in 2018 by Star Seas Company.
Publication rights for this English edition arranged with Star Seas Company through Kodansha Ltd., Tokyo.

Seven Seas press and purchase enquiries can be sent to Marketing Manager Lianne Sentar at press@gomanga.com. Information regarding the distribution and purchase of digital editions is available from Digital Manager CK Russell at digital@gomanga.com.

ISBN: 978-1-64505-525-9

Printed in Canada

First Printing: December 2020

10 9 8 7 6 5 4 3 2 1

FOLLOW US ONLINE: ***www.sevenseasentertainment.com***

READING DIRECTIONS

This book reads from ***right to left***, Japanese style. If this is your first time reading manga, you start reading from the top right panel on each page and take it from there. If you get lost, just follow the numbered diagram here. It may seem backwards at first, but you'll get the hang of it! Have fun!!

1
2
3
4
5
6
7
8
9

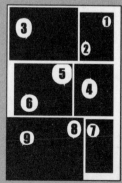

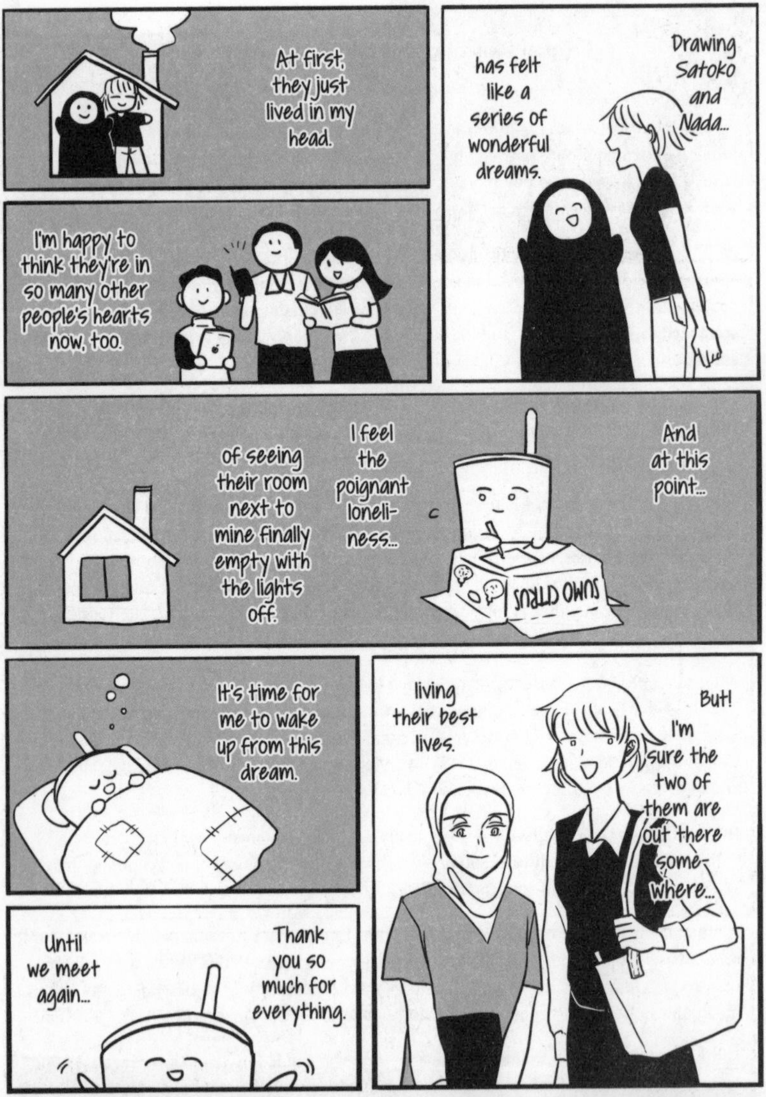
Drawing Satoko and Nada...
has felt like a series of wonderful dreams.
At first, they just lived in my head.
I'm happy to think they're in so many other people's hearts now, too.
And at this point...
I feel the poignant loneli-ness...
of seeing their room next to mine finally empty with the lights off.
But! I'm sure the two of them are out there some-where...
living their best lives.
It's time for me to wake up from this dream.
Thank you so much for everything.
Until we meet again...

To the readers, script advisor Marie Nishimori-san, my editor Hayashi-san, and everyone else who helped with the creation of Satoko and Nada: thank you all, from the bottom of my heart.

Yupechika

Upon Reaching the End – Marie Nishimori

After the terrorist attacks in 2001, and each time Al-Qaeda, the Taliban, ISIS, or other Muslim extremist groups carried out terrorist attacks thereafter, I always thought, "I have to write a book so that people will understand what 'moderate' Muslims think!" But my daily work kept me so busy that years passed and I still hadn't been able to start.

In 2009, another horrible incident occurred: this time in Texas, where I live. A Palestinian-American soldier who had been radicalized committed a mass shooting, killing fourteen people while shouting "Allahu akbar!" After this attack, the media reported that Islam was brainwashing young people, so for a long time after, I desperately tried to explain to friends and neighbors that Islam isn't dangerous.

I particularly remember explaining over and over that the phrase "Allahu akbar" means "God is greatest," and is meant to be a peaceful praise of God, not a war cry used when committing terrorism.

I decided that a book about Islam was needed now more than ever and sent my proposal for a book on the Islamic faith to Japanese publishers. But I only got negative reactions: "It's too much like a boring textbook," "It's too preachy to sell well," and so on. Even my friends who were well-informed about the Japanese publishing business said, "It might've sold if you put it out right after all those terrorist attacks, but now...isn't it a bit late for this?" I kicked myself for not taking action earlier and grew incredibly depressed.

After that, there were more incidents around the world of Muslim extremists shouting "Allahu akbar!" while committing acts of terrorism, and each time, my desire grew stronger to create a book that would dispel misunderstandings about Islam. But I couldn't think of a format that would make it fun and easy to understand. Seven more years passed, and I had all but given up on doing my book about Islam.

But then, I ended up publishing a book about the American presidential elections with Seikaisha thanks to an editor friend of mine, and as a result, I wound up becoming the supervisor for Yupechika-san's manga!

A "fun, heart-warming manga" is just the sort of format that can teach people about Islamic religion and culture without being preachy or boring! Thanks to this series, we were able to introduce readers to easily misunderstood customs and traditions, like polygamy and the niqab, through Satoko's eyes. I'm incredibly grateful for this opportunity!

Satoko and Nada is the product of a meeting that was guided by the hands of God. I hope that people who read it will expand their worldview--and at the same time, learn how wonderful Japan is, too.

Inshallah!